Craft Matters

Craft Matters

Artisans, Development and the Indian Nation

Soumhya Venkatesan

Orient BlackSwan

CRAFT MATTERS

ORIENT BLACKSWAN PRIVATE LIMITED

Registered Office
3-6-752 Himayatnagar, Hyderabad 500 029 (A.P.), India
E-mail: centraloffice@orientblackswan.com

Other Offices
Bangalore, Bhopal, Bhubaneshwar, Chennai, Ernakulam, Guwahati, Hyderabad, Jaipur, Kolkata, Lucknow, Mumbai, New Delhi, Patna

First published 2009

ISBN: 978-81-250-3682-1

Typeset in Adobe Garamond 11/13 by
InoSoft Systems, Noida

Printed in India at
DeUnique, New Delhi

Published by
Orient Blackswan Private Limited
1/24 Asaf Ali Road, New Delhi 110 002
E-mail: delhi@orientblackswan.com

This book is dedicated to my grandparents,

K Kalyan Raman
and
Rajamma Kalyan Raman

Contents

List of Pictures xi

Acknowledgements xiii

Introduction 1

Research

Involvement

Structure of the Book

1. Crafting the Subject: Craft Producers, Craft Objects and Craft 21

What is Craft? Excavating a Trope

Craft in India

Knowing Craft

Pragmatism and Romanticism: 'Developing Craft'

Imaging Craft Objects and their Producers

Dancing with Images

2. People, Place, Life 46

Early Impressions

Spaces, Changes

Labbais and Rauthers

Hindus and Muslims: Resonance, Hostility and Layered Subjectivites

3. In the House 72
Who is in the House?
Money Matters
Informal Sources of Liquidity
Fluctuating Fortunes
Leading a Good Life

4. The Work of Weaving 101
From Sedge to 'Silk': the Raw Material
Making Mats
The Politics of Space for Weaving
Learning to Weave, Learning to be a Weaver
Production and Re-production
Aesthetics and Authenticity

5. Uneasy Balances 138
Weavers and Traders
The Cooperative Society
Private Traders and the Cooperative Society
Weavers, Traders and the 'Society'
The NGO as a Trader
Choices and Opportunities
The Idea of Community

6. Production and Representation 170
The First Award: 1993
The Second Award: 1996
Active Helplessness

7. Talking About Mats 191
Mats for Marriages
'Silk Mats' and Marriages
Craft and Ritual
The Agency of Objects
Gifting Mats, Opening Doors

Superfine Mats Lead, Fine Mats Follow
Ironies

8. Selling Gifts: Mats in the Market 228
Selling Pattamadai Mats
'The Master's Best, Yours to Possess'

9. Technological Matters 243
Who Wants a Better Loom?
The Craft Enterprises Looms
Challenging the Body

10. Conclusion 266

Appendix: Newspaper and other articles 272

Bibliography 275

Index 291

List of Pictures

1.	A mat for a Queen	3
2.	A mat for a museum	14
3.	Map showing where Pattamadai is in India	47
4.	Schematic map of Pattamadai	55
5.	Rolling *beedis*	84
6.	The Kanadiyan canal, Pattamadai	101
7.	The mat weaving loom	111
8.	Indicative drawing of the reed/*achu*	112
9.	Abdul Wahab and Saad Ali lay the warp	113
10.	Separating the warp threads to create the shed	114
11.	Removing the pith after retting	115
12.	Splitting the korai into fine strands	116
13.	Hasan Fathima and Peer Mohammad finish two mats while Nanni looks on	117
14.	Hasan Fathima at her loom	118

15. A weaver's feet on the bar 119

16. Abdul Wahab and Khadeeja Beevi pack a mat 121

17. Sultan burnishes a mat with a smooth stone 122

18. Abdul Wahab compares a paper design with the finished mat 123

19. A national award made very visible 176

20. A S Peer Mohammad holds up a marriage mat in his shop 200

21. A mat for *selvi* Jayalalithaa 221

22. A mat for Prince Charles and Princess Diana 224

23. Hasan Fathima sits at the prototype new loom 261

24. Regina on the loom with her child 262

25. A brick-stick-comb-and-old-toothbrush loom 264

Acknowledgements

It is over ten years since my first visit to Pattamadai. Throughout this time, the mat weavers and other residents of Pattamadai were patient, welcoming and generous. I do not have the words to thank them enough. It is impossible to name everyone but A S Peer Mohammad, Ibrahim Beevi, Peer Fathima, Sultan and others from that family; Khadeeja Beevi, Rahmatullah, Zeenat, Regina, Abida, Khadeejammal, Arabat and other members of their family; Abdul Wahab and Peer Fathima; Hasan Fathima, Peer Mohammad, Zeenat, Nanni, Waheeda and other members of the family; S M Meeran and Sulaiman; Saad Ali and Noorjahan; Saavanna and Hair un Nissa; and Chinna Peer, Hair un Nissa and other members of their family have made possible this study and enriched my life in more ways than I can know. Hema Raghunathan became friend, interlocuter and sounding-board. This work owes more to her than I can say.

The employees and associates of 'Craft Enterprises', many of whom became good friends, cannot be thanked enough for help, cooperation and discussions. I am extremely grateful to 'Lila', Vidya Sastri, Gita Ram, Devarajan, Latha and Julie Kagti. Special thanks to the Pattamadai Labbai Fine Mat Weavers' Cooperative Society who allowed me to reproduce and use the image of the mat for the Queen. Isakki Muthu of the cooperative society was particularly helpful. My thanks also to S M Meeran, who permitted me to reproduce the image of the mat for Prince Charles and Princess Diana. Mr Harihara Iyer and Mrs Jaya opened up the marriage hall for me to stay in during short trips to Pattamadai. I am thankful to them and also to Muthu. I am also grateful to the Sivananda Hospital for putting me up during one trip to Pattamadai.

This book is based on my PhD thesis and would not exist but for the support of many institutions and people. The University of Cambridge, especially the Department of Social Anthropology and Christ's College where I was a PhD student, and King's College, Cambridge where I held a post-doctoral position were convivial, intellectually stimulating and wonderful spaces. I would especially like to thank my PhD supervisor Deborah Swallow for her generosity and rigour. Susan Bayly gave freely of her time and her knowledge. I am truly grateful. James Laidlaw, Marilyn Strathern, Rajnarayan Chandavarkar, Nikolai Ssorin Chaikov, Anita Herle and Stephen Hugh Jones listened, guided and steered my thoughts. Colleagues at the Department of Social Anthropology, University of Manchester, where the book was completed, have been a great source of intellectual stimulation and friendship. I would particularly like to thank Peter Wade, Penny Harvey, Karen Sykes, Jeanette Edwards, and Stef Jansen. Laila Tyabji has always been a source of inspiration and learning.

The award of a Hunt Postdoctoral Fellowship (2002) by the Wenner-Gren Foundation enabled me to convert my PhD thesis into a book manuscript and also to carry out some additional research. My gratitude to the Wenner-Gren Foundation is immense, as it is to all the institutions which enabled my doctoral and later work through financial and other support. These include the Jawaharlal Nehru Memorial Fund, the Cambridge Commonwealth Trust, The Overseas Research Studentship Scheme, Christ's College, Cambridge, the Smuts Foundation, the Emslie Horniman Fund at the Royal Anthropological Institute, the William Wyse Fund, Girton College, Cambridge and King's College, Cambridge. One of the mats pictured in the book is now in the collection of the Cambridge University Museum of Archaeology and Anthropology. My thanks to the museum for everything.

My PhD examiners, James Laidlaw and Helle Bundgaard, gave feedback and support on the thesis and beyond. I would also like to thank the anonymous reviewer of the manuscript for valuable comments and suggestions. I also thank participants at various seminars where parts of this work were presented. Vipul Sangoi, Anusha Subramaniam and Jonathan Woolf travelled to Pattamadai and took some of the photographs that appear in this book. Vipul Sangoi also designed the book cover and has taken the photograph that appears on it. Chris Gregory, Gillian Evans, Liana Chua, Stef Jansen and Anthony Simpson read and commented on various chapters. Marie Rostron helped scan various images. My thanks to them and also to Hemlata Shankar, Satyadeep and others at Orient Blackswan for their work in guiding this work to publication.

All my friends, especially Zamin Iqbal, Sharon and Ruth Jordan, Ben Horton, Andy Merrills, Kaveri Gill, Matei Candea, Geoffrey Moggridge, Tom de Wesselow, Stef Jansen, Rane Willerslev, Magnus Marsden, Benedicta Rousseau, Vipul Sangoi—thank you for the hours of conversation, food and fun.

To Jon, Appa, Amma, Swathi, Thatha, Patti, Bala chitthi, Chris, Linda, Rangamma, my Athais and other members of my family, especially in Madras: thank you for everything.

Needless to say, while the book itself could not have been written without any of the people and institutions named above (and others not named but nevertheless present), all mistakes, errors and omissions are my responsibility.

SOUMHYA VENKATESAN

Introduction

India, 1953. The nation has been independent for six years and whilst some are eager to banish the traces of a colonial past, others are keen to retain either economically useful or deeply felt emotional ties with Britain. Take Mr Rangan, for example: a chief agent with the Royal Insurance Company in Madras.[1] Mr Rangan seems to have been reluctant to relinquish connections with Britain. He also seems to have harboured a rather remarkable ambition to sell, according to someone who knew him at the time, an insurance policy to the Queen of England. This may be a slightly malicious comment; we will ignore it. Nevertheless it remains that he wished to commemorate the coronation of Elizabeth II on 2 June 1953, and in a way that would bring himself and the nature of his business—in insurance—to her attention.

[1] Madras was renamed Chennai in August 1996 in an attempt to banish the city's colonial past—the name Madras coming from the British, who had built Fort St George in 1640 around which the city grew. But, as it was called Madras in Mr Rangan's time, I will continue to call the city Madras here. Moreover, when I began fieldwork in 1997, many people with whom I worked referred to the city as Madras. Several continue to do so interchangeably.

Though Mr Rangan lived in Madras, a close relative of his lived and worked as the district public prosecutor in the southern city of Tirunelveli, near which is a small town (a village in those days) known as Pattamadai. Both Hindus and Muslims live in Pattamadai, though it is the latter that concern us most closely. For, among the Muslims of Pattamadai was, and still is, a sub-group known as Labbai who specialise in weaving extremely fine mats on simple handlooms. These mats look and feel like they are woven from silk rather than the lowly reeds which actually form their raw material. Finer than almost any other kind of mat woven in the region, Pattamadai mats had already won critical acclaim at the Delhi Exhibition of 1903; the entry from Pattamadai was awarded a Bronze Medal in the mats category. The Delhi Exhibition had showcased manufactures from all over British India thousands of objects were brought to Delhi, officials travelled the length and breadth of the subcontinent seeking out makers of manufactures that would make suitable exhibits (Watt, 1904).

Pattamadai mats, then, were considered of very fine quality by the colonial state and this was recognised with a medal. This mark of the colonial state's appreciation, the proximity of Mr Rangan's relative to Pattamadai, and the ability of the weavers to 'write-weave' names and numbers on the mats—all this may have influenced Mr Rangan's decision to gift Elizabeth II a Pattamadai mat to mark her coronation.

A great deal of thought and preparation went into the gift. According to weavers who remember, Mr Rangan's relative came to Pattamadai to commission the mat for the Queen. More than one weaver wanted to weave it. So the question was put to tender. The weaver willing to charge the least would have the honour of weaving the mat.[2] But the other weavers nonetheless did help the selected weaver in his effort. Mr Rangan had very precise requirements. After all, the mat was special: it would embody the connection with the Queen that he so ardently desired. The weaver was asked to use silk threads to weave the name of the Queen onto the mat, her title as Head of the Commonwealth and the date of the coronation. These

[2] The final cost of the mat was Rs 150. This works out to just under £2 in 2006. Between 1950 and 1959, £1 was valued at Rs 13.3.

would all appear at the top of the mat. At the foot of the mat would be woven Mr Rangan's name and his professional affiliation.

Mr Rangan's initial ambition, however, was to be thwarted. The protocol governing coronations was very strict. No personal gifts were to be accepted on the occasion. Mr Rangan tried to get around this by presenting himself as the intermediary through whom the entire group of weavers was presenting a coronation gift to the Queen. It would, thus, be a gift not from an individual but from a group that wished to show its respect to the head of the commonwealth. This meant changing the writing on the mat. While Mr Rangan's name and business would continue to be prominently displayed, the mat would also bear the name of Pattamadai and the 'mat weavers' association'. This association, some say, existed only in the writing on the mat. The mat finally looked like this:

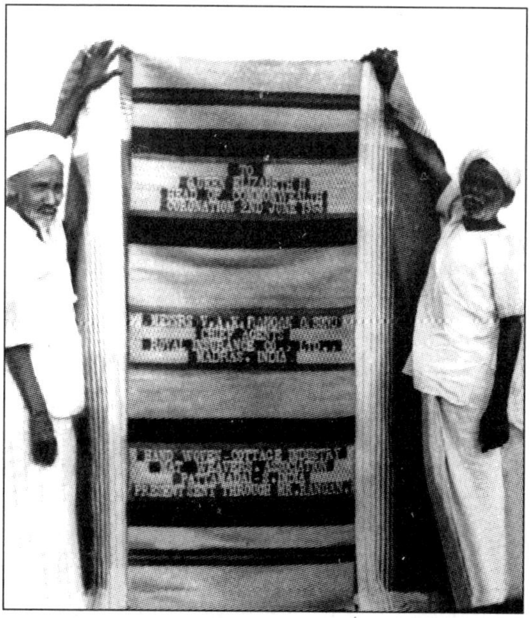

A mat for a Queen. *Photo courtesy*: Pattamadai Labbais Fine Mat Weavers' Cooperative Society.[3]

[3] The text reads as follows: top: 'To Queen Elizabeth II, Head of Commonwealth, Coronation 2nd June 1953'; middle: 'Messrs V. A. K.

A government publication devoted to the mat weaving industry of Pattamadai reports that 'the mat was duly presented to the Queen and was on exhibition along with other presents.' (1964: 6) This exhibition brought the 'superb specimen' to the attention of the All India Handicrafts Board, the newly formed central government agency for the support and development of those Indian hand manufactures identified as 'craft objects'. The chairperson of the board, Kamaladevi Chattopadhyay, visited Pattamadai in 1953 and set a chain of events in motion. These included classifying the mat weavers as a 'traditional craft community', encouraging them to form a craft cooperative society, giving them land to build houses and tools with which to weave, plugging them into state and non-governmental development initiatives and making them—a group of poor and marginalised rural Muslims—visible and desirable within the state.

The above is a composite reconstruction of a story told and retold within and beyond Pattamadai, one that, over the past fifty-odd years, many people have participated in, embellished and built on. Memories are selective, often fragmentary. Information comes in fits and starts as chance comments trigger recollections. Inaccurate, if instrumental, information abounds, especially in the popular press. This is often reiterated in different spaces and by different kinds of people.

There is another and more substantiated version of this story that did not end quite so successfully for Mr Rangan: Mr Rangan's attempt to circumvent the rules governing coronation gifts by making the mat look like a gift from the mat weavers, and himself their intermediary, did not work. According to the Inventory Clerk for the London Palaces and Residences, following a lengthy correspondence between D J C Crawley of the Commonwealth Relations Office and Major Sir Michael Adeane at Buckingham Palace (1953), the mat was, in the end, not accepted as it continued to be classified as a personal gift.[4]

Rangan and Sons, Chief Agents, Royal Insurance Co., Ltd., Madras. India'; bottom: 'Hand woven cottage industry, mat weavers association, Pattamadai—S. India, Present sent through Mr Rangan'.

4 Personal communication by email, August 2005. Unfortunately, I have been informed that access to this correspondence, held by the Royal Household, is restricted for the duration of the current reign.

But, as far as the weavers, and indeed several others, are concerned, the gift was successful. The Queen's mat continues to form part of the mythology of Pattamadai mat weaving and the weavers continue to be described over and over again in the press as a group of poor Muslims who made a gift to a Queen.[5] Indeed, one newspaper article even describes it in the following terms:

> ...Of course, no lore concerning the mat would be complete without its faery touch—way back in 1948 [sic.], out of the wealth of India's handicrafts, it was a finely textured Pattamadai mat which was chosen as India's wedding gift [sic.] to the then Princess Elizabeth.[6]

Clearly, the elements of the story that remain here are the beauty of the mat, India's handicrafts, the Indian nation and British royalty.[7] That poor and skilled weavers were a crucial part of this gift makes the story even more magical, even more able to be used as a springboard for action involving the weavers and the rest of the nation. To think these through is to open up the rich and complex world of 'craft' in India. It is to show why—for producers, for the Indian nation, for national and international development agencies, for those within and beyond India in search of 'roots', for those who seek to ameliorate poverty, inequality and other oppressions—craft truly matters. It is also to show how artisans, including the mat weavers of Pattamadai who are at the heart of this book, become visible through the objects they make.

Craft matters is a study of marginalised people who strive to be visible and valued, knowing at the same time that they stand for the past and that the future does not belong to them, indeed by definition never can. By means of development schemes and through their objects, which in many ways are as important as they are, they participate in the creation of value at the point of

[5] For a detailed discussion of this gift and how it challenges notions of reciprocity in gift-giving, please see my paper: 'How a free gift can make friends' (in preparation).

[6] Chari, 'The wonder of the Pattamadai mat', *The Hindu*, 25/02/1996.

[7] The remaking of the mat as a 'wedding gift' will be discussed in detail in Chapter 7.

production, and are then swept up into other more influential attempts to create value in locales that are closed to them or open in very narrow ways.

This book about craft and development in contemporary India is based on ethnographic fieldwork over several periods of varying length between 1997 and 2003 among Muslim artisanal mat weavers of Pattamadai town in south India and among development agents who work with the weavers. The book seeks to understand the processes and particular ways in which people like the mat weavers become visible within the Indian state and how they are created as particular kinds of subject, and simultaneously as objects of national and international concern. It asks why artisans actively participate in the shaping of images about them that they recognise as, at best, partially representative of what they do and why. The creation of artisans as objects of development emerges from the engagement of the universal and the particular, of the place of the traditional in the modern (which in itself is, of course, a modernist project). The frictions between these (Tsing, 2004) generate creative encounters that allow a group of poor marginalised Muslims in a small town in south India to reposition themselves within the nation. But there is another kind of friction with which this book seeks to engage: between the production and circulation of images of craft with their claims to universality, and craft weaving in Pattamadai as a particular kind of production system with its logics of embodiment, material concerns, opportunity costs and aspirations. Value emerges not only in consumption and exchange but also in the relations and processes of production that give rise to the objects that are exchanged and consumed. The ethnographic method, in moving from the large to the small to the large again, allows an exploration of the different spheres within which value is created, transformed and recreated. This is what this book seeks to do through an examination of the production and circulation of 'craft objects' in contemporary India and beyond.

I ask how and why the concept of 'craft' has gained such powerful purchase in twentieth and twenty-first century India, and suggest that this is because of the way in which the trope has been used to imagine a certain mode of production that has ideological appeal:

objects predominantly handmade by groups of people who may be described as forming a 'community' and who, by virtue of the production techniques as well as their often hereditary ownership of the work they do, are not simple sellers of their labour in the marketplace. Artisans are imagined to share a deep and meaningful relationship with their work, which is embedded in their social relations not only within the community but also in 'traditional' networks. Furthermore, I suggest that many people seek to resolve their feelings of unease and disquiet about the world in which they live—of industries, alienated labour, lifestyles that leave no time for enjoying the simple pleasures of making—through the consumption of objects made by 'traditional craft producers'. Artisanal craft producers are construed as deeply integrated in their natural environment, drawing both inspiration and raw materials from their surroundings. Craft, here, stands for rootedness and for an inalienable link with the natural world and the collective past. In this perspective, different craft forms materialise the collective heritage of the nation, even of humanity, and must be protected in the face of growing onslaughts from increasing industrialisation and urbanisation.

Artisans are important because they stand for important values. But they do not stand alone. The objects they make are crucial, perhaps even more than they themselves are. It is, as we saw in the case of the mat for the Queen, the objects that make a 'craft producer'. Things are crucial in social processes. The material qualities, forms and physical properties of the craft object attract, but so do the processes of its manufacture. The simple non-mechanised technologies, the body at work manipulating things, twisting, bending, lifting and materialising skilled knowledge, creating something extraordinary from extremely ordinary, even mundane raw materials—the enchantment of technology (Gell, 1999a)—render craft enchanting. Even though craft objects are made for sale, I show how they are a special kind of commodity best described as object+person+idea.

The category of craft comprises objects, skills and producers—all of which are seen to be under threat and requiring support. The loss of traditional craft is the loss of the nation's and humankind's heritage. Development is one way to protect craft. Craft development is a concern of the Indian state, pan-Indian and local non-governmental organisations, and international agencies including the United Nations Development Project (UNDP) and the United Nations Educational Scientific and Cultural Organisation (UNESCO). My focus is restricted to Indian agencies that seek to preserve and promote craft, and will explore the interactions between the guardians of objectified notions of heritage and the people who produce objects that are culturally valued.

Development is deeply implicated in the ways in which craft is seen and valued. Based on unequal relations of power between people who care about the ideological and instrumental implications of craft, and people who produce craft objects and who value their work differently from those who use their products, craft development nevertheless forms the common ground where the two interact. What does this mean for people who bear the burden of these expectations—who are proud of their skills, yet want other things for themselves and their children that they may not be able to realise independently of development initiatives?

My ethnography shows that producers participate in their own objectification, they engage with a way of thinking about them and their work that does not necessarily mirror their own understandings, concerns and aspirations. Rather than focus on the 'success' or 'failure' of different development projects, I suggest that we examine the ways in which development enhances and constrains the agency of both producers and development agents, who are too often described as cynical and self-seeking, or at best naive. This allows a nuanced examination of why different kinds of people are involved in development.

Research

I have known about Pattamadai mats all my life. My mother was given one around forty years ago and I remember many occasions from childhood holding it, bending it this way and that, marvelling at the way it felt like silk yet was made from reeds. It is fair to say the mat drew me first not only to Pattamadai, but also to craft and development. In 1993–4 I spent a year working in Delhi for one of India's foremost non-governmental organisations working with craft producers. At the same time I was pursuing a Master's degree in the History of Art. For my dissertation I focused on the ritual wall paintings of the Warli 'tribe' in western India. I had gone to study the iconography of the ritual paintings but had ended up becoming interested in the effects of a governmental initiative to generate income through the paintings by encouraging Warlis to paint on paper or cloth for sale.[8] It seemed clear that 'craft' and its 'development' demanded detached analytic attention. A subsequent degree in Social Anthropology solidified this feeling. Pattamadai, in the form of my mother's mat, beckoned.

There are many factors that made Pattamadai interesting at the time, not least of all the desire to see more mats, learn how they were made, and perhaps even learn to weave. The larger political climate in India was making, and continues to make, life difficult for Muslims in the country. But, at the same time, Hindutva, or chauvinistic nationalism based on the Hindu identity, emphasised India's ancient traditions, including its craft heritage. Craft, like many other ideological constructs, was used by both the liberals and the bigots. As Muslims, the weavers of Pattamadai were believed by some to be anti-national and, therefore, objects of suspicion. As craft producers, however, they were celebrated as representatives of the real nation. Ethnographic research would reveal how these contradictions played out on the ground.

Moreover, having heard hardly anything about Pattamadai in different craft networks and in the media, a newspaper article advertising a craft sale in Delhi electrified me. Not only were there mats from Pattamadai at the sale, there were also two weavers who had brought their products. Dashing off to the Blind School in Delhi where the sale was being held in the winter of 1993, I met two people: an elderly father and his daughter who, shivering in the unaccustomed north Indian cold, were nevertheless welcoming

[8] Venkatesan, 1994. 'The process and results of the commodification of Warli ritual wall painting'. Unpublished MA dissertation. National Museum Institute, New Delhi.

and happy to talk to me. I helped translate customers' needs and questions from Hindi into Tamil for them, and ended up spending the greater part of the day at their stall.

Almost two years later, having completed an MPhil in Social Anthropology, I visited Pattamadai in the summer of 1995. Mohammad, the man I had met in Delhi, dominated my first visit and from him I learnt of the rewards that could be reaped from manipulating the trope of craft. Mohammad's shop and his presence in influential craft networks, including the Crafts Council of India, the Madras Craft Foundation, and both state and central government craft development boards, all testified to his success. I visited his home and met his daughters, three of whom weave, as well as his son who works in the shop with him. Mohammad was at pains to point out to me that his efforts were crucial in the continued survival of Pattamadai mat weaving.

On that first short visit, Mohammad had me sussed out as a female in my early thirties, Tamil Brahmin from an urban, upper-middle-class family in Madras, and, therefore, not dissimilar to many of the development agents from non-governmental organisations he had encountered and worked with. His conversations with me in the early days reflected this awareness and also his puzzlement: what exactly did I want to do in Pattamadai if not work in craft development?

In October 1997 I returned to begin my doctoral research (on which this book builds), intending to spend a year working with weavers and their publics. By now the Pattamadai mat weaving industry was the focus of sustained interest within the craft worlds. A new NGO—which I will call Craft Enterprises—had arrived to work with the weavers. Unlike the Crafts Council of India and the Madras Craft Foundation, both of which worked with Pattamadai mats but did not have any real presence in the town, central to Craft Enterprises' work was the presence of a 'facilitator' who would live in Pattamadai for the first year, build deep relationships with the weavers and gain knowledge of their work. This was felt to be crucial to the development process. In this, Craft Enterprises was unusual among the myriad craft development agencies that exist throughout India. The facilitator, Lila,[9] and I would become close friends, sharing a house, bouncing off ideas against each other and, later, reading each other's work and collaborating on projects.

I had hoped to live in one of the weavers' homes, perhaps even Mohammad's. But Mohammad took this off my hands, arranging that I should live in the Brahmin section of town as that, he said, would be most appropriate.[10] He suggested I live with Lila, describing her as being 'like his daughter'. She agreed, and so it was. Living with Lila allowed me to gain valuable insights into the way the NGO viewed and conducted its work in Pattamadai. There were some obvious disadvantages, including the initial suspicions of traders, who saw the NGO, which was heavily involved in marketing, as competition. However, the periodic storms and also the gradual breakdown in relations between Lila and Mohammad, when he perceived that the NGO's work with other weavers threatened his dominance over the industry, did not extend to me.[11] As I visited everyone who would talk to me, I was seen as somewhat neutral, and as a useful source of information not only on what the NGO was up to, but also what other weavers and traders were doing. At any rate, Lila and I did some things together, but by no means all. As far as the weavers and traders were concerned, I was also a resource—drafted in to write letters and publicity brochures, carry petitions to senior governmental officers that I was interviewing, and to deal in other ways with bureaucratic structures. The fact that I was working towards my PhD at a British university invested me with a certain amount of glamour as it showed that even people very far away were interested in Pattamadai mats. Also, England was where the mat for the Queen had gone. I too came in time to be described by Mohammad as one of his daughters, even as Lila slowly slipped out of that category. Others, including those older than I, moved from addressing me as older sister (*akka*) or even madam to just calling me by my name. That, given the importance

[9] Tamils rarely use surnames, so I will refer to her by her given name.

[10] The spatial organisation of Pattamadai is discussed in chapter 2.

[11] This is discussed in Chapter 7.

accorded to hierarchy and the widespread recognition of unequal power relations among a people who, as objects of development, are alive to such distinctions, felt good.

Following the worsening of a chronic spinal problem, I had to leave the field in February 1998 and was unable to return until November 1999, after which I stayed in Pattamadai till April 2000.[12] Initially, this was a blow to research plans, but the longer time frame allowed a glimpse into the dynamic nature of the mat weaving industry—the shifting alliances, the arrival and departure of NGOs, those who stayed and those who left. This posed a serious challenge to wider characterisations of craft as unchanging and static.

In the early days, however, as I wandered around Pattamadai going to different weavers' houses and trying to establish relationships beyond those Mohammad saw as suitable for me, two things I had stood me in good stead. One was my mother's old mat. The other was a census publication from 1964 devoted to the fine mat weaving industry in Pattamadai.[13] Both caused no small stir. Weavers in Pattamadai had never seen an old mat before. Taking up to a month to weave, these mats are too expensive, in terms of opportunity cost, not to sell. Mats sell as luxury items in distant markets. Few return to Pattamadai. As I walked through the narrow streets of the Labbai areas when I first arrived, people (even those who did not weave) would stop me and ask if I had the old mat. They wanted to see how it had aged; also how the older technique of spinning the yarn at home affected the texture and fabric. Nowadays people use shop-bought thread for the weft. I ended up carrying this mat with me for almost the entire duration of my first month in Pattamadai. The census publication also evoked great interest. Again, people would stop me on the street and say,

[12] I have since made several visits to Pattamadai between 2001 and 2004. I also continue to remain in close contact with Lila who, despite the closing down of Craft Enterprises due to lack of funding, retains her connections and interest in Pattamadai. We have also collaborated on occasion.

[13] Nambiar, 1964. Handicrafts and artisans of Madras State: Fine mats of Pattamadai. Census of India 1961. Vol. IX. Madras. Part VII-A-iv. This is discussed in more detail in the next chapter.

'So and so told me you had a book with a picture of my father in it.' We would look together at the pictures with frequent stops and exclamations as people were recognised and others called to come and see people now dead or aged almost beyond recognition. I learned a great deal from our shared use of the book and, in the end, left photocopies of it with anyone who wanted one.

The publication was also useful because I could use it to answer the question of what I was doing there. Everyone knew I lived with Lila but they could not work out why I was in Pattamadai since it was clear that, unlike her, I was not working with weavers, developing new designs and buying mats to sell in craft markets. When I said I was hoping to write what would become a book on their work and lives, they were excited. 'Make sure you put our names in your book. We want to be remembered.'

This question of names was to crop up several times. As producers with commodities to sell, traders and weavers are very aware of the benefits of publicity. The cooperative competition that characterises the weaving industry also means that individuals want their own names to be visible in documents as they know the power of newspaper and other kinds of articles in bringing customers to the town and to specific establishments or people. This posed a dilemma for me and, throughout my time in Pattamadai, including when I took my study back to Pattamadai to show it to people and discuss my analysis, I tried to argue that they might not really want their names revealed. Mohammad, who does not read much and with whom I went through the entire document chapter by chapter, was dismissive of my worries: 'When people pick up your book and look through it, they will see our names and remember that. No one is going to read all of it!'

This reflects the way in which weavers and traders keep a copy of any publication they may find that mentions their work. In most weavers' houses and in all the mat shops in the town can be found press-cuttings carefully placed in folders or rolled up in mats and displayed at some time or the other to visitors interested in the mat weaving industry—development agents, buyers and anthropologists. Mohammad's collection of such cuttings and photocopies is impressive and formed a great resource.

To be recognised and remembered is seen as a good thing. A collection I was making for the Cambridge University Museum of Archaeology and Anthropology was greeted with enthusiasm and several people entered into plans for making special mats for the collection.[14] One couple, who wove a very fine mat and wove-wrote their names on it, were explicit in their reason for doing so: 'This will be in the museum for hundreds of years. People can just walk

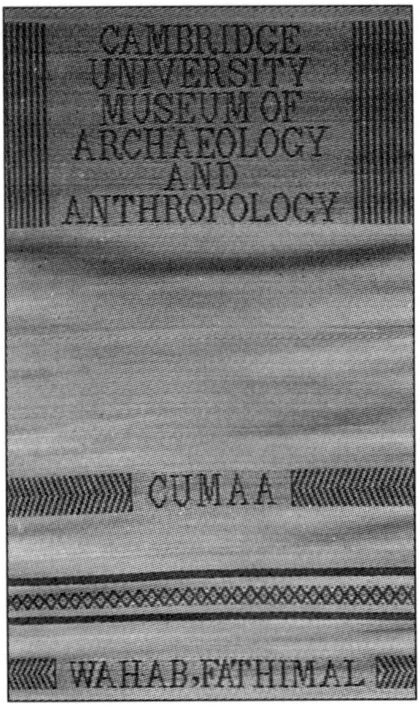

A mat for a museum. Made by Abdul Wahab and Pir Fathimal for the Cambridge University Museum of Archaeology and Anthropology, it formed part of the exhibition, Crafting culture: Pattamadai mats from south India, April 2002 to December 2003. *Photo courtesy*: Cambridge University Museum of Archaeology and Anthropology.

[14] The collection and, based on it, the special exhibition, Crafting culture: Pattamadai mats from South India, was funded by the Crowther-Beynon Fund at the University of Cambridge University. The exhibition ran from April 2002 to December 2003 at the Cambridge University Museum of Archaeology and Anthropology. An exhibition catalogue (Venkatesan, 2002) was published to complement the exhibition. I thank Anita Herle for her invaluable support throughout this project.

in and see our mat and our names. Maybe even our children's children will be able to see it there [laughter].' The laughter came from the thought that their children or their children's children would be able to visit a far-away and expensive nation and walk into a museum, an idea implausible to them, yet desirable. While no one lost sight of the fact that they would be paid for their mats, like the Queen's mat, these mats for the museum too were special. A poster from the exhibition based around this collection as well as the exhibition catalogue now form part of the galaxy of images of the Pattamadai mat weaving industry and, like other publications, are displayed to visitors as a testimony to the interest evoked by Pattamadai mats and their makers.

Involvement

Crafting culture: Pattamadai mats from south India opened at the Cambridge University Museum of Archaeology and Anthropology in April 2002. A second 'gala' opening was accompanied by a sale of mats from Pattamadai. All profits were to be taken back to Pattamadai for weavers to use as they saw fit; medical expenses were what was mainly envisaged by me, Lila and weavers with whom this was discussed. The sale was in response to a question I was increasingly asked in Pattamadai: 'You will get a degree from being with us, what will we get?' Having finished my doctoral fieldwork, I sought to address this question. It was to cause a temporary, though unsettling, change in my relationship with several weavers.

Lila had sent me mats for the sale which, after costs, raised around £650—a substantial amount of money in Pattamadai. When I took this amount back with me and met various weavers in their homes or in a newly formed cooperative society to discuss what they wanted done with it,[15] I found to my shock that I had suddenly stopped being Soumhya and was 'madam' instead. People made claims over me and thereby over the money. In the end, and after much painful discussion, the money went to pay for various cataract surgeries, a CAT scan for one woman and a child's throat

[15] This newly formed cooperative society, the CE co-op, is discussed in Chapter 5.

operation. There was still some left over. The weavers of the newly formed cooperative decided to use this as working capital to tide the cooperative over the early stages of its existence.

But the saga was not over. The mat traders also wanted a share. 'Our weavers too should get the benefits,' one argued. Smaller sums of money were given to them in the teeth of opposition from the cooperative society—these, I found out the next year, were distributed in the form of Eid presents, thereby displaying the benevolence of traders.[16] In the end, all the money was gone and all I felt was relief, even though some weavers still scolded me. One even shouted at me in anger. I became Soumhya again. I was happy that some people could see better and that one woman was able to pay for scans to find out that she did not have a fatal condition as she and her doctor had feared. But, never again would I become directly involved in 'development' in Pattamadai, I thought, or at least never in this way.

I detail this because I think it reveals something important about development and the ways in which its objects engage with it. As long as I had nothing to do with money and certainly had no power over its distribution, I was harmless. Drifting along, writing my notes, asking questions, sitting around, listening, learning to weave—none of these things really bothered anyone in Pattamadai. I was/am a source of possible publicity, a means of gathering information about others, and someone to bounce ideas off and use to reach important people to whom I was seen to have access. I was not allied to any group/faction (however temporary) in the atmosphere of cooperative competition that characterises relationships within the mat weaving industry. As soon as I decided to help more directly, I became like a development agent—someone with whom people had to match their wits to get something, someone with power to distribute scarce resources.

Anthropology and development may generate knowledge in similar ways using similar kinds of oppositions—local: global; indigenous knowledge: 'universal values'; internal: external, etc.

16 Chapter 5 discusses relationships between weavers and traders in some detail.

(see Yarrow, 2008)—but for people who are habituated to being objects of development, what each does is clearly distinguished: development has real and immediate outcomes that affect people. An organising paradigm, it generates competition and strategising. Anthropology, on the other hand, generates knowledge that may or may not be 'useful', and not necessarily directly for the people who are its objects of research. Insofar as people in Pattamadai were concerned, I had money to learn about them and write about them. This was bewildering but not of much real concern. I might generate publicity, I could certainly be used as a resource but was essentially just someone who was around—towards whom some felt kindly, even affectionately, and others more or less tolerated. Transcending this divide between anthropology and development threw up problems precisely because it destabilised relations that were based on particular understandings.

Should the anthropologist refrain from becoming involved? There is no simple answer to this question and I believe we must each work out what and how we might want to do in 'our field', keeping in mind that the decision may not wholly rest with us in any case. Given a methodology where, to paraphrase Sarah Green, it is my eyes that see and my ears that hear (1997: 4), it is difficult to predict what one might do, or feel moved to do, or regret. In my case, my similarity to, yet difference from, many development agents found me a measure of acceptance initially. By 'doing development' I briefly lost the space I subsequently managed to carve out, but learned much nevertheless. These are perhaps the pitfalls of doing anthropology 'at home' where one is recognised as a representative of a category and created as a subject in a way not dissimilar to that in which the weavers are created as 'traditional craft producers'.

Structure of the Book

Chapter 1 focuses on the ways in which the category of craft has become important in twentieth-century India and in the idea of the Indian nation. The chapter seeks to understand what 'craft' is, and how a term which first became important in late-nineteenth and early-twentieth-century Britain, has today become a dominant trope in development and nation-building activities in India.

Chapter 2 moves from the craft worlds and images of craft to Pattamadai town—a busy bustling place where weavers, traders, development agents, other townsfolk and the anthropologist encounter each other in various ways.

Chapter 3 narrows in on Labbai Muslim households where weaving forms one, though not necessarily the only, source of income. Through detailed discussions of how and when people weave and why they say they do it, the chapter seeks to contrast the lived worlds of artisans with their representations in the craft worlds.

Chapter 4 introduces the reader to the physical work of weaving. The materiality of the mats they make is what has made them so valued and given the weavers entry into the craft worlds. While weaving is a rich and oft-used metaphor in the English language, we are nevertheless faced with the inability of language to describe the embodied work of weaving. For the weavers, their mats are a source of ambivalent feelings: pride as well as disgust at the 'drudgery' involved in the work. This chapter attempts to go beyond the text to describe the work of weaving though a pictorially rich description of the weaving process. I argue that this is important if we are to understand how people feel about their work and why this may differ from idealised descriptions and furthermore affect development on the ground.

Weavers are not the only people involved in the craft industry in Pattamadai. Local traders and non-governmental organisations compete with makers over ownership of craft products and rights to sell them. Characterising the interactions between these different kinds of people as 'cooperative competition', Chapter 5 investigates the shifting alliances, negotiations and, sometimes, outright hostility within the mat weaving industry. The chapter questions the analytic value of the oft-used term 'community', arguing that this is too simplistically applied to hereditary occupational groups.

Chapter 6 returns to the craft worlds, focusing this time on interactions between weavers and craft development schemes.

Examining one prominent weaving and trading family who have achieved considerable fame and who engage adeptly with craft development programmes, the chapter examines the acceptable language of petitions and what governs their success or failure. This, it is argued, is because of the ways in which the need for development in the craft sector is conceptualised and craft development itself works—privileging the idea of the craft producer rather than the actual person.

The mat is a physical object. Its meaning and use depends on the context in which it is placed and the ways in which it is made meaningful. Through a discussion of 'craft mats', 'marriage mats' and 'gift mats', the specific forms they take and the ways in which they are embedded in social relations, Chapter 7 analyses 'commodity' and 'gift' in contemporary India. Furthermore, it shows how commodities are made into gifts even at the point of sale by Muslim traders who seek to position themselves within Hindu networks. But the chapter goes beyond an analysis of human beings acting through objects. By exploring how objects *do* things or act in the world, the chapter builds on the work of Alfred Gell (1999) to explore how agency is possessed not just be people but also objects.

Chapter 8 focuses on the sale of craft objects. Pattamadai mats, like other craft objects, compete with commodities in the marketplace. This is where contradictions between craft as livelihood and as 'timeless tradition' are most clearly seen. The chapter examines the implications of these contradictions and examines if they can be resolved within the framework of 'craft' as it is now.

It is all too easy to forget that the term craft refers to a series of nested processes—physical, technological and social. Often it is impossible to separate these; indeed it would be absurd to do so. Chapter 9 both pulls together issues from the previous chapters and furthers an oft-neglected area: the anthropology of technology. Through an analysis of attempts by development agents to 'improve' the mat weaving loom, the chapter shows that unchanging technology is not a sign of tradition or stagnation; rather it is the result of (active and passive) choices made on the basis of complex ideas about work, the body, gender roles and suitability. I follow Tim Ingold (2001) to suggest that in skilled craft practice, persons and tools constitute a single totality.

The concluding chapter suggests that we think about craft as a heterotopia (Foucault, 1967), or the attempt to realise utopia. This gives us a rich way of thinking through the contested, selective and attractive idea-thing-practice that is craft in India. The detailed and grounded ethnography of the workings of traditional craft, I hope, will also make a contribution to understanding this little considered yet important part of Foucault's oeuvre.

There are several themes that run through the book and the chapters mirror the ways in which these are interlinked and inform each other. For the reader who wishes to pursue a particular theme, the following map may be useful. The question of craft: how and why it has become important is addressed in Chapter 1; the ways in which craft is imaged reappears in a more practical sense in Chapters 6, 7 and 9 where we see how different members of the mat weaving industry engage more or less successfully with their idealised objectifications. The question of technology appears first in Chapter 4 and then again in chapter 8. In the latter, it is linked to development through a focus on attempts to encourage weavers to change the ways in which they organise weaving, both in terms of raw material procurement and by modifying the very loom on which they weave. Chapter 2 moves away from the questions of 'craft' and 'development'. It introduces the reader to the town of Pattamadai and locates the Muslim mat weavers within the context of the town and other groups with whom they share it. This sets the scene for discussions in Chapters 3, 5 and 6, which focus on individual households, the 'craft community' and the use of the mats in deflecting suspicions that arise from the fact that the weavers are Muslim.

1 Crafting the Subject: Craft Producers, Craft Objects and Craft

What is Craft? Excavating a Trope

The United Nations, 'Report on the Inter Governmental Group on Tariff Reclassification' gives the following guidelines to identify handmade and, within this category, handicraft or craft products:

> The term handmade articles should be taken to cover those produced with or without the use of tools, simple instruments or implements operated directly by the craftsman mainly by hand or by foot... Within the group of handmade goods, some such as Handicraft often have identifying features such as, (a) traditional or artistic features deriving from the geographical region or country of production, (b) production by craftsmen working generally on a cottage industry basis. (cited in the *Report of the Task Force on Handicrafts for the VIII Five Year Plan*, 1989: 6.)

The guidelines focus on technological aspects of craft production, that is, the fact that craft products are made primarily by hand, using simple tools;[1] it touches on the possible 'artistic' qualities of craft objects,[2] and on their 'traditional' nature, without any allusion to the problematic nature of these two terms. The uses of craft objects are also left unclear—are they decorative or are they useful, or are they sometimes both? Most crucially, this definition does not even hint at the complex history through which 'craft' has come to be represented and defended in discussions at various levels (academic, political, economic, and in the popular press) and produced as a self-evident kind of product and activity imbued with a particular kind of moral value.

In fact, the term craft defies exact definition. Most usefully thought of as a trope to be excavated, the use of the term from the nineteenth century is made up of various strands of thought that are intertwined and difficult to tease apart. Over the years it has acquired several layers of meaning. These meanings do not necessarily sit well together (Dormer *et al*, 1992: 9). Describing craft as an 'empire' which subsumed within it several disparate things, Greenhalgh (1997) seeks to provide an archaeology of the term craft as it is used today. In nineteenth-century Britain, when the term first came to be used in its contemporary sense, three distinct elements were subsumed within the one category of craft, but had little in common: (i) decorative arts; (ii) the vernacular; and (iii) the politics of work.

1 The entry for 'craft' in the *International Encyclopaedia of Social Sciences* describes crafts as including 'all activities that produce or modify objects by manual means, with or without the use of mechanical aids.' (Sills, 1968: 430).

2 The distinction between art and craft has been the subject of debates between different kinds of scholar, practitioner and other 'expert', at least since the nineteenth century; as Firth notes, '...the distinction between art and craft may depend primarily upon social and not aesthetic parameters.' (Firth's 'Introduction' to Coote and Shelton, 1992: 17.) Also see Gell, 1999: 193–4 for an illuminating summary of Danto's thought experiment on what constitutes art through two examples of groups who might equally be called craft producers—the pot people and the basket people.

The decorative arts had become a disenfranchised category following eighteenth- and nineteenth-century debates about the nature of art, and the distinction between the fine arts, or art for art's sake, and skilled productions, or crafts which had a function. The function, in this case, was that of adornment, be it of the body or of physical spaces. The prestige items characteristic of the decorative arts—enamelling, gem setting, ivory work, fine weaving—had, for centuries, been produced and traded in highly sophisticated environments. These kinds of production served the same elite clientele as did fine art painting and sculpture. As luxury products, they were often made for distant markets. Their designs and demand were affected by fashions. These kinds of item existed in contrast to the vernacular crafts—functional objects of everyday or ritual use, sometimes decorated, and usually traded locally, if at all. The vernacular and decorative arts make uneasy companions within an encompassing definition of craft. Described as the cultural produce of a community, the vernacular carries the mystique of symbolising the authentic voice of society.

> The work of country craftsmen was believed to have evolved 'naturally' as the direct and honest expression of simple functional requirements and solid virtues. This vernacular tradition was construed as something static and timeless, in contrast to the dynamic and progressive modern world. (Greenhalgh, 1997: 31)

Greenhalgh points out that the beginnings of vernacularism as a cultural phenomenon can be clearly identified to the beginnings of the nineteenth century as urbanism and industrialisation took their toll on older forms of life. The vernacular was of great symbolic importance to the founders of the Arts and Crafts Movement, and the revival and preservation of the 'authentic tradition' was one of the utopian visions of the movement. This was coupled with another concern of the movement: the politics of work.

During the nineteenth century, work was a key area of politico-economic debate. Resistance to mechanical and political control of the worker went back to the origins of the Industrial Revolution. The nature and relationship of work to human-ness became subjects of intense debates in the nineteenth century. Key figures of the age sought to highlight the alienation of the worker from the work with the onset of the machine age. John Ruskin's insistence that a man could not be part of a mechanised world and still remain human,[3] and William Morris' emphasis on creative work which would improve the environment, lead to an equitable distribution of wealth and generate psychologically fulfilled people, were especially influential. From this position, Morris, in particular, generated what may be termed a politics of craft. The metaphysics of work provided craft with its moral core (Greenhalgh, 1997: 33).

These three elements were brought together in the nineteenth century by thinkers of the Arts and Crafts Movement to form the term 'craft' or 'handicraft'. They did not necessarily belong together, but were brought together because 'the historical moment was right, the combination in this context dynamic and compelling' (Greenhalgh, 1997: 35). The politics of work provided craft with its moral core. Vernacularism gave craft its nostalgic and nationalistic character. The inclusion of the decorative arts, especially the top end of the category, made craft a matter of elite concern and consumption.

Craft in India

Selected Indian manufactures had already achieved critical acclaim in Britain following their display in the Great Exhibition of 1851. Prominent designers and thinkers in Britain, including Owen Jones, Henry Cole and William Morris took up the cause of the preservation and protection of Indian artisans from imperialist exploitation and from decline, which they attributed to the flooding of Indian markets with mass-produced manufactures.[4] India, with

[3] While Ruskin was not particularly sympathetic to Indian art and manufactures, his essay *Unto this last* (1862) influenced Gandhi deeply, especially in his thinking about politics and the economy. Gandhi, who described the effect this book had on him as 'a magic spell', paraphrased it in Gujarati under the title *Sarvodaya* (1908). This was translated into English by Valji Govindji Desai (1956) and is available online on www.forget_me.net/ Also see Brantlinger, 1996.

[4] A representative sample of the writings on craft by Morris, Havell, Birdwood and Ashbee may be found in the Foreword and Appendices

its 'living traditions of craftsmanship', became one of the utopias of the Arts and Crafts Movement (Mitter, 1977).[5]

The ideals of the Arts and Crafts Movement were taken to India by, among others, George Birdwood,[6] E B Havell, and Ananda Coomaraswamy.[7] The following rather long but extremely revealing extract from Birdwood's *Industrial arts of India*, shows how the category of craft was applied to selected aspects of rural life to create a compelling picture of traditional Indian village life and its destruction due to industrialisation.

> ...in every Indian village all the traditional handicrafts are still to be found at work. Outside the entrance, on an exposed rise of ground, the hereditary potter sits by his wheel moulding the swift revolving

---

of *The Indian craftsman* by Ananda Coomaraswamy (1909). The book illustrates how the ideals of the Arts and Crafts Movement shaped thinking about 'craft' in early twentieth-century India.

[5] Much has been written on Ruskin's and Morris's opposed stances on imperialism and especially on whether or not Morris believed that British rule in India should end, even though he condemned the destruction of Indian arts and crafts by imperialism and industrialisation (see Brantlinger, 1996). What is clear is that Morris read and drew upon the writings of Birdwood for his ideas about Indian arts and crafts and was an important influence on Ananda Coomaraswamy. Both Birdwood and Coomaraswamy are discussed in this chapter.

[6] Sir George Birdwood was professor of Anatomy and Physiology in Bombay, though his interests extended far beyond medical practice and study. Inspired by the ideals of the Arts and Crafts Movement, Birdwood contrasted the evils of Western industrialism with the ideal village communities of India and formulated policies for the preservation of crafts skills in India and the protection of artisans from Western influences (however, see McGowan, 2005, who argues that this concern with preserving tradition led to a new definition of Indian traditional design). Sir George Watt, Director of the Delhi Exhibition of 1902–3 (at which a Pattamadai mat won a medal), described Birdwood as 'the pioneer and chief advocate of the art crafts of India' (1904: viii).

[7] Ananda Coomaraswamy (1877–1947) wrote extensively on what we would today call South Asian art and craft (1905, 1909, 1912, 1956). He has been hailed as 'an inspirer of Indian renaissance' (Rao, 1980).

clay by the natural curves of his hands. At the back of the houses, which form the low irregular street, there are two or three looms at work, in blue, and scarlet and gold, the frames hung between the acacia trees, the yellow flowers of which drop fast on the webs as they are being woven. In the street the brass and copper smiths are hammering away at their pots and pans; and further down, in the verandah of the rich man's house, is the jeweller working rupees and gold mohrs into fair jewellery, gold and silver earrings, and round tires like the moon, bracelets and tablets and tinkling ornaments for the feet, taking his designs from the fruit and the flowers around him, or from the traditional forms represented in the paintings and carvings of the great temple, which rises over the grove of mangoes and palms at the end of the street above the lotus covered village tank. At half past three or four in the afternoon, the whole street is lighted up by the moving robes of the women going down to draw water from the tank, each with two or three water jars on her head: and so going and returning in single file...Later the men drive in the mild grey kine from the moaning jungle, the looms are folded up, the coppersmiths are silent, the elders gather at the gate, the lights begin to glimmer in the fast-falling darkness, the feasting and the music begin...The next morning with sunrise, after their simple ablutions and adorations performed in the open air before their houses, the same day begins again. This is the daily life going on all over Western India in the village communities of the Deccan, among a people happy in their simple manners and frugal way of life.

But of late these handicraftsmen, for the sake of whose works the whole world has been ceaselessly pouring its bullion for 3000 years into India, and who, for all the marvellous tissues and embroideries they have wrought, have polluted no rivers, deformed no pleasing prospects, nor poisoned any air; whose skill and individuality the training of countless generations has developed to the highest perfection, these hereditary handicraftsmen are being everywhere gathered from their democratic village communities in hundreds and thousands to the colossal mills of Bombay, to drudge in gangs at manufacturing piece goods, in competition with Manchester, in the production of which they are no more intellectually and morally concerned than the grinder of a barrel organ in the tunes it turns out. (Birdwood, 1880: 58–9)[8]

Beautiful though this word picture Birdwood paints, it is highly implausible that members of different occupational castes would gather together in this way to 'feast' every evening. Indeed, the passage recalls Said's (1978) point that the orient is not a place, it is an idea which stems from the concerns of the person describing it. Birdwood's representation 'operates as representations usually do, for a purpose, according to a tendency, in a specific historical, intellectual, and even economic setting' (1978: 273). His concerns about the displacing, dehumanising aspects of industrialisation here find vent in an excessive romanticisation of village India.

In India, the term 'craft' acquired new layers of meaning, stemming both from the colonial encounter and from older ideas about work, ritual and the nature of objects (see C A Bayly, 1986). Embroiled in debates about the existence or not of fine art traditions in India, it also quickly became a contested site (Guha-Thakurta, 1992; Mitter, 1994). These debates and, indeed, the ideology of craft, remained the province of elites, both British and Indian.

While Birdwood claimed that India did not have a fine art tradition and was concerned with preserving the industrial arts or crafts, Havell and, more particularly, Coomaraswamy laid stress on the central role of the Indian craft producer in the socio-religious order. In his influential book, *The Indian craftsman* (1909), Coomaraswamy characterised craft as a 'sacred mystery, a sacrament [rather] than a secular trade' (ibid.: 72–3). He located the craft producer at the centre of a complex social and religious

[8] The general appreciation for Birdwood's work can be seen from Sir George Watt's decision in his catalogue of the Delhi Exhibition of 1902–3, to merely give brief descriptive accounts of objects even though this would mean the neglect of the 'beauty and poetry that appertains to the art crafts [of India] as...in Sir George Birdwood's *Industrial art of India* the student already possesses a work that so completely meets that feature as to render it undesirable that the ground should be traversed a second time' (1904: vii–viii).

order. Using several Hindu and Buddhist texts, temple and court inscriptions, grants, charters and stories from different periods and drawn from all over the subcontinent including Sri Lanka, he built up an essentialised picture of the craft producer in an idealised Hindu order. Coomaraswamy's Indian craftsman upholds the order of things with little concern for financial gain, 'the wage asked by the traditional craftsman in *unspoilt districts* today represents no more than a bare living for self and family' (ibid.: 92, my emphasis). His work was a 'calling', something greater than himself. Like Birdwood, Coomaraswamy too lamented the gradual erosion of Indian crafts and ways of life, often laying the blame not only on the colonial state and its policies but also on the urban upper and middle classes who actively 'aped' modern fashions and lifestyles—buying foreign cloth and having it made up in westernised styles, using Western-style furniture and ornaments in their homes (1905).

We can make a connection between the increasing influence of the ideals of the Arts and Crafts Movement and the increasing purchase of nationalist ideals in the late-nineteenth and early-twentieth century. In this period, Goswami argues that in Latin America, East Asia, South Asia and Europe, nationalism became not only 'one of the most legitimate articulations of collective identity...but also one of the most pervasive and entrenched forms of modern particularism' (2004: 15). Nationalist discourses, she shows, worked in and through their similarity with, and difference from, other nation-states and nations (ibid.).

One of the key arenas where emergent Indian nationalism asserted its particularity and difference from others was that of material production using pre- or non-industrial technologies, or in modern parlance, 'craft'. Art and, subsumed within it, craft became 'an ideal agent to bind the fissiparous languages and cultures of India' (Mitter, 1994: 223). Thus, in 1912 E B Havell published a series of letters in *The Hindu*, an English language newspaper published in Madras, arguing that art and national identity were crucially intertwined.[9] For him, 'an art which is truly great strikes

[9] Ernst Binfield Havell (1864–1937) was Superintendent of the Madras School of Arts in 1884 and later moved to the Calcutta School of Art where he was a close associate of Abanindranath Tagore and

down deep into national life and permeates the whole national character.' India's development lay not in slavishly industrialising but in being sensitive to its artistic and manufacturing traditions and in working with its hundreds of thousands of craft producers (1986 (1912): 5; 9). Similar arguments continue to hold sway today, at least in certain quarters.[10]

The tension between industrialisation and Indianness, and especially Gandhi's coupling of industrialisation with colonialism and the rejection of both, saw powerful movements promoting Indian hand manufactures and village industries to stem and replace the growing distribution of foreign made products in India. Handspun and woven cloth, *khadi*, became one of the most important components of the nationalist movement (Cohn, 1996: 147). *Khadi* and village industries became material symbols of a movement which not only felt that the Indian nation could and should be allowed to stand on its own, but which also sought to embrace a responsible and ethical consumption that eschewed showiness in favour of simplicity and self-sufficiency.[11] Important in this context are the attribution of a national identity to Indian craft, the identification of artisans as representatives of fading 'traditional Indian values',

---

supported the Bengal School. Guha-Thakurta divides his career into two separate phases: the art teacher and the scholar-aesthete. In the former phase, his main concern was with the revival and support of crafts and decorative arts and he argued forcefully for the establishment of cooperative credit societies for weavers so that they could increase production through mechanisation. In the latter phase, as a 'scholar and aesthete', he became more concerned with a spiritual approach to Indian art (Guha-Thakurta, 1992: 149–59).

[10] I am not unsympathetic to this viewpoint but believe that the ways in which it has been sought to be applied need analysis.

[11] There is a large and diverse literature on the importance of khadi and other textiles, village industries and crafts for the nation. See for instance, C A Bayly (1986); Channa (1975); Chattopadhyay (1980); Cohn (1996); Fisher (1972); Greenough (1995); Guha-Thakurta (1992); Mitter (1994); Misra (1993); Liebl and Roy (2004); Roy (1993, 1996); Sethi (1989); SRUTI (1995); Sundar (1995); Wilkinson-Weber (1999).

and the powerful ideas of crisis in Indian manufactures under the twin processes of colonial rule and industrialisation.[12]

In a manner that recalls Greenhalgh's analysis of the expanding constituency of craft in Britain, over time and as a result of the conceptual oppositions between industrial and non-industrial manufacture, and fine art and decorative art, other hand manufactures, including luxury weaves, certain kinds of jewellery manufactures, sculpture and traditional painting, also came to be incorporated into the category of craft. Since independence in 1947, the constituency of the term craft has continued to expand and now includes many different kinds of manufacture from all over the country.

Knowing Craft

While, on the one hand, the crisis in Indian manufacturing was attributed to colonial policies, colonial ways of knowing were crucial in gaining a picture of Indian crafts or industrial arts (as they were then known) in the nineteenth and twentieth centuries. We have already seen, in the Introduction, the importance of the Delhi Exhibition for Pattamadai mats and other 'art crafts', for instance. Census knowledge was useful, whether for legislative, judicial and executive purposes in India or to address 'scientific' concerns of European scholars with regard to questions about race, primitive customs, archaic industries, etc.[13] In many ways, the censuses of

[12] However, see Bean (1999) who suggests that not all craft were affected adversely by colonial rule. Clay sculpture in Krishnanagar, she argues, flourished in the period of colonial rule and continues to do so [although she is not so sanguine about the condition of the craft producers today]. She suggests that, conditioned to think about decline in the arts and crafts of India arising from colonialism, we are perhaps unwilling or unable to see instances that contradict this trope (ibid.: 99). It will be recalled that Pattamadai mats first came into prominence when a mat was awarded a bronze medal at the Delhi Exhibition of 1903–4.

[13] See for instance, *Man*, 1901, wherein an extract is published from the Proceedings of the Government of India in the Home Department (Public) on the uses and logistics of an ethnographic survey of India

independent India carried on the concerns of earlier censuses, especially with regard to collecting information that could be put to use by governments. Indeed, colonial censuses and gazetteers continue to be used as important sources of knowledge.

Following independence in 1947, the census of India turned its attention to the developmental needs of the nation and embarked upon 'studies in such vital and important fields as ethnography of Scheduled Castes and Scheduled Tribes, traditional crafts, fairs and festivals besides the socio-economic surveys of about five hundred villages all over the country' (Padmanabha, 1978). The handicraft surveys aimed to document craft traditions in order to foster economic and social development.

> ...Household industry should be separately investigated for a proper accounting of the nation's manpower resources and its specific contribution to the national income...However, an enumeration of the total number of establishments and their industrial classification would be incomplete without a proper description of what they produce and how they produce...It was important...to make an assessment of the limits of flexibility that traditional skill is capable of because *the transformation of traditional skills may well reveal that it is perhaps cheaper from the social point of view to develop industrial skills from scratch than to try to graft traditional skills on to alien soil*...The primary aim was to obtain a picture of the artisan himself and of his craft in his social and economic setting, the extent to which tradition bound him and the winds of change ruffled him...*how far he was able to pierce his own caste-tribe socio-economic cocoon and make a break through to new opportunities* promised by the Five Year Plans. The aim was to hold up a mirror to hereditary skills struggling with the dialectics of tradition and change. (Nambiar, 1964: Foreword; emphasis mine.)

The broad aims of the project, therefore, were to assess how static were the skills of 'traditional' artisans and how best to serve national socio-economic goals, including that of industrialisation. The project thus conformed to the ideals of the 'modernisation

---

(Simla, May 23, 1901). The link between census enumeration and description, and the ethnographic project is also an important one (Risley, 1891a and b).

theory' of development in that 'tradition' was seen as an obstacle to progress and 'break-through'. However, it also confirmed the importance of craft to the nation-building project. It encapsulated the dilemmas of the newly formed nation state: small-scale hand manufacture versus industrialisation, tradition versus modernity, and the place of the past in the future.

The census monograph entitled *Fine mats of Pattamadai* (1964), which came out of this project and forms part of the 'Handicrafts and Artisans of Madras State' series, furnishes us with a comprehensive account of the mat weaving industry from the 1960s. It continued the traditions of earlier censuses by focusing on caste and occupational groups and on detailed descriptions of production processes. Though field research was undertaken, the publication draws heavily on the 1917 *Gazetteer of the Tinnevelly district* written by H R Pate, Collector of the Tirunelveli district within which administrative region Pattamadai was then located. It thus reiterates earlier modes of thinking about craft production and craft producers.

Handicrafts, then, have been long important in the nation-building project. And indeed, 'one of the earliest acts of the new government in India was to set up a national board for identifying and development [sic.] of crafts' (Chattopadhyay, 1980: 56). It was as head of this organisation, the All India Handicrafts Board set up in 1952, that Chattopadhyay visited Pattamadai in 1953. The importance of craft to the nation is emphasised over and over again in policy documents. Thus, 'Handicrafts are not only a part of the country's rich cultural heritage but have also been a unifying factor in the national life' (Eighth Five Year Plan, 1992–7, quoted in Greenough, 1995: 241).

Now, six decades after independence and faced with a raft of new problems, including fears about globalisation, separatism, growing inequalities and loss of identity, the revival and support of craft continue to be important in contemporary India, embraced by both the state and the public sphere. Identified in opposition to industrialised, faceless, mass-produced manufactures, support for craft producers and objects, it is believed, can halt the relentless spread of capitalism and new forms of imperialism. At the very least, 'ancient India' and 'modern India' can march hand-in-hand into the future. The state-of-the-art mobile phone can be carried in a hand-made embroidered, mirrored case sourced from a 'traditional Indian producer group'—one often described in need of support and development to continue to exist with dignity in the contemporary world.

But craft does not merely allow the reconnection of the past and the present, it is also conceptualised as building bridges between disparate sections of society—rich and poor, low and high caste, Hindu and Muslim. As the objects move from one group to the other, fulfilling desires and, in some cases, enabling the successful performance of rituals, Chattopadhyay suggests that 'The craftsman...combines within his being the tradition that embraces both the producer and the consumer within the social fabric' (1995: 2).

Both within India through the medium of institutions such as the Crafts Museum, craft *melas* (fairs), bazaars and festivals such as *Apna Utsav*, and overseas, especially through the Festivals of India,[14] the Nehruvian ideal of 'unity in diversity' is reinforced and celebrated.[15] This has sometimes tended to mean, as Durrans points

[14] Pupul Jayakar (1915–97), popularly known as the 'czarina of Indian culture', started her public career as secretary of the Indian Planning Commission chaired by the then prime minister, Jawaharlal Nehru. She followed Chattopadhyay as chairman of the Handicrafts Board (1974–7) and was also chairman of the Handicrafts and Handloom Export Corporation. In 1982 she took up the post of vice-president of the Indian Council of Cultural Relations and organised the Festivals of India: *The Festival of India*, Britain 1981, USA 1985; *Shilpakar: Continuing Traditions of Indian Craftsmen*, USSR, 1986–7; *Indian Craftsmen*, Sweden, 1987; *The Tribal Arts of India*, Japan, 1988; *Indien Festspiele*, Germany, 1992. Jayakar also wrote extensively about craft.

[15] Singh discusses the emphasis on arts and crafts laid by the first prime minister of independent India, Jawaharlal Nehru, as India's cultural ambassadors through the analysis of correspondence between ministers and bureaucrats regarding the organisation of a parade to mark the third year (1953) of India's becoming a republic: 'I should also like that procession to contain some more civilian element...more especially representatives of arts and crafts. Indeed some of our tableaux may

out, 'No potter can be allowed to fashion a pot, but that his soul, a fragment of India's own, flows through his hands.'

Pragmatism and Romanticism: 'Developing Craft'

Romanticisation of craft is harnessed to a pragmatic core: craft forms an important part of the economic landscape. There are over 20 million artisans in India; they are generally poor, live in rural India, and are marginalised by their low social status and their poverty. Their importance to the idea of the nation cannot be overestimated. Neither can the economic benefits of the work they do. According to the Ministry of Textiles, under whose aegis the offices of both the Development Commissioners of Handicrafts and Handlooms function, the handloom and handicrafts sectors are the second largest employers in rural India.[16] The high demand for Indian craft objects and other kinds of items made using craft technologies, including cloth,[17] mean that the sector is a significant source of foreign exchange.

Furthermore, support for crafts is not only perceived by planners, politicians and bureaucrats as advantageous in larger economic terms, it is also seen to fulfil social and developmental goals. Commercial handicraft production is encouraged among non-

---

represent the arts and crafts of India' (Nehru, 09/09/1952, quoted in Singh, 1998: 97).

16 Publicity material, 2000; also see the editorial on crafts in the *Economic and Political Weekly*, 2006, Vol. 41, No. 37, 16/09/2006. However, as Greenough points out, the number of artisans is greatly influenced by the definition of artisans used. According to the Planning Commission, in 1991–2, there were 26.4 million workers employed in the 'traditional' industries, i.e. khadi cloth weaving, handloom weaving, village industries like grain husking. The Indian census, however, includes artisans within the category of household worker and counts only the workers whose principal income derives from the home-based production of handcrafted products. This is a problematic assumption and does not in any way approach the numbers of persons employed in the sector. The 1991 census estimated the number of handicrafts workers at 10.4 million (Greenough, 1995: 244).

17 See, for example, Swallow, 1982; Neve, 2002.

artisanal groups (especially minorities, lower castes and women) as part of employment generation and social welfare schemes.[18] Craft production with its imputed advantages of low capital requirements, simple technology, relatively little need for training, and domestic production is seen as allowing 'the large-scale involvement of women, weaker sections and minorities' (*Report of the Task Force on Handicrafts for the VIII Five Year Plan*, Government of India, 1989: 5). There is also a belief that supporting rural craft can stem the ever-growing tide of migration from rural to urban India.[19]

Development is an enormously powerful set of ideas, which has guided thought and action across the world over the second part of the twentieth century. As well as being a series of interlinked concepts and ideals, it is also a set of practices and relationships (Gardner and Lewis, 1996: 2). Development projects are designed in terms of a number of conventional rationalities. These rationalities are performative—they define goals, fields and mechanisms of project activities and are of two different but mutually dependent kinds. Project goals refer to implicit values, which are to be achieved through the specific objectives of the project (Craig and Porter, 1997: 52). Organisational structures can be explained both by the nature of the tasks they undertake and by their ideological underpinnings (Curtis, 1991: 11).

The ideological grounds on which craft development organisations are based are well established and recognised in India. These organisations draw on the established stock of discourses,[20] images

[18] Thus, as mentioned in the introduction, members of the Warli 'tribe' in western India were encouraged to translate their ritual wall paintings onto paper and to sell these paintings in craft bazaars and other venues (Venkatesan, 1994). Also see Rajasekhar, 2002.

[19] However, see Solanki (2002) for a critical analysis of this belief based on his study of artisans in two districts in north India.

[20] Foucault uses the term 'discourse' to refer to a group of statements linked to a 'referential', itself consisting of 'laws of possibility, rules of existence for the objects that are named, designated or described within it, and for the relations that are affirmed or denied in it' (cited in Grillo, 1997: 12). Discourse includes both language and what is represented through language. A developmental discourse of craft

and ideas about crafts and craft production. They are paradigmatically similar both in their conception of the position of crafts in India in the past (i.e. before colonial rule) and their vision for crafts in the future.[21] The ways in which producers, development agents, the state, and interested others, engage with, seek to shape and negotiate through the category of craft and through craft objects is an important focus of this book. The study recognises that development forms an important organising paradigm for groups such as the weavers of Pattamadai and other artisans. It asks what development does and how and why people—both development agents and objects of development—want to engage with it, and why craft producers accept, even actively seek out, development agents and their schemes.

Development opens up new avenues. It facilitates contacts with elites which, however circumscribed, are nevertheless valuable. It also distinguishes craft producers from the faceless millions whose names (individual or collective) never make it into the national, regional or local media. It brings in money and opportunities. All these, however, are predicated on a certain level of cooperation with the development mechanism, which has its own aesthetics, its own histories, commitments and justifications. The embodied skill of the artisan is harnessed to the powerful discourses of craft and development—both work together to produce objects (and persons) that comply with the dominant craft aesthetic and which will sell.

Greenough's paper on the National Crafts Museum in Delhi, where selected producers are invited to stay for a month and demonstrate their skills as well as sell their wares, makes the point about the making of the craft producer clearly:

---

identifies appropriate and legitimate ways of speaking and thinking about craft. This in turn, I suggest, affects development practice.

21 See, for instance, the publicity brochures of organisations working with craft development, e.g. the Crafts Council of India, Dastkar, Craft Enterprises, Government of India, Office of the Development Commissioner (Handicrafts); also see Bundgaard (1999) for an analysis of similar issues. Actual working practices, and the specific discourses from the available set that each organisation chooses to emphasise, vary.

> The artisans spoken of here [i.e. in the paper] are the *official* artisans...at least a dozen men could be found daily preparing beams and poles for the new buildings, laying brick, spreading plaster and paint...These were recognisably workmen because of their soiled clothes, their indifference to visitors, their freedom to address each other loudly and to move around the site, whereas the invited craftsmen sat in clean clothes at assigned spaces, producing steadily while conversing with visitors. Next to each official artisan was a neatly lettered sign not unlike those placed before animals in a zoo, stating the artisan's name, medium, village, district and state.[22] Clearly, the crafts museum has the authority to define which artisans are worthy of attention... (Greenough, 1995: 246)

Many artisans I know are keen to have their names included in the museum's list of craft producers and to be invited to the museum to sell their wares. An artisan whose objects do not sell has little incentive to continue producing them. A large part of craft development on the ground involves intervention in selected groups identified as craft communities and the manipulation of the forms of artisanal products in order to make them more desirable to contemporary urban audiences. These objects, when identified as examples of craft, are crucial mediators in relationships between artisans and influential others. It is their existence that makes a person or group 'craft producers'—craft objects are thus both valued items and sources of value; they may also be described as having a kind of agency or the ability to make changes in the causal milieu (following Gell, 1998).

Many craft objects have been reinvented in response to urban Indian and non-Indian consumption needs. An advertisement for a sale of embroidered clothing describes the wares as 'Ethnic. Trendy. Medieval. Modern' and invites buyers to 'wear an irony now' (Banascraft poster, 2005). Craft bazaars teem with buyers. Several try and bargain with the artisans who have come to sell their wares. For artisans, invitations to these bazaars, usually organised by non-governmental organisations or by the state, are

[22] This seems like an overstated analogy made with an eye to maximum polemic impact; comparison with exhibits in a museum might be more appropriate.

important sources of revenue and exposure. In Pattamadai, where a mat can take up to a month to weave and its sale is crucial for household subsistence, urban designers and developers are crucial for the survival of the industry. Invitations to craft bazaars are keenly sought after. Bargaining is usually prohibited but that does not prevent people from trying to cut prices on the grounds that sellers and/or development agents inflate them. No one wants to be cheated, and the perception that this is likely when one is buying at such venues is rife. On the other end of the scale, some organisers of bazaars too suspect artisans of under-representing their sales and over-representing their expenses. Here the seller, who is also a producer, is identified as 'crafty'. This, as Herzfeld (2004) points out, is not a positive identification.

Craft producers, as much as the things they fashion, are objects of development. The prevailing assumption is that craft producers need the kind of help that can only come from the outside; they can better themselves but only with help from others. They are skilled but not knowledgeable. The few dissenting voices within the development circuit are influential (e.g. Tyabji, 2003),[23] but there are many more who favour an instructional approach. Governmental policies and schemes continue to emphasise the helplessness and lack of knowledge of craft producers and the need for 'designers' and others to intervene and help. Politicians, bureaucrats, museum staff, academics, civil society organisations and other authoritative figures join makers and traders to form what, following Becker (1982), I will call the 'craft worlds'. The various individuals and institutions that make up the craft worlds do not necessarily work together, though their paths, intentions and methods do occasionally coincide. I will discuss the workings of the craft worlds in some detail later. For the moment, suffice it to say that different members of the craft worlds wield power in ways that reflect their standing in wider Indian society. Usually poor, living in rural India and marginalised in more ways than one, producers have little influence over the ways in which they are described. The paradox here is that

[23] Some of Tyabji's articulate and passionate writings on craft are listed in the Bibliography.

while craft is important and patronised by the rich and powerful, craft producers are neither rich nor important. This is a paradox that producers have to live and engage with in all their interactions in the public sphere, especially if they wish to benefit from craft development programmes.

Imaging Craft Objects and their Producers

Lisa Bakewell (1998) makes a powerful case for extending the idea that words do things (Austin, 1962) to images as well. She includes within the category of image 'all kinds of *humanmade* images:...from body gestures to great works of art and everything in between' (Bakewell, 1998: 22). Images, she writes, rather than being descriptive representers of reality, can be more accurately categorised as actions: they do things or cause people to act in certain ways. Thus, one can write not only of 'speech acts' but also of 'image acts' (ibid.). Pictures of large-eyed, starving children spark a reaching into wallets to support the charities that say they can help with our help. Pictures and words also act on each other. Verbal and visual descriptions of craft producers and craft contexts, I suggest, can best be seen as composite images that communicate a picture of how craft production and craft items are, or at least ought to be.

> The craftsman is not an individual expressing individual whims, but a part of the universe, giving expression to ideals of eternal beauty and unchanging laws, even as do the trees and flowers whose natural and less ordered beauty is no less God-given. (Coomaraswamy, 1909: 75)[24]

> It is not easy to trace the origin of Pattamadai silk mats, *a real work of aesthetics rather than the vision of the mat-weaver*. (Syed Muthahar, 'University bid to revive dying skill', *The Hindu*, 23/11/1995; emphasis mine.)

> In the metamorphosis of the green korai growing wild on the banks of the Tamaraparani, into the wonder that is the Pattamadai mat lies the genius of the *paramparic* [traditional] Indian craftsman.

[24] This quote continues to be commonly cited by governmental, developmental and other publications on craft, for example, *National awards for master craftspersons and weavers*, Government of India, 1999; Chari, 'Weaving craft into dance', *The Hindu*, 15/02/1998.

> His conceptual harmony which so effortlessly weaves function and aesthetics together into objects of superb craftsmanship, his empathy with the moods and rhythms of nature, from which much of his work is crafted, as well as total dedication to his calling spells the very essence of India's craft heritage, be it the minakari and jadau jewellery of Jaipur, the namdahs and carpets of Kashmir, the shola pith craft of Bengal or the stone carving of Karnataka. Or the serene allure and brilliant workmanship of the fine Pattamadai mat. (Chari, 'The wonder of the Pattamadai mat', *The Hindu*, 25/02/1996: 15).

> The function of art and craft in providing a livelihood, even today in India, is often surpassed by its more important function on major ritual events such as birth, initiation, marriage, [and] death as well as annual and seasonal festivals. Here, both the craftsman and his craft serve as important ritual contributors in the ceremonies. On all these occasions an assortment of textiles and garments, vessels and utensils, toys, games, props and furniture is used. What is noteworthy, however, is that the same object used for mundane purposes attains a ritual value, a sacrosanctity, which then elevates the craft, and consequently its maker, to the realm of the sacred. These are therefore not items of 'craft' made for the sole purpose of marketing; in reality, they form an integral part of the socio-religious order of traditional and contemporary tribal and village India. (National Crafts Museum brochure, cited in Greenough, 1995: 225)

The word craft may be seen as a multi-layered image made up of words and visuals.[25] The image builds on and evokes nostalgic longing for a gentler past, rural idylls and work that satisfies the soul. It offers a palliative to the losses incurred by modern life: people wrenched from age-old ways of life by a world that moves too quickly and harshly for them; a nation that, having shaken off foreign shackles, is in danger of losing itself in eagerly chasing after a mirage called 'progress through modernisation'; and, the erosion

[25] I use the term 'word images' to refer to the ways in which crafts and production contexts have been described in India since the end of the nineteenth century. These paint a vivid picture. A good example is the quote from Birdwood cited above. Word images will later be discussed in more detail.

of traditional skills that are undervalued and irreplaceable. It offers an outlet for the urgent need to do something to make the world a better and more beautiful place.

Bakewell (1998) writes about the word 'mother' in Mexico: 'Madre, a word. A world. An object that turns into action when it rolls off a tongue.'[26] Craft too is a powerful word, and English is the language of craft in India. In India, even those who do not speak English rarely seek to translate it into the languages that they do speak. Rather, the word carries with it not only its own particular transnational history and with it the echoes of a desired world, but also the whiff of power that the use of English still contains in India. This makes utterances about craft fall into certain patterns, especially if, as in Tamil, there is no clearly equivalent word. In Pattamadai, weavers and traders use the English word in specific contexts, including at craft bazaars or in newspaper interviews. They rarely use the word among themselves, or after the first few weeks to me.

It is mainly in English language newspapers, magazines and reports that certain kinds of artisanal work become reified and represented as traditionally Indian. The literature on craft and craft production in India is aimed at a large and diverse audience. This is reflected in the number and range of publications on the subject. Craft is a regular feature in the columns of newspapers like *The Hindu*, a Madras-based broadsheet in English. This newspaper even dedicated an issue of its Sunday magazine to the subject ('Craft' in *Folio,* 21 March, 1999). There is also a niche for craft and craft products in the glossy publications genre ('coffee-table books'). These combine glossy colour photographs with brief descriptive accounts of the context of production. The number of reports, surveys and studies on the economics of craft production, preservation and regeneration reflects the economic significance of craft production in contemporary India. The majority of reports are published or commissioned by relevant government agencies, though publications

[26] Bakewell, 2005. Excerpt from MS *Madre: Travels with a Spanish N(o)un*. http://www.wordswithoutborders.org/article.php?lab=quepadre, accessed October 2006.

non-governmental organisations and research bodies are also important. There is also a large unpublished literature, which includes reports and internal documents of governmental and non-governmental agencies. In addition to ethnographic research among the mat weavers of Pattamadai and among development agents, this study also examines published and unpublished materials in different media—development reports, newspaper and magazine articles, sale posters and advertisements, websites and governmental publications—to explore how the category of craft has been described into being and is reinforced and contested.

Description is a creative process and the objects of description are transformed in the act of representation. People have to be made into 'craft producers'. As this is dependent on the recognition of their manufactures as craft, objects have to be *made* into craft objects. In public speech, written acts and visual images, Pattamadai mats are grouped with other 'craft' items. This affects the ways in which they are described, and what is expected of them and their makers. These descriptions lead to particular kinds of relationships and collaborations; it spawns discussions about authenticity, creativity and ownership that both seek to shape the forms the objects under question take, and the ways in which they are received within, and beyond, the Indian nation. Furthermore, as the descriptions of these objects and the people are continually generated in different media, they are creative, multi-layered and mutually reinforcing. To seek a true meaning of the objects or to try and recover 'original or true contexts' is to deny the power of these many descriptions. It is to assume, falsely, that craft production and descriptions about craft inhabit separate spheres and that it is possible to understand the former without reference to the latter. I suggest, however, that craft producers do indeed have little choice but to engage with descriptions about them, if they want to access the craft development apparatus and the visibility, money and markets it brings to them. Descriptions of craft, ideologically loaded as they are and reflecting unequal relations of power, often highlight some features while masking others. They reify selected aspects while rendering others irrelevant, even wrong. Engaging with craft development and with the images of craft serves to simultaneously enhance and constrain the agency of not only producers but also development agents.

Dancing with Images

Visual images of Indian craft objects and craft producers abound in various media.[27] Posters and articles in newspapers advertising craft sales show intricate objects. They also show producers—dressed in traditional clothing, smiling at the camera or engaged in making objects. Pleas for support for craft often have haunting pictures of dignified solemn-faced artisans accompanied by texts that discuss their pitiful helpless plight. These kinds of picture conjure up a series of economically and politically loaded images of craft producers in contemporary India. Verbal and textual descriptions of craft producers and their work also do the same by rarely deviating from dominant modes of representation, especially in the popular media, but also in the development literature. Both subjectified and objectified, artisans and their work appear in the following ways:

- the craft producer is a natural being: not dissimilar to trees and leaves; his creativity is located in the mists of time and in the ephemeral yet strangely powerful world of traditional aesthetics; the craft producer is a vessel of authenticity rather than an author of his own strategies of production;
- craft is a national resource;
- craft production symbolises village life and the simple technologies of simple people who are the innocent victims of colonial rule, industrialisation, and the modern world;
- the isolated, anachronistic, tradition-bound rural craft producer, unable to adapt yet needing to in order to better serve himself and the nation;
- craft—an economic and political problem;
- The craft producer who, uneducated, unthinking and/or helpless, wishes to stop working at his rightful occupation

[27] A quick search in Google images for Indian craft in March 2007, for instance, shows hundreds.

and turn to other work;
- The 'crafty' artisan who seeks to make an unacceptable profit from his work;
- the craft object materialises the collective heritage of the nation and is a means of uniting all Indian people;
- the craft object embodies relations between the past and the present, between socially and physically distant people, and between disparate social groups.

Most people believe they know what traditional craft is and believe they can recognise it, and values associated with it, anywhere in the world.[28] For artisans and for those who sell their work, craft becomes more than a way of producing objects, means of self-expression, livelihood or application of skilled knowledge; it becomes a dance with images. But the images do not all segue together, or in harmony. It takes a skilled dancer to make them work.

Cut off from the personal, often contradictory, experiences of people who work in craft, these images seem, like the fetished commodity, to have a life of their own. Whether on the part of people who feel moved to develop crafts and/or consume craft objects, or on the part of artisans who want to work in craft production and/or engage with craft development, these images produce particular kinds of actions. The images are not, however, discrete. Rather they coexist in the same time spaces. They do not always make harmonious juxtapositions, often creating contradictions and paradoxes which pervade dealings between craft producers and others. The images about craft and craft production are best described in Mabro's (1996) evocative phrase as 'veiled half-truths'. I suggest that this is widely recognised, if not directly acknowledged. I aver that hardly any one innocently accepts these images as true or buys into them wholesale. Artisans, traders, the state, development

[28] 'Crafts: handskills, works of art, symbols of tradition, the cultural ethos of a place, community, expressions of the interconnectedness between humankind in a culture specific paradigm and the related environment, thick mythology and visions of the earth' was one woman's response to a question on what was craft. Questionnaire placed in different craft outlets, Madras, 2000.

agents, buyers and other members of the craft worlds play with them and utilise them for the purposes of strategic production. This is an important point.

The diverse images—verbal and visual—that make up the term 'craft' participate in what Herzfeld (2004) has powerfully termed a global hierarchy of value. Like Goswami (2004), Herzfeld is interested in the relationship between the universal and the particular. His focus, however, is on the ways in which certain ways of doing things and thinking about the world come to be seen as natural and commonsensical so that even 'diversity can become a homogenous product. So, too, can tradition and heritage: the particular itself is universalized' (2004: 2). The ways in which 'craft' is seen: the peculiar combination of the 'pedestal and the tethering post' (ibid.), which both idealise the craft producer and shackle him, that Herzfeld describes in Crete, is resonant with the Indian context.

The next chapter relocates our gaze to Pattamadai—a small Tamil town in south India where Muslim weavers make the famous silk-like mats on simple handlooms.

2 People, Place, Life

Pattamadai town is located in Tirunelveli Kattabomman district, one of the southern-most districts of Tamilnadu state in south India. In 1991, its total population was 12,993 with 6,275 males and 6,718 females.[1] Although described as a 'sleepy hamlet' in some descriptions at craft sales and in newspaper articles, it is classified as a town.[2] In 1995, agriculture was the main occupation in the town. Other occupations include cow herding, carpentry, petty trade and services, and mat weaving. [3]

[1] 'Total population and population of Scheduled Castes and Scheduled Tribes in Town Panchayats, Municipalities and Municipal Corporations in Tamil Nadu', *1991 Census*, Directorate of Census Operations, Tamilnadu, Madras, 1995.

[2] Pattamadai is classified as a Class IV town. These have a population of between 10,000 and 19,999 persons. Class I towns have a population of 1,00,000 and above, while Class VI towns (the smallest) have a population of below 5,000. As a Class IV town, the form of local government in Pattamadai is a town panchayat with elected members.

[3] Pattamadai Town Panchayat Report, 1995, unpublished.

Around 40 per cent of Pattamadai's population is Muslim. Of these, the Rauther Muslim group is the larger, representing around 35 per cent of the total population. The Labbai group numbers around 650 persons. It is primarily Labbais who weave the famous fine and superfine mats of Pattamadai, though some Rauthers are also engaged in this work. The Labbai sub-group of Tamil Muslims will be discussed in some detail later.

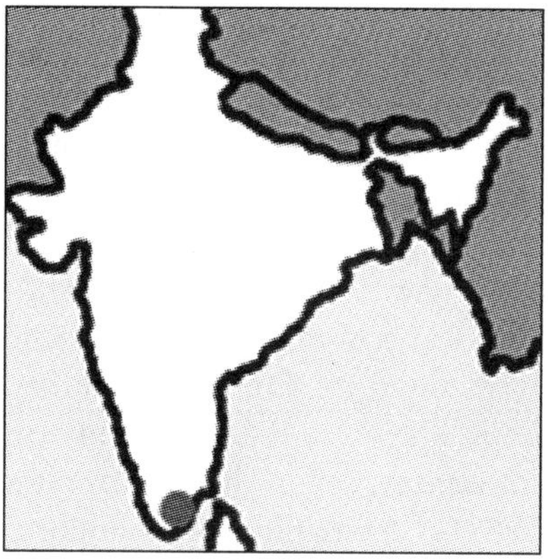

Map showing where Pattamadai is in India,
the approximate location indicated by the large dot.

The nearest large railway station—Tirunelveli junction—is around 25 kilometres to the north-west and easily accessible by bus or taxi. A state highway connecting Tirunelveli to towns further south runs past Pattamadai. Tirunelveli junction is an important nodal point connecting the town and surrounding areas not only to the state capital Madras and other Tamil cities, but also to other parts of the country.

The Tirunelveli region has a long and complex history and has been the focus of significant scholarly activity. Prehistoric remains found here, dating from the fourth millennium BC, are archaeologically important (Ludden, 1989). Tirunelveli town was an important seat of Brahmanical culture which, as in other Tamil wet land agrarian areas, had its roots in the medieval period in the spiritual legitimisation of kingship and land ownership by ritually powerful Brahmins (ibid.). As one-time capital and important centre of the Pandya dynasty (800 to 1300 AD), the region abounds in inscriptions providing evidence relating to kingship and the use of temples as institutional means of gaining and maintaining power. Between the tenth and fifteenth centuries, the Nellaiappar temple in Tirunelveli town, for instance, was the centre of a transactional web that covered much of the southern Pandya country (ibid.: 43).[4]

As a result of its long history, relative stability, and its location in the fertile Tamaraparni river valley at the confluence of major trade routes, the Tirunelveli region displays remarkable demographic diversity. Arab traders visited the Coromandel coast and settled there from the eight century. After this, Muslim communities were established initially on the coast, later spreading inland through inter-marriage and conversion (S Bayly, 1989; Fanselow, 1989). Thirteenth-century migrations from the Central Asian steppes into north India triggered waves of migratory movement southwards into peninsula India from about the fourteenth century. These included Muslim horse troops, known as Rauthers, and artisans, particularly cloth weavers, who were crucial in the lucrative international textile trade (Ludden, 1989). Christianity too is important in the region and Palayamkottai near Pattamadai is well known for its many churches and church-related educational institutions.

Although the system of Brahmanical land control persisted, new settlements were formed and there was marked urbanisation from the fifteenth to the eighteenth centuries. European trading companies came to the region in the late-sixteenth century, and by the eighteenth century had trading settlements along the entire Coromandel coast. Mission and mercantile records form important sources about European expansion in South Asia (see S Bayly, 1989) and about the region and its inhabitants more generally. Today the region attracts many visitors—both on pleasure and business.[5] There is an important Siva temple in Papanasam and also large cloth mills. Kuttrallam town is famed for its waterfalls where many tourists refresh themselves in the heat of summer. Nagercoil is an important

[4] For a discussion about temples and their place in political activity, also see Stein (1978; 1996).

[5] See for instance, T S Subramaniam, 'Promise and potential', *Frontline*, volume 19, issue 19, September 14–27, 2002.

Tamil Christian centre. None of these is very far from Pattamadai, and indeed numerous vehicles traverse the highway that runs past the town. Few, however, halt here unless their occupants wish to buy mats or to visit the birthplace of Swami Sivananda, founder of the Divine Life Society, which has a world-wide following.[6]

Early Impressions

Between Tirunelveli and Pattamadai, beyond the densely clustered small towns and villages along the road, the countryside is characterised by paddy fields and banana, coconut and palm groves where there is water, and thorny scrub where there is little. In the background loom the hills of the Western Ghats. The water in this part of the country is provided by the Tamaraparani river. This is one of Tamilnadu's few perennial rivers and its water is a precious resource in this semi-arid land located in the rain shadow of the Western Ghats. I was here first during the short rainy season and everywhere there were pools of water, birds dipping and soaring, children playing in the shallows and groups of women washing clothes. Subsequent visits at other times of the year have revealed dry, dusty vistas, except in the vicinity of the river and the intricate system of canals it supports.

As one approaches Pattamadai, the Tirunelveli-Ambasamudram highway curves past two large ponds and a small Sufi grave shrine; pink and green houses loom up ('money from the Middle East', says a man) and the dome of the Pattamadai mosque comes into view. A long road (Bazaar Road) greets the eye as the vehicle turns into Pattamadai from the highway. Pattamadai is situated on a south-north axis. The Kanadiyan canal cuts across the northern part of the town and beyond it, a couple of kilometres or so away, numerous paths cut through the paddy fields and banana plantations to the Tamaraparani river.[7] Shops and a few houses of

[6] For an account of the life and teachings of Swami Sivananda, see *Sivananda: biography of a modern sage*, published by the Divine Life Society, Sivanandanagar, 1985. Pattamadai is referred to as a 'holy city' by the followers of the Swami.

[7] The Kanadiyan canal is part of a network of canals that were built after the thirteenth century (see Ludden, 1989: 53–54, 115). In

brick, concrete or mud and thatch construction line Bazaar Road. Frequent traffic of people, bicycles, bullock carts, cows and a few large vehicles, including town buses, means that there is usually dust on this road. Dust lands lightly on arms and clothes. The air is filled with its sharp tang, to which are added occasional food or rubbish smells. Music blares from the various tea-shops that are, more often than not, adorned with large posters of Tamil film stars. The temples compete with devotional music played on loudspeakers. The periodic call to prayer from the mosques adds its own punctuation. Pattamadai engages all the senses.

Early in the mornings, Bazaar Road is full of people heading north to work in the fields or to wash in the Kanadiyan canal. A little later, the office and college goers (many from the brahmin area in the northern part of town) head south to take buses into Tirunelveli town. At around the same time, streams of children, the younger ones often escorted by adults, head to the town's primary, middle or secondary schools. The Ramaseshier Higher Secondary School, located in the brahmin section of the town, is famous throughout the region and boasts many illustrious alumni, including bureaucrats occupying high positions in government; it is even mentioned in Pate's *Gazetteer of the Tinnevelly district* (1917: 365). Some Muslim men in the town also attended this school, though few Labbais went on to tertiary education or to finish their school leaving exams. As the day wears on, Bazaar Road, though never fully deserted, becomes somewhat somnolent—with a few people out on errands, and goats, pigs and dogs rummaging in bins and near the many tea stalls. It starts to get busy again around 4 pm when the glare of the sun has abated somewhat. It remains full of life until twilight, when the cows that have been pasturing elsewhere are herded back for milking by their herders. As darkness falls, few women are to be seen on Bazaar Road, though groups of men stand around talking. On occasion, late in the evening when I have walked by, coming back from a weavers' house or from one

---

Pattamadai, the canal is said to have been dug by a devout Brahmin, and its course to have been based on the perambulations of a sacrificial cow that was set free and followed by the Brahmin.

of the two places where I can make national or international phone calls, they have fallen silent and then resumed their conversations once I have passed. They are probably just surprised to see a woman alone out after dark.

The Kanadiyan canal cuts through the northern part of the town. People grouped according to caste and gender stand in its rushing waters, washing themselves and their clothes, chatting as they carry out their waterside chores. Upstream and close to their houses, early in the morning, some Brahmins wash themselves ritually in the waters of the canal. Before them, between 3 am and 5 am, groups of sexually mature Muslim girls of marriageable age go downstream to wash under cover of darkness. After marriage, they will be free to make the same trip in daylight. Throughout the day, the canal is a busy place as individuals and groups from all over Pattamadai use its waters for various purposes. For the mat weavers, the canal is important as they soak bundles of korai in its waters in preparation for weaving the sedge.

Spaces, Changes

Caste and religion are both important factors in the social and spatial organisation of Pattamadai. The town has mainly Hindu (over 55 per cent) and Muslim (around 40 per cent) populations, besides some Christian households. The president of the town panchayat in 1997, Khadeeja Beevi, a Muslim herself,[8] listed in a conversation with me over eighteen castes (Tamil: *jadhi*) that she said were represented in Pattamadai. I reproduce the information as she gave it to me:[9]

[8] The 1992 Panchayat Act provides for a system of reservation of seats for women and backward castes. The specific panchayats for which the presidency is so reserved changes every term (five years) on a rotating basis. During part of the fieldwork period (1997–2001), Pattamadai panchayat fell into the women's reserved group.

[9] Interview, December 1997. The words have been translated from Tamil. I have not placed the above in quotations marks as it was extracted from a larger discussion and some explanations have been omitted.

> Iyer and Iyengar (Brahmins); Illavar (who sell leafy vegetables, betel leaf, etc.); Pallar and Paraiyar (mainly agricultural labourers); Chakkiriyar (Adi-dravidar, scavengers and cleaners); Thevar (of whom she identified three subdivisions: Agumpadinar, Kallar, Siramaravar) and Pillaimar (two subdivisions: meat-eating and vegetarian)—both Thevars and Pillaimars are predominantly involved in agriculture); Kuyavar (potters); Reddimar (three subdivisions: Natukottai, Chettiar, Vannigai Chettiar); Nayakar (forest workers: firewood and honey-gathering); Koravar (gypsies), Pattariyar (cloth weavers: Saurashtra and Tamil); Achari (smiths: stonesmiths, blacksmiths, goldsmiths, carpenters); Vannar (washermen); tanners and leather workers; Konnar (milk producers) and Nadar (merchants). The numerically dominant caste in Pattamadai are the Pillaimars. Agricultural land is owned by the Pillaimars, Thevars, Rauther Muslims and the low-caste Paraiyars.[10]

Housing is segregated on the basis of caste or group affiliation, but the spatial divisions are gradually becoming less rigid. Thus, while people speak in terms of the Brahmin area or *gramam*,[11] the Thevar sections of town, the Pariayar and Pallar *cheris*, the potters' section and the weavers' streets, it is not only members of specific groups/castes that live in the sections identified with them. A Tamil Christian household lives in one of the two Brahmin streets as do some other non-Brahmin households, including Thevars, and Vannigar Chettis live in the weavers' streets. In part, this is due to migrations out of the town. For instance, the brahmins were once

[10] Censuses do not do caste-based enumeration, nor does the panchayat office maintain such records, and so I could not get actual numbers. Detailed discussions of relationships between the different castes are not relevant to my study of the mat weaving industry. There is, of course, a large and theoretically varied literature on caste in India (see for instance, Beteille, 1974; 1979; 1991; 1996; 1997; Dumont, 1980; Quigley, 1993; Srinivas, 1966; 1976). S Bayly (1999) and Fuller (1997), in particular, are useful for a general overview on the subject. Nicholas Dirks' excellent article in the volume edited by Fuller describes the politics of caste and race in Tamilnadu and highlights the difficulties of writing about so complex a subject (Dirks, 1997).

[11] Referred to by non-Brahmin Tamils as *gramam* and by Tamil Brahmins as *agraharam*

the largest landowners. Many have now either migrated to large Indian cities or abroad (primarily USA). Young Brahmin men leave either to study or to find white-collar jobs. Young women leave the town after their marriages. Older people leave to join their children, especially sons. Some return periodically, spending part of their time in Pattamadai. Most Brahmins have sold their lands to other castes; nevertheless they continue to be an important presence as will become clear in later discussions relating to patronage in the mat weaving industry.

Streets are still clearly visually marked by their associations with specific occupational castes or groups and religions. All the Hindu areas of Pattamadai have rice flour patterns (*kolam*) outside each house. These are renewed morning and evening by the women of the house or by their unmarried teenage daughters. The potters' area is identifiable by the elevated communal firing area which is piled up with brushwood; also visible are orderly rows of pots drying in the sun. Similarly, the weavers' streets have communal troughs for starching yarn.

Ten years ago, when coarse cloth weaving was still an almost viable occupation in Pattamadai, the front verandahs (*thinnai*) of most houses on the weavers' street were used for drying yarn, the grey skeins of undyed yarn making a pleasing contrast with the whitewashed walls and red tiled roofs of the houses. Also audible was the constant *clack clack* of shuttles traversing the width of the handlooms. The looms are now silent, a sole elderly man who is the president of the cloth weavers' cooperative society weaves towels on one of his two looms. The decline of coarse-cloth handloom weaving throughout India is reflected on the cloth weavers streets in Pattamadai.[12] Many young men of the weaving caste have left Pattamadai to work elsewhere as short- or long-term economic migrants, while the women and others work as agricultural labourers in the surrounding paddy fields.

[12] Analysts—academics, NGO activists and journalists—place the sharp decline of coarse-cloth weaving at the door of the government and the National Textile Policy of 1985 (discussed in Misra, 1993). However, the decline of coarse handloom weaving is a more long-standing issue (see Baker, 1984)

The Muslim areas, both Labbai and Rauther, are mainly located around the mosque (Tamil: *Pallivasal*). The Labbais are by and large concentrated on the eastern side. Here, as in the other residential areas of Pattamadai, the streets are narrow and winding and the houses are set close to each other. Unlike the Hindu areas, however, few houses have verandahs (*thinnai*) which front directly on to the street. Rather, the houses are more inward looking: high walls enclose houses with courtyards; smaller houses are separated from the street by walled or fenced front yards. The houses are generally made of brick and have tiled roofs. Most are whitewashed and gleam blue-white in the bright sub-tropical light. Some houses are built of concrete and sport bolder colours on their façades. There are a few dry goods and grocery shops where women do their daily shopping.

The Labbai colony, where there is a preponderance of weavers, is not located in the streets around the mosque. Established in 1973 as part of common-land (*paramboke*) redistribution under a craft development scheme by the state government to mat weavers who did not own houses, the Labbai colony is marked by houses built in close proximity to each other. During the research period, of the 45 or so houses in the colony, weaving was carried on regularly in around fifteen. Strands of sedge used in mat weaving are strewn in front yards and in the lanes outside these houses. Children play in the lanes, which are too narrow to allow the passage of vehicles. Front doors are usually wide open and, during the daytime, the streets are rarely empty. A further allocation of land for houses was made in 1979–80 and some Labbai and Rauther households were among the beneficiaries. This area, referred to as the New Colony, has a mixed population as land allocation was made with poverty as the main criterion rather than craft development.

On the long main road is a small shed where the blacksmith works, a busy spot. Men congregate here with their agricultural and other tools needing repairs. In the streets lying to the east of the shed are the houses of the smiths. Their work-spaces are also located in the same area and are marked by piles of materials—wood, tools, and work in various stages of completion. The mat weavers visit the work sheds of the carpenters and blacksmiths when loom parts need repairing or when they wish to commission new pieces. In such cases, cash payments are made.[13] The sole goldsmith in Pattamadai works in the local bank, though he also practises goldsmithy outside office hours. Throughout Pattamadai, as in other parts of the country, members of different occupational castes and groups are making livelihood choices based on new opportunities, changing circumstances and personal preferences.

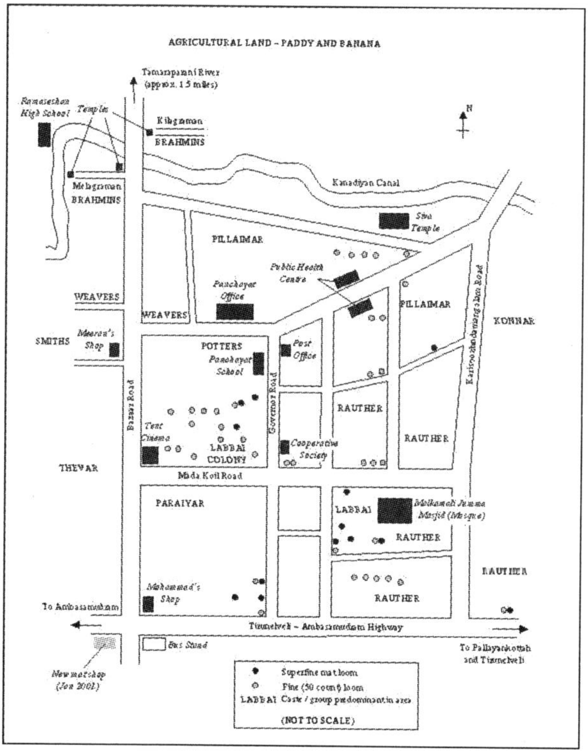

Schematic map of Pattamadai.[14]

[13] I did not conduct detailed investigations of customary prestations among the artisanal and other caste groups in Pattamadai as the Muslim mat weavers do not form part of these. For a description of caste-based patron-client relationships in Tirunelveli villages, see Good (1982).

[14] There are two main qualities of Pattamadai mat. The superfinc quality feels like silk and requires more skill and labour than the fine variety,

Many people helped me with my map, which I started to draw quite soon after my arrival in the town and kept adding to over time. I worked on large sheets of paper and each sheet replaced a cruder, less complete one as the spatial organisation of the town and my knowledge of individual homes became clearer to me. One man, Saad Ali, frequently drew pictures or maps on the ground to help me understand what he was talking about. Another, Raza, who was an elected member of the town panchayat and whose knowledge was, therefore, quite subtle, would use the map to discuss alliances between different groups in the town. Thus, he said, the Rauther Muslim group and the Hindu Konnar caste areas abutted each other and the relationships between the two groups was characterised by friendly relations to the extent that when it came to local elections, the groups would support each other's candidates against candidates from other groups.

Labbais and Rauthers

The majority of Pattamadai's craft mat weavers are Labbai Muslim, though at the time of fieldwork one Rauther woman and her daughter were beginning to weave mats of this high quality. Both Labbais and Rauthers are Tamil-speaking Muslims who claim different origins. However, naming practices are not straightforward, in the sense that there seem to be moments when the two groups are clearly distinguished and others when they are not. This, in part, depends on who is doing the identifying (so the Labbai Muslim or Rauther Muslim is just a Muslim to the Hindu observer), and on the politics and economics of colonial and post-colonial naming practices.

The history and use of the term 'Labbai' is a case in point. Pandian (1978) shows how it was used by some Tamil-speaking Muslims to signify their Arabian descent, at the same time as delineating a category of Muslims speaking Tamil. According to More (1997), the word 'Labbai' made its first appearance in the seventeenth century. Based on readings of Tamil literary sources

---

which is nevertheless of higher quality than mats woven elsewhere in Tamilnadu.

from the medieval period, he argues that until the sixteenth century, three terms were commonly used for describing Muslims: Sonagan (*Sonagam*: Tamil for Arabia); Ravuttar or Rauther from the Tamil *irauttar* or horseman, meaning Tamil Muslim military men; and Tulukkar from the Tamil for Turkish, a term still in use in use in Tamilnadu. Later, 'Sonagan' was split in the seventeenth century into the two categories of Marakkayar and Labbai, the richer Tamil Muslims coming to be called Marakkayar in reference to their control over seaborne trade (*Marakkalam* and *Raayar*: Tamil for boat and ruler respectively) and the poorer ones, Labbai. [15]

This association of Labbais with poverty and lack of prestige forms the subject of a government report on 'backward classes' (1971):

> The exact connotations of the term 'Labbai' puzzled us at first, as generally it is not considered to be a term of respectable address...But reference to the Census Report of 1921 and of earlier decades confirmed the fact that this term was intended to cover all Tamil-speaking Muslims, as distinguished from Urdu-speaking Muslims...Thurston who is generally referred to on caste matters, also confirms that Labbai covers Tamil-speaking Muslims. (*Report of the Backward Classes Commission of Tamilnadu*, 1971: 3, cited in Pandian, 1978: 146)

It is interesting to note the reliance of the commission on colonial censuses and classifications, and the consequent confusion arising from the difference between contemporary usage and textual sources from the colonial period. However, as Pandian points out, a Muslim member of the Commission emphasised the etymology of the Tamil word 'Labbai', arguing that it derives from the Arabic root word *Labbe*, meaning 'here I am, and at your service.' For him, this referred to the readiness of the response of early converts to the

[15] A detailed discussion of the arguments relating to Marakkayar, Labbai and issues of hierarchy among Tamil Muslims is beyond the scope of this study. For in-depth discussions please see S Bayly, 1989; Fanselow, 1989; 1997; and More, 1997. Also see Pandian, 1978. For early-twentieth-century description of Muslims in south India, see Thurston, (1909: 198–205) and Pate (1917: 97–100).

divine call (ibid.). The implication seems to be that Labbais were early Tamil converts to Islam and, though some might claim Arabic descent, this was by no means the case for all. Pandian's central argument is that, notwithstanding the common characterisation of Tamil-speaking Muslims as Labbai, the label signifies different things in different socio-political contexts and has been used differently in different parts of Tamilnadu.

In Pattamadai, Labbais claim that the term was originally used for religious men. This corresponds to both Fanselow's and More's understanding of the term. According to Fanselow (1989), 'Labbai' was originally the Tamil word for imam or priest. As imams serving in mosques, Labbais were found throughout Tamilnadu wherever a Muslim community was present. But, as payment for their services in mosques and at household ceremonies and life-cycle events was irregular and sporadic, this thus placed them within the poorest section of Muslims.[16]

Certainly, the Labbais of Pattamadai are not wealthy. Hardly any own agricultural or other land, jobs are precarious, and the line between monetary comfort and indebtedness is thin. This is exacerbated by the lack of financial safety nets.

A middle-aged weaver, Hair un Nissa, whose husband is skilled in ritual practice and in much demand when in town (he normally works in Bombay) said that the traditional occupations of a Labbai male include officiating and reciting from the Quran at ritual events and life-cycle ceremonies, laying of foundation stones of buildings, and slitting the throat of the sacrificial goat at festivals. A small payment is made to the Labbai for the performance of these services and food sent to his family. Labbai women also officiate at ceremonies for and by women. A Rauther woman told me that at weddings Labbai women are invited to tie the *thali* (the necklace with marriage symbols worn by a woman as a sign of her married

[16] However, it does not seem clear that all Labbais were poor or considered to be of lower rank (see More, 1997: 23). S Bayly too writes about rich Labbais from Melapallayam near Pattamadai, who in the seventeenth and eighteenth centuries and at the time of Turnbull's *Dehzada* (1823), controlled the town's extensive carpet trade.

status) around the neck of the bride.[17] The woman invited to tie the *thali* represents a marital ideal: she has to be a married Labbai woman with children.

The same Rauther woman described her community as being like brahmins, a higher caste than the Labbais. But Mohammad, one of the most prominent men in the Labbai community and in the local mat industry, disagreed. He compared the different divisions among Muslims to the different divisions among Brahmins or to the divisions among Achari (smiths). According to him, there are no hierarchical divisions among Muslims. It is significant that the examples he used were of divisions within a caste group rather than between castes—there is both an implication of hierarchy here and of endogamy, though not of barriers to commensality.[18] Both the Labbais and Rauthers form part of the same *jama'at* or mosque congregation and the mosque committee is constituted of men of both groups. Many Muslims in Pattamadai averred that intermarriage between Labbais and Rauthers would be acceptable to both groups and that all Muslims would eat together. In effect, they were denying any caste-like qualities of the subdivisions. I personally came across no instances of Labbai-Rauther marriages.[19]

[17] The *thali* is a Tamil Hindu symbol of marriage. That the Labbai women of Pattamadai wear the *thali* is indicative of the transformation and Islamicisation of what can be termed 'Hindu symbols'. Young men influenced by reformist ideas are increasingly questioning certain practices they see as Hindu in origin or problematic in other ways.

[18] The debate about whether caste or a caste-like structure is present among Muslims in India has occupied many scholars. Mines (1973), for instance, argues that Tamil Muslims do not exhibit a hierarchically ranked caste-like structure. Other scholars, including Ahmad (1973: 3), disagree with Mines and are unwilling to rule out the presence of hierarchical ranking and caste considerations among Tamil Muslims. It is obvious that the issue of caste in Islam is a loaded one. Also see Fanselow (1997), whose paper exploring the question of caste among Indian Muslims through contrasting Hindu, Muslim and anthropological viewpoints, is an extremely interesting attempt to address a vexed question.

[19] Fanselow (1997) reports a similar tolerance towards marriage alliances between Rauthers and Tarakanars in Kalakkadu town, also in Tirunelveli

Debates over such questions or about whether a certain practice is Islamic or not, acceptable or not, etc., often take place in shops, tea stalls and other places where men gather. I was told that people also talk about these things outside the mosque as well, after prayers, but I have never been present on these latter occasions, though sometimes someone will tell me of a particularly vexing or interesting discussion.

By and large, though, the consensus seemed to be that Labbais were of low status, relative to other Muslim groups. Some Labbais linked this with their poverty and landlessness. At the time of fieldwork, only one Labbai in Pattamadai was said to own any agricultural land. But other reasons were also given. Abdul, a weaver in his fifties, told me that Labbais were considered inauspicious by others. This was because, he said, that while Labbais perform rites at auspicious occasions such as marriages, they are also called upon to officiate at funerary rites. His description seemed to place Labbais in an ambiguous position within Muslim society—necessary but not socially desirable. He said: 'Rauthers need Labbais to officiate at ceremonies but also treat us with reserve. Some Rauthers even avoid the sight of Labbais before commencing any important business.'

Among the tasks of Labbais, Abdul listed leading congregations in prayer, performing marriages, effecting reconciliations between estranged marital partners, and exorcism. A Rauther who learned and performed the above ritual tasks would be *treated like a Labbai* and other Rauthers would say of him, 'He has become like a Labbai' (*Labbai pola aayittu*).[20] Abdul added that he himself had not learned how to perform these tasks because as a boy he had felt ashamed of being a low-status Labbai and wished to disassociate himself from the 'traditional' Labbai occupation. He sometimes regrets this decision as he feels he has closed himself off from livelihood opportunities that other members of the group fruitfully

district, where he did fieldwork. According to him, the trend among Tamil Muslims in Kalakkadu is to move towards a collective Islamic identity with the stress laid on divisions among groups gradually disappearing.

20 Abdul's statement brings to mind Dumont's characterisation of purity and pollution as the important ordering principles of caste (1980).

exploit. Abdul's is one of the only households in Pattamadai where mat weaving forms the sole source of income. Most other Labbai households derive their income from a variety of sources. We will examine this in more detail in the next chapter.

The Labbais of Pattamadai are kin endogamous and many, though not all, marriages are arranged within the town. Furthermore, the idiom of kinship, frequently used, is inclusive and people frequently say, 'We are all related.' A result of this, and of the densely housed streets of the Labbai areas, is a high level of information sharing and contact between households. Almost every member of the Labbai group is invited to festive and ceremonial events as and when they occur, some even as far away as Thiruchirapalli, over a 100 miles from Pattamadai.[21]

I was in Pattamadai when a man in the Labbai colony was having a building constructed. The entire colony was invited to watch the builders (*mestri*) raise the corner post. We all stood in the narrow lane and watched the event. A few specially invited, elderly Labbai men chanted from the Quran. After the corner post was raised, the builders received a customary offering of betel leaves, betel nuts, coconuts and bananas.[22] The spectators were given betel leaves and nuts and sweets. Similarly, at a house-warming feast, the entire Labbai group in Pattamadai was invited and members of the host's household darted through the Labbai streets inviting and, in some cases, playfully forcing guests to come to lunch.

Contacts between Labbais and Hindus, unless they live close to each other or have business interests in common, is less frequent or close, though some men can be seen in the company of individuals from other groups. Khadeeja Beevi, former president of the Pattamadai town panchayat, is a Labbai and her circle of acquaintances outside the Labbai group is unusually wide compared to other women of her group.

[21] Mines, writing about Tamil Muslim merchants in Madras city also stresses on the importance of kinship ties, and on kinship as an organising factor (Mines, 1976).

[22] Hindu groups too make a similar offering to the *mestris* who are Hindu themselves.

Hindus and Muslims: Resonance, Hostility and Layered Subjectivites

2002. A shop in Pattamadai selling fancy goods. I am talking to the shopkeeper about something I need when I catch sight of his table-top display case and freeze in shock. Alongside sundry articles were a range of small pictures intended to be slipped under the numbers and the hands of watches as decorations and visible symbols of appreciation of the wearer's favourite film star or politician. It was one such watch face that caught my eye and rendered me briefly speechless. It depicted a plane flying into a large building. Part of the building was collapsing. The shopkeeper noticed my interest (though, perhaps, not my shock) and told me that he had ordered several, thinking that Muslims in the village would like to buy them. No one had. His reason for this lack of interest was not that people did not celebrate the events of September 11, 2001,[23] but that without enough smoke or dead bodies in the picture, it was not graphic enough to appeal to a bloodthirsty people!

His idea that this was an appropriate image for the Muslims of his town was unshakeable, even though he shares the same physical spaces as them and interacts with them in his shop, and even though the lack of sales did not bear out his convictions about them. This suggests that the descriptions of Muslims found in newspapers and television as well as in conversations around this shopkeeper are so powerful, they override his personal knowledge of individual Muslims in his vicinity.

Walking through the town another day I pass a small tailoring shop run by a young Muslim man and see Raza inside. He pops out to say hello, and we both go into the shop to sit and chat. They ask how my work is going, and I tell them it is fine. The tailor and his assistant who have seen me before but have not spoken to me ask what I do in Pattamadai and we talk about weaving for a while

[23] On this day planes hijacked by members of Al Quaida, an 'Islamic terrorist group', were flown into the World Trade Centre in New York killing thousands. I place the words 'Islamic terrorist group' in inverted commas because this kind of naming is a form of depoliticisation, privileging religion as the main point of contention. Much has been written on 9/11 as it is commonly known and I will not go into this here.

before moving on to talk about events in the world. I ask them what they think about the latest attempt to try and bring some of the perpetrators of the violence against Muslims in Gujarat in 2002.[24] Raza and the other young men seem to close up instantaneously. We are all suddenly aware that even though all of us detest what happened in Gujarat, we do not have the words to describe this. I am female and, to them, Hindu. They are young and male and Muslim. Our angers may not mesh—indeed, we each might be rendered uncomfortable by the other's articulations of outrage, anger, distress. If Raza and I were alone, we might have been able to talk. The presence of the tailor and his assistant, both of whom I barely knew, made this difficult if not impossible. Shortly after this, Raza left town on work and I never had the opportunity to follow up this conversation. Indeed, there were few people who explicitly discussed these issues with me—some of the women I knew well and a handful of men, many of whom were much older than I. And yet, the politics of religion penetrated everyday life almost imperceptibly and certainly came to the fore at particular times of the year: December, for instance, around the anniversary of the demolition of the Babri Masjid mosque in Ayodhya,[25] and on important Muslim festival days.

[24] In 2002 the western Indian state of Gujarat was torn by violence. Claiming 'revenge' for the deaths of a number of Hindu activists who were on their way to Ayodhya (see following footnote) and whose railway carriage was burnt, large numbers of Muslims throughout the state were killed, raped and otherwise assaulted by Hindu 'mobs'. There is strong evidence for the connivance and active participation of the Gujarat state government in these attacks. See Varadarajan (2003).

[25] On December 6, 1992, 'Hindu mobs' inspired and organised by prominent Hindu supremacist organisations destroyed a mosque, the Babri Masjid, which had stood on its site in Ayodhya since 1530. Claiming that the mosque had been built on the deliberately destroyed ruins of a temple that marked the birthplace of the important Hindu god, Rama, these organisations desired the building of a temple on the site. They demanded that the state and Muslim populations of India should acknowledge the rightful ownership of Hindus to this site. Riots rocked the country and every year since then, the beginning of December has been treated by law enforcement agencies as an explosive

The growing religious tensions in India have affected the entire region.[26] Hindu and Muslim fundamentalist groups were active in Pattamadai especially in 1998–9. The murder of a local Hindu Munnani activist in December 1998 escalated tensions, especially with the discovery of his body in a Muslim section of the town.[27] Over a dozen young Muslim men from the town were arrested. Most of them were eventually acquitted.[28] While the heightened tension has since gradually dissipated, the aftermath of the murder still affects relationships. A prominent brahmin, in the course of a discussion with me, referred to the Muslims as 'terrorists' and to the Muslim areas as 'terrorist dens'. He seemed to have no hesitation in saying this to me. The same man would praise the Muslim weavers for their skill in weaving mats and often bought mats for ritual and other purposes. He would frequently drop into one of the mat shops and chat a while before leaving his bicycle there for safety while he caught a bus to town. Clearly, for him the Muslim could be both terrorist and resource, friendly acquaintance and threat. Conversations like these make uneasy listening but are crucial in understanding the ways in which the Muslim person's

---

time. Muslims are particularly vulnerable in this period. The issue is too complex to enter into here. See Gopal (1993) and Ludden (1996b).

[26] See for instance, *The Hindu* (online edition), 17/12/2000 (http://www.hinduonnet.com//2000/12/17/stories/05171344.htm).

[27] This is a Tamilnadu-based Hindu fundamentalist organisation that has been accused of stirring up communal trouble in Tamilnadu. See Syed Muthahar, 'Target of Hate', *The Hindu*, 17/12/2000.

[28] The murder in Pattamadai was widely reported in several local newspapers and linked to the bomb blasts allegedly by Muslim fundamentalists in Coimbatore town. Also see an article on the rediff.com online news server dated 12/02/1999 (http://www.rediff.com/news/1999/feb/12tn.htm). An idealised, and to my mind extremely problematic, account of the events in Pattamadai following the murder of the Hindu Munnani activist was written by a craft developer, who worked with the mat weaving industry in Pattamadai. The paper attempts to relate the events in Pattamadai with larger dilemmas facing the Indian nation (Ananthanarayanan, 1999) and celebrates both the craft and the village for promoting harmony.

subjectivity emerges through diverse interactions and instances of positioning.

A majority of people in Pattamadai, Hindu or Muslim, live in situations of financial precariousness. As described above, neighbourhoods, though segregated by caste and religion, are not rigidly demarcated and different people can live in reasonably close proximity to each other. In such cases, there is some give and take between Muslim and non-Muslim households.

Once the children and a couple of women in Ibrahim's household came down with chickenpox. When the self-imposed quarantine period was over, I was in their house talking to the women when one said, 'It has been a very difficult period for us with this illness. We saw the doctor, we prayed. One of our Hindu neighbours said to us that we should make an offering to the pox goddess at the outskirts of the town. We sent some fruit and flowers to the goddess through them.' When I expressed surprise, another woman said, 'We are Muslims, but they said she is a powerful goddess and it seemed like a good thing to do. After all, we wanted the illness to go away.'

Unni Wikan makes a strong case for going beyond words and getting to the commonalities of feeling and experience that people share in their everyday lives. 'Resonance...demands something of both parties to communication...an effort at feeling-thought; a willingness to engage with another world, life, or idea; an ability to use one's experience...to try to grasp, or convey, meanings that reside neither in words, 'facts', nor text but are evoked in the meeting of one experiencing subject with another...' (Wikan, 1992: 463).

Wikan uses the example of a learned and devout Muslim woman in Bali who describes herself as a 'fanatic Muslim' but who listens to a Hindu healer who suggests that the troubles her family is facing is due to an unfulfilled vow made by her ancestors. The woman in explaining this to Wikan says, 'He says *karma pala*, I say *taqdir*—it's all the same!' (ibid.)

Wikan knows, and so does this woman, that the Hindu *karma pala* (the idea of actions in past lives affecting this life) and the Muslim *taqdir* or destiny are not at all the same thing. For a Muslim, she points out, there is no past life. There is only this one life and taqdir refers to God's omnipotence in deciding what the course of that life will be. Nevertheless, there is a resonance born out of the woman's appreciation of the fact that the Hindu healer wants to help her. Wikan is at pains to point out that this is not just about an afflicted woman grasping at straws and justifying this. What is going on here is the reaching beyond words to commonalities of experience, concern and human feeling.

Following Davidson as used by Rorty, Wikan adopts a pragmatic rather than a literal view of language: 'words as ways of producing *effects* rather than as entities having or conveying intrinsic meaning' (Rorty, 1989: 15 in Wikan, 1992: 464). How do we transcend the words and go beyond their precise meanings? By paying deeper attention to the speaker's intention, and the social position from which the words emanate, says Wikan. How do we know these things?

Again Wikan turns to Davidson and Rorty. When we interact with someone, we resort to a number of guesses about what the other person will do under the circumstances, and so would they in response to us. For Davidson, this is a 'passing theory about the noises and inscriptions presently being produced by a fellow human.' Such a theory is passing in the sense that 'it must constantly be corrected...' (Rorty 1989: 14 in Wikan, 1992: 468). So, people meet, each has an idea or set of ideas about themselves and the other and, when these converge, they communicate. Wikan's 'fanatic' Muslim friend and the Hindu healer, for instance, did manage to communicate: he, by showing his concern; she, by taking it in the spirit in which it was meant and deciding to act on his suggestion. The words *karma pala* and *taqdir* suddenly became commensurable.

To most members of the Muslim household who wanted respite from illness, sending offerings to the goddess's shrine through the friendly Hindu neighbour did not represent a problem. It did not seem to have thrown into jeopardy their knowledge of themselves as Muslims. For many anthropologists of Islam, this is inconceivable. They would be far happier and reassured to hear about the one member of this household who has a more stringent notion of what is permissible and what is not and for whom the offering to the shrine would have represented an incommensurable problem (the household's women did not tell him what they had done). These women sent the offerings in the full knowledge that Muslims do not do these things.[29] It was not part of any model of Islam they followed. Nevertheless, the suggestion of their Hindu neighbours in this difficult time struck a chord on which they chose to act. The long-term debilitating consequences of illnesses to household incomes are a shared and common concern. When women and unmarried girls fall ill, people worry about their marriagablity and reproductive ability.

Another woman named her daughter after a Christian missionary she met while pregnant. 'She was a very good woman,' she told me when I asked, 'and I wanted to remember her.'

But, too many things jeopardise this resonance. In 1999 there were some bomb blasts in Coimbatore, a large industrial city in Tamilnadu some distance from Pattamadai. Some policemen came to the mat shop run by Mohammad and his son, both Muslim. The shop also employs a Hindu and a Christian, and another Hindu odd-jobs man frequently stops by to see if there are any errands he can run. Mohammad said, 'The policemen did not come for anything in particular, they just came. The Hindu odd-jobs man who was present said, unasked: "Those two are Muslims."' Mohammad was stunned. He had never thought this man would say such a thing: so clearly give up, as it were, Mohammad and his son to the police. The police did nothing—indeed, it was never made clear why they had stopped by—but, for Mohammad, the memory lingers.

Holland and Leander (2004) suggest that a person or a group is offered or afforded a social position which creates them as a subject. These positions could treat the person as classed, gendered, raced, as a member of a particular religion or as a 'traditional Indian crafts producer'. Subjectivities—actors' thoughts, sentiments, embodied sensibilities and their senses of self and self-world

[29] However, see S Bayly (1989: 133–7) for a very detailed analysis of the incorporation of the Muslim saint cult and the south Indian goddess tradition.

relations—are created by experiences of being positioned and, in turn, contribute to the production of cultural forms that mediate subsequent experiences (ibid.). A person may wholly or partially accept or reject positionings offered to them. Perhaps Raza and his friends' silence was an implicit critique of my raising a topic that they felt reflected my awareness of them as young Muslim men. This was perhaps why they remained non-committal. However, given the nexus between power and knowledge, sometimes people may have no choice but to engage with the ways in which they are positioned.

The back and forth micro-production of subjectivity is likened by Brenneis to the process by which cymbals are made. Rather than being cast in a single process using a mould and molten metal, cymbals are laminated layer by layer, being wound from the inside of the cymbal outward.[30] This layering results in a musical instrument that resonates differently to one made from a single piece of metal. For Holland and Leander, lamination is a useful metaphor to think with. 'Episodes of positioning', they write, 'create what we might think of as a laminate. They leave memories laced through feelings, bodily reactions, and the words and glances of others...they also leave behind tangible artefacts...' (2004: 131). They inhere in one's sense of self. I would add that they do not inhere smoothly, rather some layers are imbricated overlapping other layers, leaving them partly exposed.

Let us return to the Muslim artisans of Pattamadai. To be identified as a traditional Indian crafts producer is one kind of a good thing.[31] To be a Muslim craft producer is another kind of a good thing, *especially if* one can show that craft can unite people

[30] The papers in the special issue of *Ethos* (Vol. 32, Issue 2, 2004) on positioning and subjectivity were presented at the 2003 Biennial Conference of the Society for Psychological Anthropology. Don Brenneis served as discussant and his comments find a place in the introduction to the special issue. (Holland and Leander, 2004)

[31] Although, as a craft producer, one may also be characterised as anachronistic, hide-bound, helpless and dependent. As manual workers, most craft producing groups in India occupy a low status compared to those who do not work with their hands.

of diverse persuasions and social standing.[32] This is something both craft developers and mat weavers/traders seek to emphasise in various contexts, especially focusing on the use of Pattamadai mats in Hindu rituals. But, to be Muslim can in some situations be a very bad thing.

Mohammad, an elderly man now in his seventies, prominent trader and member of Pattamadai's *jama'at* committee, and widely accepted as a devout Muslim, has accepted the first two of the above positionings and fashioned a stable persona around them.[33] The third—that of the suspect Muslim—has perforce been thrust upon him. However, and this is important, while it changes the ways in which he sees himself in the gazes of others, it does not obliterate his, or their, other understandings of himself.

Every encounter Mohammad has shapes him in some way as he sees himself reflected in the eyes of others and thinks about what he sees. Some things he likes. Others he does not, but must still engage with. And each encounter allows him to generate more passing theories about what people may say or do in relation to him. His choice has been to ignore or explain away unsavoury incidents. The Hindu man still runs errands for Mohammad. 'He must have just got scared seeing the police' is his charitable explanation.

Mohammad describes himself as a devout Muslim: he prays every day, attends the Friday mosque. He would also call himself a liberal Muslim who is interested in commonalities between religions. Others acknowledge this, and he has been invited to speak at a local Hindu ashram (the Swami Sivananda Ashram) on religion and what makes a 'good person' irrespective of his

[32] This may not always work. Jhala (2006) writes of meeting a Muslim artisan-trader in Gujarat who made figurines of Hindu gods but was afraid to say he made them, merely saying he sold them. He was afraid of negative repercussions if the Hindus who bought these figurines realised that they were made by a Muslim. However, unlike the weavers of Pattamadai, this man was not classified as a craft producer by the state or public sphere (on this, see Greenough, 1995).

[33] Holland and Leander define a persona as 'a culturally elaborated social identity that may be taken up by some as a personal identity' (2004: 128).

religion. He is proud of his having been asked to give this talk and mentions it frequently. When in his shop, this is accompanied by his gesture towards a photograph displayed prominently on the wall: Mohammad presenting a Pattamadai mat to the head of the Divine Life Movement, a Hindu movement with an international following, founded in the mid-twentieth century by Swami Sivananda who was born in Pattamadai.

One year when I was briefly visiting Pattamadai and had nowhere to stay, Mohammad took me to the Sivananda Ashram. 'She is like my daughter,' he said to the monk who heads the ashram, 'and she needs somewhere to stay for a week. Can you give her a place in your guest house?' They did.

Mohammad may be described as having an intellectual approach to religion. He actively seeks in his conversations to abstract what he sees as essential features of different religions and to focus on them. In doing so, he feels he can communicate with people of different persuasions and can do things in ways that please them without compromising himself.

Others around Mohammad, equally unhappy being casually identified as terrorists or as potential terrorists, react variously depending on their age, circumstances and means. This recalls Hansen's excellent paper (2000) on the reactions of different kinds of Muslims in Bombay who, depending on their class position and resources, either became actively political or withdrew into reforming their religious practice in the private sphere after the anti-Muslim riots in Bombay.

Young Muslim men would routinely be arrested 'on precautionary grounds' in early December and released after a few days. Police presence would intensify in the Muslim areas of town. Weavers/traders who had been invited to sell mats at craft bazaars in Delhi or elsewhere (the winter months of December and January are most popular for these events) would ensure that their bundles were packed in such a way as to ensure easy opening and repacking in case of police inspections on the trains they were taking. Selecting mats for one such bazaar in Delhi, Mohammad said: 'We are Muslims, they will search us. What can we do?' It was ironic that the bazaar to which he and his daughter were travelling was to celebrate master-craftsmanship and the nation's rich craft heritage. It seems one can be celebrated and suspected at one and the same time.

It is important to ask who is identified as a Muslim, when and by whom. For our purposes, it is also important to note what role this plays in craft development and in the ways in which the weavers are packaged as 'Hindu-friendly'. One of the tasks for those who seek to develop Pattamadai mat weaving is to show that the Muslim weavers and Hindus have lived 'for ever' in harmony and are embedded in exchanges that are mutually profitable and form an intrinsic part of social life of the region. This is not untrue, albeit instrumentally mobilised. This will be discussed in Chapter 7. Positionings such as Muslim or craft producer intersect and are imbricated at some times and in some kinds of space, at others they remain separate. Sometimes, it is possible to bring them together fruitfully; at other times, it is felt better to let one positioning come to the fore while another is allowed to recede. But other kinds of positionings too, like mat weaver and craft producer, become visible or invisible, emphasised or disregarded according to the context. The next chapter shifts our focus to the household where weaving is carried on and forms one among other livelihood strategies employed by the Labbai Muslims of Pattamadai.

3 In the House

This chapter moves away from the street and the shops to the insides of people's homes. Almost all the weaving is carried on in homes and it was primarily in the houses of weavers, seated beside them as they worked, that my information was gathered and issues of the day—whether pertaining to the household, other households or the world—were discussed.

In their book *Society from the inside out*, in which they make a plea for paying greater attention to households in analyses of South Asian societies, Gray and Mearns ask: 'how [do] the structure, practises and meanings of the ... household as a distinct unit have implications for larger-scale social realms such as the hamlet, village, region, state and cosmos?' (1989: 20).[1] It is too easy to position the Labbais of Pattamadai purely in relation to their religious affiliation, economically marginal status, rural background and 'traditional' occupation of mat weaving. It is certainly true that the fact of being Muslim, male or female following socially established gender

[1] For a fuller analysis of the implications of the 'outside-in' and 'inside-out' strategies, see Gray and Mearns (eds.), 1989: 9–34.

norms, poor and partially educated do, to a large extent, inform their lives. Yet within these broad categories differing strategies are adopted by individuals and households, which in turn inform Labbai society in Pattamadai as a whole. The 'inside-out' approach privileges the household as the primary building block in South Asian society. However, as Gray and Mearns emphasise, this approach is complementary to the more common 'outside-in' approach. As households are shaped by larger structures, so they shape them. An example of this is the growing importance of dowries in Labbai marriages—something that seems to have emerged fairly recently and which both affects the strategies of individual households and is affected by these strategies.

As mentioned in the previous chapter, Labbai homes are concentrated in two main areas of the town—the first is what is commonly known as the Labbai colony. This was established in 1973 when the state government gave weavers who did not own their houses land on which to construct houses. The other, and older Labbai area is located in the streets near the mosque. Photographs in the 1961 census monograph show weavers living in mud houses with thatched roofs. When they saw these photographs, many people exclaimed in shock, '*Tchah*, see how they used to live!' The money from migrations, the possibilities of government jobs for some, as well as state-government land and housing schemes, mean that few houses are now of mud and thatch construction. Almost all the houses described above have either tiled or partially thatched roofs. Few houses have running water so water has to be brought from public taps and stored in buckets or big vessels. With few exceptions, houses do not have lavatories, nearby waste lands are used instead. Bathing and washing of clothes is usually done in the waters of the Kanadiyan canal.

There are few artefacts in Labbai houses. Some houses have televisions, a few with cable channels and it is not uncommon to see children and a few adults from neighbouring houses sitting in these homes watching TV; fewer still have telephones. A few have sewing machines. Furniture is at a minimum and coarse mats bought from itinerant traders or mat shops are used for sitting and sleeping. When not in use these are rolled up and stood against corners.

Old mats are used to store clothes and other articles. Things are rolled up inside a mat, which is then suspended from, or tucked into, the ceiling beams. When a visitor arrives in a Labbai home, he/she is greeted with the word *vanga* (please come) and a mat is immediately unrolled on the floor on which the visitor can sit. The quality of the mat differs with the status of the visitor and sometimes an old mat that is already spread on the floor may be put away and a newer one substituted.

The room where the loom is placed in weavers' houses is also the main living space where people sit, eat and sleep. In most weavers' homes spaces are not distinguished as male or female. In the kitchen all activities are carried on at floor level. Pots and pans—mostly of earthenware and aluminium—are stacked on the ground and food, where the households can afford to buy in bulk, is stored on open built-in shelves or placed within vessels on the floor. Wood fires and kerosene oil stoves are the main cooking appliances. Wood is bought from the local timber merchant often on a daily basis; kerosene is distributed under the Public Distribution System (ration) and its procurement can sometimes be delayed due to bureaucratic hold-ups and inefficiencies. Informants speak of days spent waiting, sitting in the hot sun, outside the ration shop until supplies arrive. Women cook every day meals, men often cook or direct the cooking of feast food.

Most houses have yards. Some people have sweet-neem or drumstick trees in their yards and use the leaves and fruit in cooking; very few households cultivate food or flowering plants. Few weavers had stored supplies of food or other daily necessities in their homes with the exception of some rice. Finances did not necessarily allow this. Most bought provisions on a daily basis. Children or married women, sometimes men, would go out to the various shops—some Labbai owned—and buy things as and when needed.

Certain parts of houses are simultaneously public and private spaces. Doors were rarely shut during the daytime and women especially would sit chatting on verandahs and thresholds. Children run in and out of homes collecting and imparting information in their wake. Coordinators of ROSCAs (Rolling Savings and Credit Associations) or 'correspondents' as they were called would call in to collect payments—most Labbai households seemed to be involved in at least one ROSCA at any given point in time. Traders and their employees would drop in to check on the progress of a mat on the loom and to ensure that a weaver who habitually supplied mats to them were not tempted by someone else.

The prevalent and frequently voiced claim that all the Labbais in the town were related to each other meant that people did drop in on each other for pleasure or business. Among other things, this means that there is a high level of knowledge about people's actions whether acquired directly or indirectly through other people. Indeed I too was caught up in this flow of information as people would tell me about others and also seek to elicit information about them. The fact that hardly anyone gave 'interviews' (Tamil: *paetti*) and did not want to be tape-recorded meant that conversations were not necessarily directed—ebbing and flowing with our various current interests and preoccupations.[2] Only a couple of people have ever dropped in on me in the house I shared with Lila in the Brahmin section of the village—this was partly because of where it was located although some people I know did walk past the house as they took their children to the school that lay beyond it, it was also partly because I was rarely in during the day. On any given day I would go to at least two or three houses—sometimes being called in to people's homes as I walked past them on my way somewhere else. In a few homes that mainly had females present, if I happened to be around at the time of the midday meal I would be given food and then a mat would be unrolled for me to sleep on if I wanted, like anyone else in the house, to take a nap. In many homes, there

[2] By and large, people were reluctant to have interviews tape-recorded or even to answer questions about landholding, number of household members, etc. Formal surveys and the presence of a tape-recorder seemed to make them very uncomfortable. 'For what purpose' they would ask, 'can't you just write things down?' One man suggested that people were fed up with answering various government surveys that never amounted to anything as far as they were concerned. Only one interview—with the District Commissioner of the region—was tape recorded.

were few men present—they lived for part of the year in other Indian towns or even abroad working and sending home money. This will be discussed. As darkness drew on houses would gather their members in and begin to close up.

Most evenings I would end up in Mohammad's shop at the entrance to the town and unless I had something to ask him or he had something to tell or ask me, we would sit in companionable silence—Mohammad and whichever of his employees was around working on something or just sitting looking at the world go by, occasionally talking to each other or to a passer-by; weavers would sometimes come in for mats, or looking for advances on mats still on the loom. The ways in which Mohammad dealt with them will be discussed in Chapter 5. I would be writing in my notebook though looking up and listening and sometimes joining conversations that neither included nor excluded me. Sometimes Mohammad or someone else would deliberately draw me into a conversation by explaining something to me or asking me a question. Occasionally he would ask me to read out something from my notebook. If he found what I read out interesting or worthy of comment he would expand and a conversation would begin. This happened in some houses as well, especially if I was drawing something.

Who is in the House?

As Gray and Mearns point out, the household in south Asia is a specific confluence of three forms of social relations—kinship, production and consumption—including the functions and meanings co-implicated by them (1989: 22). In Pattamadai, kinship is not only at the core of the structural and conceptual dimensions of the household, it also affects choice of marriage partners. The Labbais of Pattamadai are kin endogamous. Marriages are normally arranged either to someone whose family lives in the town, or to someone who has relatives in the town though they themselves might live elsewhere. Even though virilocality is upheld as the norm, it is not uncommon for a married daughter to live with her parents in their home if her husband works elsewhere and is away for a few years. This is sometimes true even when the daughter's parents-in-law live in Pattamadai.

A household, therefore, might comprise grandparent(s), parents, sons and their wives and children, unmarried daughters and, sometimes, married daughters and their children. Divorced daughters return to their parents' houses. Men who work in other parts of India return periodically, almost always during Ramadan but also at other times of the year. Men who work in the Middle East are away for up to three years at a time. They send back periodic remittances and sometimes speak on the phone or send messages through other men returning to Pattamadai. By and large they play hardly any role in the day-to-day running of the home, including everyday financial decisions. These are handled by the women in houses where there are no men present. Larger decisions, particularly marriages of household members, await the return of men.

Marriage is a central institution, which marks a significant turning point in the lives of women in particular. Labbai females can be divided into three categories on the basis of their marital and sexual status. Female children who have not attained puberty are free to play on the streets and lanes around their homes along with their male siblings. Both male and female children are sent to school though girls are usually stopped from attending school after menarche. This propels them into the next phase of their lives.

Between menarche and marriage the girl stays mostly within doors learning household tasks, and helping with the cooking and cleaning. Her life is spatially restricted and largely confined to the house. I once visited a weaver's house with a Tamil novel that I was taking to the town library to return. The weaver's sixteen-year-old daughter, Abi, asked if she could borrow the book. Her ten-year-old niece (sister's daughter) instantly pointed out that she could not go to the library to return it. The niece, who subsequently became my 'research assistant' taking me to the houses of all the weavers in town, allowed herself to be bribed with some sweets by Abi to take the book back to the library for her.[3] Boys in the

[3] This girl, 'little Khadeeja' was my guide throughout the survey of weavers' houses in Pattamadai. Her grandmother, a weaver and then president of the town panchayat, thought she would be most suitable for this role because, being female, she could freely enter houses and talk to women; also, as she had not yet attained puberty her

same age group continue to attend school. A few go on to take diplomas in vocational courses, though most begin to work in their late teens.

After her marriage, some of the restrictions on the female are lifted. She can go to the canal in daylight hours and move around in the Muslim areas of Pattamadai, though her movements continue to be monitored by her in-laws, her parents and other members of the Labbai group. As she grows older and becomes a mother and then a mother-in-law, her mobility tends to increase and one can see women travelling to Tirunelveli or to other nearby towns on work or to visit relatives. A few women travel on their own and one of them even worked briefly for the state government teaching mat weaving at various income generation schemes to women across Tamilnadu. This same woman, Khadeeja Beevi, even successfully stood for the post of president of the town panchayat, as an independent candidate defeating candidates fielded by the two main parties in Tamilnadu. She suggested that this was because most people in the town were fed up with the major parties especially in the wake of growing communalisation of politics, and also because of corruption scandals. A councillor on the town panchayat had a different explanation: as an independent candidate any money she made on the side would not be diverted to the parties, some of it might be redistributed among the other councillors!

The transition from girl to bride is one of the most financially difficult periods for her natal household. Although several people have said that the practice of giving and taking dowry (*rokkam*) is against the teachings of Islam, significant amounts of money (equalling two years or more of the natal household's income) are demanded by the parents of the groom and usually have to be paid before the marriage takes place. In addition, gold ornaments, new clothes and gifts have to be purchased for the bride, groom and members of the groom's family. Other expenses include the cost

---

movements outside the house were not restricted. Like other Labbais of Pattamadai, she knew every Labbai household and was able to take me to all the weavers' houses; she was recognised by almost all the members of households we visited.

of a marriage feast.[4] With the birth of the first child come more expenses, the parents of the new mother have to pay medical costs; they also have to buy both bride and groom new clothes for the first *Eid* festival after the marriage.

The above expenses are usually borne by the entire household to which the girl belongs though some help (in the form of cash contributions, *moy*, which are usually returnable at a future date), may also be extended by close kin. Households with unmarried girls try to save money for marriages. However, this is not always possible and the marriage of daughters causes major indebtedness and financial difficulty. Other culturally defined expenditures include male circumcision and female coming of age ceremonies, births and deaths. Households also have to bear miscellaneous contingency expenses including medical and hospitalisation costs when necessary. The household's productive resources in the form of both male and female labour are harnessed in an effort to provide for the expenses detailed above.

Money Matters

In many houses worries about money dominate conversations. How little there is, how to make more, how to arrange for a large amount quickly for the various events that punctuate everyday life: illnesses/marriages/funerals/menarche ceremonies. So, there are two distinct kinds of conversations about money. The first involves getting enough to lead a comfortable albeit not lavish life—to be able to eat reasonably well with enough rice, some vegetables, the occasional bit of meat, curds; to be able to buy firewood or other

[4] People say that, in keeping with trends among other groups in Pattamadai, there has been a significant increase in dowry demands over the years. An 80-year-old woman said that a nominal amount of Rs 1.50 was paid at her marriage 60 years ago; for her grand-daughter's wedding in 1998, the dowry demanded was Rs 50,000. Another woman in her late forties said that the dowry for her marriage 21 years ago was Rs 150 while for her daughter's marriage in 1998, it was Rs 30,000. Even with the fall in the real value of the rupee, this represents a significant increase.

cooking fuel, to buy oneself or the children or guest the occasional cup of tea or savoury snack. Sometimes one has to borrow money even to meet these basic needs, but not often. And then there are the obligations that swallow as much as a household can muster and then some more. For these events money has to be found through ROSCAs, loans or other means.

The Labbais of Pattamadai, both male and female, are primarily involved in the informal and unorganised sectors of the economy even though they hold government jobs and jobs in the formal sectors in high esteem. However, their access to such jobs is restricted by structural factors, including their socio-economic status, which affects access to education and other opportunities.

We can make a distinction here between men's work and women's work. Women's work, which comprises household-based income generation tasks, mat weaving, *beedi* rolling, tailoring, etc., brings in small but regular amounts of money that should suffice for day-to-day living. Some men's work also brings in regular amounts of money—mat weaving being one of these, but also regular employment in shops and, if they can get them, jobs in the formal sector. A few men hold government jobs and their families are spoken of as 'people with means' (*vasadhi ullavanga*). Some kinds of work bring in more money than others though they are also risky or difficult: these include migrations to the Middle East and other places, setting up small businesses and trading in various kinds of goods, including mats, whether in Pattamadai or elsewhere.

Short-term economic migration is an important strategy for men throughout rural towns and villages in India (Racine, 1997) and the Labbais of Pattamadai are no exception. This is both because it is difficult to find jobs in Pattamadai and because the possibilities of earning more are greater outside Pattamadai. Even in households where the men can weave mats, they seek other sources of income primarily from petty trade—shops, tea-stalls, small businesses such as selling ready-made clothes on pavement stalls in Tamil towns and cities and beyond. These men return to Pattamadai periodically for a few months when work is slack or to attend festivals and marriages.

Saida's husband for instance, spent part of the year with his brother in a nearby tourist town selling clothing from a pavement stall during the tourist season. When the season ended he would return to Pattamadai briefly before moving to another town and continue selling clothing. Saida and her children live with her parents-in-law, her husband's elder brother's wife, and their small child. She says that during the tourist season, business is good though at other times, the men are not able to send home much money. Saida is frequently in her parents house, sometimes cooking meals with her mother and brother's wife (who is also Saida's father's sister's daughter).[5] She can weave but stopped when she became pregnant and was breast-feeding. Saida's husband's brother's wife whose natal home is not in Pattamadai, told me that she did not weave because her father was well off and there was no need for her to learn mat weaving, or indeed any other income generation skill. She now rolls *beedis* or Indian leaf cigarettes at home. Saida's parents-in-law are both elderly and do not work. The family depends on the income sent home by the men. The dowry given for Saida's marriage was Rs 50,000 (in addition to gold jewellery). This contributed positively to finances in her marital home, but has plunged her parent's household into considerable anxiety. She is keen to help them but is constrained in her new role as a daughter-in-law and young mother.

It is men who aim for the highly valued but scarce jobs in formal sectors of the economy. These often require higher levels of education than is the norm. This is expensive and when a household decides to educate a child it is usually a male child who benefits. The decision to educate a child beyond the age of around fifteen is a high-risk strategy because it is by no means certain that the education will result in a job. Young Peer, as he is widely known, for instance obtained a diploma from a catering college in a Tami town further south. He found it very hard to get a job and even

[5] It is common to find marriages arranged between the children of cross-sex siblings in rural Tamilnadu, though this practice is losing favour in urban areas and among the professional classes.

tried phoning me in England to see if I could help. In the end, he went to the Middle East on a three-year contract to do work unconnected with his training. His family had to borrow a huge amount of money to finance this—work permits, tickets and visas are not cheap. Young Peer was not happy about having to be away for three years and do work that was not commensurate with his training, but was resigned.

Other men who have been to the Middle East say they did not enjoy the experience. In order to get a job and a visa to enter these countries, the applicant has to go through an agent who takes a large commission, the price of the plane ticket and the price of the visa. It is only on arrival at the destination that the nature of the new job is known. If the job is not acceptable, the only choice is to return to India. Making that decision means losing all the money spent as there are no refunds. Nor does the work permit issued allow the person to find a different job. Even if the job is acceptable, the worker cannot usually leave the country for the duration of his contract, i.e. if he goes on a work visa for three years he cannot leave the country during that period and return. Many men who have worked in the Middle East describe their experience as a trial and as a necessary evil. One elderly man who went many years ago when he needed to find money for something said: 'I had to clean bathrooms, do all kinds of work that I never imagined. When you go there you never think what it will be like. I had to go and now I have returned. I will never go back. My son is there now as he has to earn money.' The man is now a trader in coarse mats, and says he is happy.

Certain occupations are considered 'traditional'. These include mat weaving and acting as ritual specialists. Gender roles inform livelihood choices and also play a part in the performance or rejection of 'traditional occupations' (*paramparai thozhil*). A man might choose, for economic reasons and personal preferences, to work or engage in petty trade outside Pattamadai rather than weave mats or act as a ritual specialist. Women's choices are more restricted to income, generation activities based within the house though some women have worked outside their homes.[6] In most households, women and unmarried teenage daughters are financially active and participate in productive activities in the domestic setting. *Beedi* rolling and mat weaving, which are the main occupational choices open to Labbai females in Pattamadai, bring in income on a more or less regular basis as the woman produces objects for immediate sale and usually, barring illnesses or any social reason such as marriages or festivals in the home, works every day.[7]

Beedis are hand-rolled Indian cigarettes. *Beedi* workers or their relatives (in the case of teenage girls whose movement outside the home is restricted) bring home tobacco dust (*thooll*), tendu leaves in which the tobacco is rolled and string to tie the leaf cigarette from the *beedi* company or shop. The tendu leaf is first wet to make it supple, it is then removed from the water and cut to shape and size with the aid of a stencil, the tobacco dust is then placed in the centre of the leaf which is rolled and tied with a string. Finally one end of the *beedi* is folded over with a metal stick.

Beedi rolling is skilled work and requires nimble fingers. It is a highly mobile task as all the implements required to roll *beedis*, including the raw materials, can be placed in one small basket and carried to wherever the worker wants to work. Some beedi companies offer certain benefits to *beedi* workers including periodic bonuses. At the time of fieldwork, the Killadi *beedi* company based in Melapallayam and by whom many Labbai women are employed, gave a bonus to any worker who had rolled a specified number of

[6] Thus, Khadeeja Beevi, a mat weaver in her fifties, said that twenty years earlier she had been employed by the government to work with an income generation programme and travel around Tamilnadu to teach mat weaving to selected groups of women in different towns .

[7] Tirunelveli is among the most important centres in India for home-based *beedi* rolling and many *beedi* companies operate in the area including in Pattamadai (M Gopal, 1999). It is not only Labbai women who roll *beedis*; throughout the town women can be seen sitting in their houses or at doorsteps with busy fingers and baskets of *beedi* materials on their laps. Lila was telling me about one teenage girl she knew who was so adept that she could assemble bundles of fifty *beedis* each without once looking down at her hands.

*beedi*s within an eight-month period. This bonus was over and above the normal piece rate. For women who rolled a thousand *beedi*s a day, the company withheld Rs 3 from the daily wage and put in a share to make up a fund that is given to the woman after ten years of rolling *beedi*s. Many females say they prefer rolling *beedi*s to weaving mats.[8] This is especially true of the younger generation and it is not uncommon to see small groups of teenage girls rolling *beedi*s together. They sit companionably on verandahs, and chat as they work. This is unlike weaving which takes place within the home and isolates the weaver from others of her age, unless there be sisters or other young women in the home. Despite frequent complaints about *beedi* work especially relating to raw materials and to health problems,[9] I noted a strong preference for *beedi* work over mat weaving among many young women.

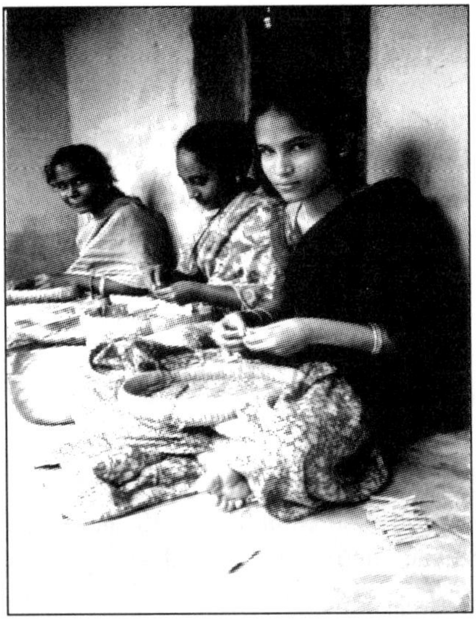

Rolling beedis. *Photo courtesy*: Vipul Sangoi.

[8] In 1999–2000 five hundred *beedi*s fetched between Rs 21 and Rs 23 depending on the *beedi* company. A very skilled worker can roll up to a thousand beads in a day. However, see M Gopal (1999) for a critical analysis of problems and exploitation in the *beedi* industry in Tamilnadu.

[9] These tally with M Gopal's findings (1999).

Mat weaving has a negotiated status in Pattamadai. Many Labbais describe it as their traditional profession. One woman said, 'Mat weaving is steeped in our blood.' (Tamil: *raththilie oori irukku.*) This is a difficult phrase to translate but roughly means 'mat weaving is something we can always turn to whether we do it now or not. It is an occupation that we are raised to know we can do.' Nevertheless, mat weaving is often the first thing to be abandoned when a household gains enough wealth through other sources so that it becomes unnecessary for the women to work. Mat weaving is often described as low-status drudgery.

The choice of occupation—whether to take up *beedi* rolling or mat weaving—is usually left to the woman, though especially in the case of unmarried girls, it is dependent on the availability of a person (usually the mother or a close female relative) from whom she can learn the requisite skills. Teaching within the home is informal. Girls learn by watching their mothers and other relatives, and occasionally receive direct instruction. So important is it for a girl to learn income generation skills that teenagers are occasionally shouted at or slapped by their mothers for not showing enough interest. [10]

The girls are also taught income-generation skills as an insurance against future need. One weaver and mother of a teenage girl said, 'a female child must know some handwork. Boys can manage somehow or the other.'[11] It is to give the girl some choice that she is taught skills she can use to earn money without venturing out of her home. Post-pubescent girls usually give all their earnings to their parents. After accounting for subsistence needs, the remainder is put away, invested in gold, in Rolling Savings and Credit Associations (ROSCAs), or used to fund migrations.

Daughters by and large leave the house after their marrriages, their productive capabilities are diverted away from the natal home.

[10] The physical processes and feelings about mat weaving are discussed in the next chapter.

[11] *Penn pillaikku kai thozhil theriyannum, aann pillainga yeppadiyavadhu pozhaichuppanga.*

However, in some cases a daughter contributes directly to finances in her natal home. Divorce (*talaq*) though uncommon is not rare. Women are sometimes are deserted by husbands. At other times disagreements break out. If these are serious women return or are sent back to their parents' homes often with their children if there are any.[12] Parents and others strive for reconciliation and this does happen but sometimes does not.

Kasim is a mat weaver in her late thirties/early forties. She returned with her one-year-old son to her parents' house in Pattamadai in the early 1980s after her husband deserted them. Her husband has since remarried, and does not send her any maintenance. Kasim's now adult son works in a shop in the Andaman islands and sends between Rs 300 and Rs 400 per month to his mother.

Kasim learnt to weave mats before her marriage; both her parents used to weave. In 1999–2000, her parents had long stopped weaving and told me that they were too old to weave as their eyes and arms had become weak. They are wholly dependent on Kasim's earnings from weaving and from her son's contribution to the household.

Kasim's parents' house is on the periphery of the Labbai colony. It is larger than the houses in the colony and has a cemented front yard with two looms. The yard is roughly thatched to provide shade and protect the two looms on which mats are woven. Kasim described the second loom in the house as a '*coolie*' loom (*coolie thari*). This term, commonly used throughout Pattamadai refers to

[12] Emma Tarlo (1997) writes of a woman in 'Jalia' who returned to her parents' home after a disagreement with her parents-in-law about whether she could or could not wear a cardigan over her saree. In the end the dispute was resolved and the woman returned to her marital home. In Pattamadai, a newly married young woman was sent back to her parents' home by her husband who accused her of having an affair. His 'evidence' was that the household was receiving a great many phone calls from someone who hung up whenever the husband answered the phone. Mohammad who was trying to resolve this said, 'When there is a phone in the house, people with bad intentions might just phone to cause trouble. See how the poor girl gets blamed. In my house too there is a phone and if the men are not at home, the women do answer. Can you blame them?'

a loom which is used by a person to whom it does not belong and who gets payment for the work she does without having any control over the final product, its design or even the colours used. Kasim owns the loom, prepares the warp, and is responsible for all the raw materials including buying, preparing and dyeing of the korai. The hired weaver was paid a piece rate for every mat, and Kasim sold the finished mat. '*Coolie* weaving' seemed to be a common practice in Pattamadai and I met around five hired weavers, one of whom actually did *coolie* weaving for her mother. Almost all the hired weavers were female, most did not own fully working looms which explained why they needed to use others' looms, although one woman claimed that she did not want to take on all the extra work involved in weaving mats on her own account.

All the mats woven on Kasim's are the 'fine' or second highest quality of mat woven in Pattamadai. these are quicker to weave than the highest quality.[13] Kasim sold her mats to any who wanted to buy them. She said that she made around Rs 400 a month from both the looms after meeting all raw material costs and the wages of the coolie weaver. I have sat in Kasim's house several times watching her and the *coolie* weaver at work. In the background were her elderly parents and sometimes, her younger sister, who was married and lived in the neighbouring town of Veeravanallur. Kasim's sister had never learned to weave, and preferred to roll *beedi*s as a teenager.

Kasim has been able to use her knowledge of mat weaving to earn her living and to support her parents who cannot weave anymore (although they were weaving when she first returned to Pattamadai). The divorce, while it has affected the course of her life, has not taken away all her choices. Girls in Pattamadai are strongly encouraged to learn either weaving or *beedi* rolling or both. If possible, they are also encouraged to learn sewing, wire-bag making and any other income-generating activity that can be done within the house. This, as one mother of teenage daughters said, was in order to give them a choice later in life. To this extent, household industry is treated as a resource which may be called

[13] This is discussed in detail in the next chapter.

into use at any stage in a woman's life especially in the case of any misfortune such as widowhood, divorce or poverty.

Today, Kasim sees herself as someone who works, who has been able to hire someone else to increase the productive capacity of her looms and who is able to exercise choice over selling her mats.[14]

Kasim's household has no young men (apart from her son who had not lived in the house for many years now). Should the household need money suddenly, say for medical expenses for her elderly parents, it is to the rural non-formal credit sector than she, like many families, turn.[15] ROSCAs or chit fund schemes (Tamil: *cheetu*) as they are known in India are among the most popular ways of raising money in Pattamadai and many households participate in one or more concurrently. But, it is not only people like Kasim who turn to ROSCAs. Almost every household I know in Pattamadai are members in one rolling savings and credit scheme or the other, sometimes in more than one concurrently. This is as true of households where some men are in the Middle East or somewhere else and send back regular remittances, as it is of households like Abdul's where all the income comes from weaving.

Informal Sources of Liquidity

Labbais join exclusively Labbai ROSCAs—indeed, each caste and Muslim sub-group has its own set of ROSCAs. This is not unusual and can be seen as a function of the ways in which ROSCAs intertwine the economic and the social. Their effectiveness lies in shared concepts about social expectations and need, and trust or at least some idea of control that members feel they have over

14 It is women like Kasim (those without the support of a husband) who are exemplified in the discourses generated by traders in Pattamadai as 'the typical mat weaver'. This discourse serves to position the weaver as a pitiful figure. The woman is made voiceless and her image is managed in ways that allow her little agency. See Chapters 6 and 9.

15 Some banks including the local bank in Pattamadai gives loans against gold ornaments as collateral. Few Labbais I met have as much gold as is required for this

each other through shared membership in marriage and other networks.[16]

In a chit fund scheme a group of people make regular payments to a central fund which acts as capital to make lump sum loans to members of the group. A description of the working of the Pattamadai chit fund schemes allows us a glimpse of the elements of competition, cooperation, and primarily, anxiety which characterise the way Labbais in Pattamadai (and other groups with similar constraints, not only in Pattamadai but elsewhere in India) manage their consumption obligations, shortage of liquidity and lack of financial security.[17]

Let us assume the commencement of a chit fund scheme with twelve contributors, including the organiser, which lasts for a calendar year. Each contributor pays Rs 1,000 per month. Assuming the scheme is inaugurated in January, in the first month a collection is made of Rs 12,000 from all the contributors (Rs 1,000 each). The organiser (or correspondent as (s)he is called in Pattamadai) gets a commission of ten per cent or whatever has been fixed by joint agreement. After this amount has been taken by the correspondent, there remains in this case, Rs 10,800. This sum is now distributed to one of the twelve contributors. In order to decide which of the twelve contributors can lay claim to it, a lottery method or an auction method may be adopted. In the lottery chit fund scheme, names are put in a box and one name is picked out. The person whose name is randomly selected gets the money that month.

In the auction chit fund scheme, the amount is thrown open for bids. *A*, whose daughter is getting married in January, may bid Rs 100 for the amount; *C*, who needs the money for hospital costs, may bid Rs 200 and so on. The one who makes the highest bid gets the lump sum *less* the amount that was bid by them.

Assuming that the winning bid was Rs 300, then the winning bidder gets Rs 12,000 less Rs 1,200 (commission for the

[16] For detailed studies of ROSCAs see Ardener, 1964; 1996 (ed.); Fessler, 2002.

[17] For anthropological analysis on ROSCAs in India see Mayoux and R M Sethi in Ardener (1996).

correspondent) less Rs 300, i.e. Rs 10,500. The winning bid amount is divided up among the other contributors and given to them. In this case each contributor thus gets Rs 300/11, i.e. approximately Rs 27.

In February, all the twelve contributors pay in Rs 1000 each, the correspondent gets his or her commission and the remainder is again thrown open for bids; this process continues for the agreed period of twelve months with the proviso that no person can take the monthly lump sum twice. This ensures that every contributor gets a lump sum exactly once. The sum each contributor obtains over the whole year in this example can be written as: 12,000–commission–own bid + 1/11(other's winning bids).[18]

Sometimes, depending on the needs of the various contributors, there can be a fair amount of competition for the lump sum. The winning bid may consequently be very high. This reduces the lump sum that the winning bidder gets considerably and increases the amount redistributed to the other contributors after the lump sum has been given. Occasionally contributors may recognise that one person's need is the greatest and allow them to take the lump sum without fierce bidding.

The obvious problem with joining chit fund schemes (unless one is the correspondent) is the commitment to paying a sum of money every month for a number of months without the possibility of getting more money than one has put in. This is unlike saving schemes in banks where one receives interest on the principal. Some chit fund schemes go on for over two years and the chit amount may be quite large—even up to Rs 2,000 per month, i.e. each

[18] In more general terms, this can be written as:

$(x-c) + \Sigma j \neq i \, (b_j - b_i)/(n-1)$

where,

x = the total monthly sum collected from all the contributing members of the chit fund,

c = the commission taken by the correspondent,

n = the number of contributors,

b = winning bid,

i = each contributor's winning bid, and

j = the winning bids of other contributors.

participating household is committed to paying Rs 2,000 every month for two years. This is a difficulty for a group characterised by the lack of any financial safety nets or economic security due to its involvement in the informal sectors of the economy.

It is clear from the above description that chit fund schemes, (particularly auction chits), despite their main disadvantage of losing the person money overall, allow him/her to access a large sum of money at short notice. There is nothing to prevent a person from joining more than one chit at the same time. Even if one has already got a lump sum from one chit fund scheme and is, therefore, barred from getting it again, (s)he can join another and bid for the money there in cases of need.

It would appear that the correspondent gains the most out of chit fund schemes as (s)he is automatically entitled to the commission on every month's collection. As the chit fund schemes are informal and not subject to government regulation, the commissions are high ranging between ten and fifteen per cent. Contributors agree that this is a problem, but justify high commissions on the grounds that the correspondent is taking a certain amount of risk. Should a contributor default after taking his share of the lump sum, it is the responsibility of the correspondent to pay the defaulter's monthly share for the remainder of the duration of the chit fund scheme.

Within the Labbai group in Pattamadai there appear to be enough community controls to minimise the risk of default. The correspondent has discretionary powers over who is to join their scheme and this, coupled with the high level of information sharing and kinship networks among the Labbais of Pattamadai, ensures a high degree of success of various chit fund schemes. Correspondents are often women and it is not uncommon to see them coming into people's houses and asking for monthly contributions that have been delayed. I was sitting in one weaver's house when a chit correspondent came by to demand the monthly contribution, which was over-due. The weaver, who did not have the money, placated her by saying he would bring it round before the day was out. He had to borrow money to make good his promise and bitterly remarked to me, 'She looks [placid] like a cow but sees to her work like a tiger' (*paarkka pasu pola iruppaanga aanaal puli pola velai paarpanga*).

Contributors often take loans from neighbours or advances from traders to keep up with their chit fund contributions. This is partly motivated by the fear that, if branded as unreliable by a chit correspondent, they may find it difficult to join other chit fund schemes later. Interest charged on even small loans constitutes an additional burden.

Another way of raising money in times of need is borrowing from money lenders (or 'brokers' as they are called) with houses as collateral. This is among the most exploitative forms of lending. Interest rates are as high as three per cent per month. The borrower is frequently required to repay the principal and the amount in one lump sum at the end of the loan period. It is not uncommon to find households that have entered the rent market, having had to give up their own houses due to inability to pay back loans borrowed against them.

Fluctuating Fortunes

In this section, I examine the interplay of the above strategies and issues on the day-to-day lives of individual actors through the detailed discussion of one household over a period of four years (1997–2001).

Bibi is a weaver of high quality mats. Her husband, Bhai, can also weave though he rarely does so and is frequently out of Pattamadai. All of their children are now married. The last marriage was in 1998. Bibi is in her late forties.

Bibi is the main weaver in the house. Her husband has worked in several places outside Pattamadai. In the second half of the nineties, he started a small business in a town in south India along with his son and one of his sons-in-law. The business failed and the group dispersed, the son and son-in-law moving to Bombay in search of jobs, and Bhai returning to Pattamadai. Bibi's son and son-in-law have since found jobs but these do not pay very well and neither is able to send much money back to their parents after meeting their own subsistence costs.

The failure of the business imposed severe financial strain on the household. This was exacerbated by the fact that Bhai's sister wanted her daughter, who was betrothed to Bhai's son, to be married soon. This was particularly important since Bibi's son had moved to the city where Bhai's sister lived with her husband and daughters, and could live in their home after the marriage. The marriage, however, could not take place until Bibi and Bhai's second daughter was married. A marriage was, therefore, arranged for Bibi and Bhai's second daughter in 1998.[19]

The household was unprepared for the marriage expenses. Bibi's income from mat weaving amounted to around Rs 1000 a month, her husband's and son's regular contributions until the failure of the business meant that the family could save a small amount after subsistence needs towards the marriage of the youngest daughter. The marriage itself was not an event that anyone was expecting for a few years. Bhai and Bibi received a dowry from the marriage of their son. They used this to pay part of their daughter's dowry though it did not cover the cost of gold ornaments and other expenses.

Bibi and Bhai borrowed over 50,000 rupees from a local Labbai moneylender and pledged half their house as collateral for the loan. They joined two ROSCAs. Bibi stepped up her production of mats; she says this has exacerbated an eye condition. Bhai tried his hand at other ways of making money including going abroad. These, though eventually succesful, meant that his contribution to the household income was sporadic for a while. When the money came, it went again almost immediately into paying debts.

Shortly after her marriage in 1998, Bibi's youngest daughter became pregnant. In keeping with local practices Bibi and Bhai have to bear all the costs of their daughters' first pregnancy and give gifts of gold to the new born child. This imposed more debt on the family. There is a high premium placed on the birth of the first child and while subsequent pregnancies may be terminated,[20]

[19] Marriages of males, while their sisters of marriageable age are unmarried, are frowned upon throughout India.

[20] Sometimes, as I discovered in the course of a conversation with some young women, on financial grounds, at other times on grounds of health. One young woman wanted to have herself sterilised after the birth of her second child. She had had the child in a private hospital

the birth of the first child is a much-awaited event. Large sums of money are spent on fertility treatments in cases where the woman does not become pregnant shortly after her marriage.

During the six month period between mid-June 1999 and end-January 2000, Bibi earned an average monthly income from mat weaving of around Rs 2,800. However, her household's monthly chit fund contribution of over Rs 1,200 subsumed a large proportion of her earnings. Further, by this time, the household was indebted to the tune of Rs 75,000.

In addition to borrowing money from moneylenders and participating in ROSCAs, the household also looked to the formal sectors of the economy for loans. According to the terms of a craft development scheme running at the time, loans of Rs 10,000 each were available to members of specially formed 'self-help groups' of female mat weavers. Both Bibi and her second daughter joined a self-help group and took out loans that utilised in debt-servicing. Bibi's daughter does not weave, nor do many of the women who are members of the self-help groups. They are able to receive the loan because craft development discourses emphasise the community aspect of craft production and focus on craft as inherited knowledge ideally practiced by every member of the occupational caste or group. The Labbais of Pattamadai are classified as a traditional

and this had cost a lot of money. This meant her household could not afford the cost of the sterilisation immediately after her delivery. She believed, like many others in Pattamadai, that the procedure could only be carried out immediately after delivery and feared that she would have to have another child in order to be sterilised. I asked a gynaecologist about this and was told that this was not necessary. When I brought back the information to the young woman she was delighted, but sceptical. In all cases, the women told me that decisions were made in consultations with husbands, parents-in-law and parents. For a discussion on fertility and contraception in Islam in general and South Asian Muslims in particular, see P Jeffery and R Jeffery (2002). The group is highly medicalised and frequently go to private doctors eschewing if possible public hospitals. Once when I had grazed my arm, a weaver told me that I should go and get a penicillin injection immediately!

craft community and mat weaving as a traditional Labbai activity. Therefore all Labbai females, whether they weave or not, are able to get loans under the terms of the women's self-help group loan scheme.[21]

Leading a Good Life

Leela Prasad's (2007) central question in her sensitive study of a small (and famous) south Indian town, Sringeri, is: 'what relationships do individuals envisage between generalised moral imperatives, moral reflection and acts in everyday life?' (ibid.: 225–6). While her study focuses primarily on high caste Hindus, her conversations with different Sringeri residents with whom she has built up enduring relations and whose houses form the settings of their many discussions is inspiring. Her approach emphasises the lived experience: everyday acts and the ways in which people reason through them. Like her informants, the Labbai Muslims in my study too engage with diverse concerns that inform the ways in which they live their lives. What it is to be a good Muslim, how to fulfil one's obligations to others, what are one's own ambitions, how do other people position one, can one resist these positionings, work with them or opt out? These are all questions that are raised at one point or another, usually in response to a particular situation. Within the house, most conversations are carried on against the backdrop of other things—work on the loom, in the kitchen, minding the children, dealing with visitors, etc.

In Chapter 2, I suggested that being identified as a Muslim by non-Muslim others was rather different from the ways in which one saw oneself as a good Muslim. While abstract conversations on these questions were rare, when specific dilemmas arose, decisions would have to be made that would sometimes be justified. When the women of Ibrahim's household sent offerings to the shrine of the goddess on the outskirts of the town, they told me that they had hidden this from their brother who is increasingly strict about

[21] At least forty Labbai women in Pattamadai joined this scheme and were about to or had already obtained loans in early 2000. Few used the loan amount to invest in mat weaving.

ridding himself and his family of what he considers unIslamic practices that come from Hinduism. They do not always listen to him though some concessions are made towards him. In 2003, during Eid ul Fitr which marks the end of Ramadan, they waited for him to leave the house before asking Ibrahim's father to say prayers over the new clothes bought for the festival. 'It does not feel good to wear clothes that have not had a *dua* said over them. He does not like it, but we feel bad' said Ibrahim's father. The brother's wife too placed her clothes on the pile.

Few Labbai women in Pattamadai wear the *burkha*, the all-enveloping garment which veils the wearer from head to foot. Their narratives reveal a tension between their adherence to Islamic tenets about female modesty and their poverty which requires them to be wage earners. Two sisters, Ayesha and Ali Fathima said, 'If you wear a burkha, you have to have nice clothes and jewellery on under it so as to give respect to the garment. Poor people like us can not wear burkha because we are not "decent" [they used the English word] enough.'

The women's emphasis on their poverty which makes them not 'decent enough' implies that the problem stems from their need to work in order to sustain themselves and their families, this in turn bars them from wearing fine or restrictive garments.[22] Most women wear sarees in such a way that they can pull one end over their heads when the call to prayer is heard from the mosque, or when certain categories of male relative come to their houses (or when a photograph is taken).[23] In neighbouring towns, teenage girls who wish to continue their studies are increasingly adopting the *burkha*. One nineteen-year old, who lives in a neighbouring town and was visiting relatives in Pattamadai when I met her was doing a degree in Computer Science in Tirunelveli town and wore the *burkha* to her women's only college. She said that the *burkha* allowed her to do things that would previously been barred to her as compromising her modesty. Here it is a freeing rather than a

[22] Ahmad discusses similar beliefs among Muslim groups elsewhere in India (1976: xxix).

[23] Most people welcomed photographs and often asked for copies.

restraining device. In fact, she saw the lack of a *burkha* as leading to the denial of higher education for Pattamadai girls and argued that this was a 'backward' (she used the English word) attitude: their clothing kept teenage girls at home home when they could be getting an education.[24] But higher education also costs money and there is not often enough of that around.

Like the above, discussions about dowries are carried on against multiple claims and realities: the larger backdrop of the household's resources, teachings from religion, customs (*pazhakka vazhakkangall*), hopes for direction from the state and the mosque, obligations towards one's children and hopes for their future, one's own abilities and ambitions.

I was frequently told that the mosque committee in the neighbouring town of Melapallayam had successfully reduced the burden of dowry on the parents of girls by denouncing it as anti-Islamic and by banning specific practices including the giving of large feasts.[25] In Pattamadai, the mosque has successfully curtailed the use of loudspeakers and a few other lavish practices but has not managed to curtail the amount of dowry demanded and given. The two women above who spoke about wearing *burkhas* have said that the government should step in and remove the practice of dowry. In fact, there is legislation against dowry in India. Placing the responsibility on the state or the mosque is, of course, a way of shifting it from one's own shoulders. But if no dowry is given, a daughter or sister will not get married. This is unthinkable. Only

[24] Half-saree: long skirt, short blouse and a rectangular piece of cloth that is tucked into the waistband of the skirt, encircles the hips and is then thrown over the left shoulder to dangle down the back. See Banerjee and Miller (2003: 65) for a picture. Muslim girls in Pattamadai start wearing the half-saree once they reach menarche and continue to wear these through their teens. When married or when they reach their twenties they switch to wearing sarees. One girl complained bitterly about having to abandon the long skirt and hip-length blouse she wore before puberty in order to wear the more restrictive half-saree and later, saree.

[25] See Ashraf (1997) for a discussion on Islam and the question of dowry in India.

one young man I know refused to take a dowry on his marriage. His father, while praising this decision, ended up marrying his young granddaughter to the brother of the young man's betrothed. With no money forthcoming from the young man's marriage, where would money be found for the girl's?

Within households arguments sometimes erupt. In other cases, people do what they think is right and no one says very much. One man who normally works in Bombay but had returned to Pattamadai for the second half of Ramadan was telling me about a dilemma he had faced. In Bombay that year, he said, people had started the Ramadan fast one day later than people in Pattamadai had. In order not to be out of step with the Muslim community around him, even though he had started his fast a day earlier than them (following what people in Pattamadai were doing), he had kept quiet about this. 'This means', he said, 'I can break the fast with people in Pattamadai where I will be for *Eid*, but have not shown myself to be out of step with my Muslim neighbours in Bombay.' His wife who lived in Pattamadai thought this was a good way to do things.

What I want to emphasise here is that people try and do the best thing for themselves and their household as well as for the larger 'community'. Sometimes, though the right thing is not clear and there are competing claims. I will end this chapter with one example that pertains directly to mat weaving. One of the aims of Craft Enterprises in Pattamadai was to encourage more teenage girls and women to weave. The NGO was keen that girls stop rolling *beedis*—this was seen as bad for their health by both NGO and by many *beedi* rollers who complained that the fine tobacco dust got into their throats and affected their breathing. A teenage girl Meerall whose interest generally lay in mat weaving was inspired by the NGO and more especially by Lila's passion for weaving. She gave up *beedi* rolling and started to weave mats, becoming more ambitious with her designs and careful about the texture of her mats. She said: 'I want to be a great weaver who weaves different and beautiful mats. I will get married in Pattamadai and continue weaving after my marriage.'

Meerall's mother was pleased. The girl was both bringing in a good income and applying herself to a useful skill. But her mother also wanted Meerall to get married and it was by no means certain that a groom would be found in Pattamadai.

One day a male weaver and I were returning from the vicinity of Meerall and her mother's house. I was telling him how excited she was about her weaving and he agreed that her mats were indeed good. I said it would be a pity if she stopped after her marriage. He turned to me in surprise and slight annoyance: 'Are you saying she should focus on weaving rather than on marriage and more important things? She will marry whoever is right, i.e. whoever her parents choose for her and that is good. That is important.'

Meerall was married and left Pattamadai and stopped weaving mats, she had children and from all accounts did not miss weaving very much. Now, with her husband away in the Middle East, she has returned to Pattamadai and is weaving mats again. She may continue doing this after he returns, equally she may not.

I bring this up because I think it reveals some very interesting tensions that people like Meerall negotiate. Inspired by the NGO and her own interest, Meerall saw weaving as an important element of her future. She did not say she did not want to get married, but she wanted to stay in Pattamadai and continue weaving after her marriage. For various reasons, of which I am not fully cognisant, her parents accepted a groom who was based in another town. She moved away, stopped weaving but did return to Pattamadai after a few years and has now resumed weaving.

Meerall was unusual in expressing a marriage preference. Few other girls do even in such general terms. Women do reminisce about their early days of marriage especially if they moved with their husbands to Tamil towns far away from Pattamadai where they say they feel a bit freer: 'not so many relatives around to see you.' Ahmadall who is in her late thirties and now lives in Pattamadai with her four children while her husband works in the Middle East spoke longingly one afternoon about 'how "jolly" we were when we lived in Erode. I would sit on the back of his bicycle and we would go watch films. Those days are gone: too many daughters, he had too many young unmarried sisters, we needed money. He had to go to the Middle East. He hates it there but what to do?' She now weaves mats in Pattamadai. One of her daughters got married in 2004 and another is fast-approaching marriageable age. Ahmadall is feisty, speaks her mind, and is resigned to many more years without her husband and many more years of leading a hand to mouth existence and worrying about money.

Not all women enjoyed leaving town as Ahmadall did. Nissa did not move up to Bombay with her husband even though he has a permanent job with the railways as she felt happier in Pattamadai where she knew people and felt she could do things. There, she said, 'one would have to observe *purdah* and be restricted whereas here, everyone is kin.' From the way she put it, it sounded like this was her personal choice and indeed other women have said this in very similar terms. One woman said: 'I went, but I was "bored" there (*ange bore adichidhu*) so I came back.' And finally, one mat weaver in talking of why she did not join her husband in Madras said: 'I have work here and can earn. I do not have to live in expectation of my husband's income, (*inge yen thozhil irukku, avanga samballathai edhirparthu vaazha vendaam*).

To conclude, *mats* are produced in the home against the larger backdrop of household, individual and what might be termed local concerns, even if these extend as far as jobs in the Middle East. *Crafts* are produced outside the home in the public sphere that embraces not merely national but also liberal concerns about what is worth celebrating and saving. There is a slightly disorienting feel in moving between the two. Indeed, few weavers move between these two sets of concerns, though traders and some development agents who work closely with the weavers have to and do, with varying degrees of success. In this chapter by locating the production of mats firmly within the concerns of the household and the larger Labbai group, I have sought to move away from the images of craft that pervade public speech acts about mats. This serves to situate weaving as one Labbai activity among others, albeit a special one.

4 The Work of Weaving

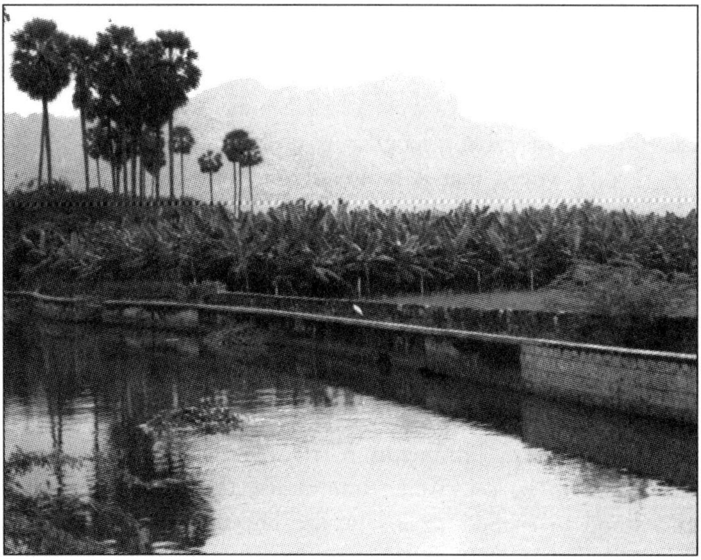

The Kanadiyan canal, Pattamadai. On the far shore can be seen banana groves. *Photo*: Soumhya Venkatesan.

> Many years ago ('In my grandfather's time' said one weaver who was then in his sixties), an elderly Labbai man was walking with his bundle of reeds on his head near the canal that cuts through Pattamadai. He was on his way home to weave a mat. At that time the mats we wove were coarse mats like those woven by others throughout Tamilnadu. The reeds were thus merely dried and split vertically into two long thick strands. A gust of wind blew his reed bundle into the canal. Fearing that he had lost all his reeds the man walked on. A few days later, on an impulse he returned to the canal and fished out the bundle. He found that the water had rotted the reeds in such a way that he could scrape out the pith at the heart of the reed and also split the reed further into several long fine strands. The mat he wove using these fine strands in the weft was much softer and finer than any other mat he had seen. Word spread and more and more of our people started to weave these fine mats. People made more innovations, increasing the number of the warp threads and modifying the loom suitably. This is how our mats are softer, finer and silk-like in texture (*pattu pola*).

A mat can be described as a fabric of woven or plaited fibres—grass, sedge, bamboo, leaves or other plant material—which have been treated in different ways to make them pliant and durable.[1] Mats are usually rectangular in shape and come in various sizes though the breadth of a woven mat is almost always dependent on the naturally occurring length of the fibre used in the weft. The length of a woven mat is more variable and depends on the type of loom used. Mats can be woven on both hand and power looms. The handlooms for mats are generally of simple construction and the various components of the loom are commonly available locally, as are raw materials. Historically, therefore, handloom mat weaving has frequently been a low-cost cottage industry and a complementary source of income for agricultural and other rural workers.

Mats are, or at least used to be, integral to the requirements of domestic space in Tamilnadu. They are spread on floors and used to sit and to lie on. When not in use these mats are rolled up and stood in corners against walls. The use of mats in this way

[1] It is also possible to find mats woven or plaited with strips of plastic.

can be linked to the lack of specifically demarcated sleeping areas (or 'bedrooms') in Tamil houses of the old type. In such houses, which are still found today, mostly in rural but also in some urban areas, rooms are used for various purposes during the day and in the night are made suitable for sleep by the simple expedient of unrolling a mat on the floor. This corresponds to the lack of furniture in many rural, Tamil houses—something that has not changed much in the last century:

> Tables and chairs are not to be found in a Tamulian [sic.] house, and ordinarily a rush mat serves as bed, chair and table. A few earthen and metal pots, and a box for keeping cloths and jewels form the whole of the house furniture. Latterly rude bedsteads have been introduced among the better classes. (Maclean, 1987 (1885): 100)

Special mats called *pandhi pai* are used during meal times, especially when large numbers of people need to be fed. *Pandhi pai* are long and narrow (approximately 9' × 1'). Diners sit in rows on the mats with banana leaves or plates placed on the ground in front of them. Changing eating habits including the use of tables and chairs and buffet style service at social events have meant that *pandhi* mats are being rendered obsolete in urban areas but there is still a large demand for them in rural areas and on ritual occasions. *Puja* or prayer mats are used in some Hindu homes as seats during the daily prayer ritual. Muslims also use mats during prayers. Such *namaaz* or *roza* mats are manufactured in Tamilnadu in large numbers and exported as far as Saudi Arabia.[2]

Maclean's *Manual of the administration of the Madras Presidency* (1885) mentions mats woven in the administrative district of Tirunelveli (or Tinnevelly as it was then called) but does not make any mention of the fine mats of Pattamadai. It is possible to speculate that it was between 1885 and 1903 [when a fine mat from Pattamadai won a bronze medal in the Delhi Exhibition (Watt, 1904)] that the above innovation in mat weaving took place in

[2] Pate remarks on the export of Tirunelveli mats to Burma and the Straits settlements by 'Mohammadans' from the port towns of Tuticorin and Nagapatnam (1917: 219). Both places had large Tamil populations.

Pattamadai. At any rate, from 1917 Pattamadai mats find regular mention as noteworthy examples of the mat weaving technique in many governmental records of the region including Pate's *Gazetteer of the Tinnevelly district* (Pate, 1917; also Rao, 1929). It also finds mention in numerous later publications on Indian craft including Kamaladevi Chattopadhyay's *Indian handicrafts* (1963).

What makes fine mat weaving quite to specific to the Labbai group of Pattamadai? Labbais living outside the town do not weave mats of this quality. Nor does anyone try to prevent from weaving, or even compare unfavourably the skills of, Labbais who were raised outside Pattamadai but who moved to the town on their marriage. While one elderly woman (Nanni) referred to mat weaving as her 'mother tongue' (*tai mozhi*), Quasim who can weave but does not was candid in a different way: 'you need patience and poverty to weave. No one who can afford not to weave would.' Each was only saying what the other may have said at another time or to another person. Indeed pride in one's skill and regret at one's misfortune at having no real alternative to drudgery are like a picture illustrating figure-ground reversal. Both are present, appearing and disappearing, dependent on the current viewpoint of the speaker and the identity or affiliations of the listener.

In part this is a problem of embodiment: the work of the body on the loom and the emotions about weaving as work which pervade weavers' experiences. This is particularly important in a place like Pattamadai where weavers rarely talk about the bodily aspects of their work—the tactile sensual physical pleasures and pains that it involves. Yet these are important and influence both what weavers do, and want to do. How to explore and represent weavers' embodied experience is a problematic that defies resolution yet must be attempted. In this chapter I will both describe the work of weaving,[3] and the ways in which people learn how to weave and simultaneously, though not always, become weavers.

[3] The description of the raw material preparation and the weaving process are pictorially rich, and I am grateful to Vipul Sangoi who has taken most of the photographs in this section. Vipul's website is: http://www.raindesign.info

FROM SEDGE TO 'SILK': THE RAW MATERIAL

'There are fewer articles of everyday usefulness than the common korai mat' (N Rao, 1929: 148). The material used in Pattamadai fine and superfine mat weaving, as well as in most mats made throughout Tamilnadu is known in Tamil as *korai*.[4] Korai, commonly misidentified as a grass, belongs to the sedge family of plants—cyperaceae. The Cyperaceae family comprises about 5000 species of grass-like plants of wet regions throughout the world. Unlike grasses, cyperus plants have solid stems. Members of the sedge family of plants are used in basketry and mat making throughout the world as well as in thatching, fencing, and rope making.[5]

Of the various cyperus species found in Tamilnadu, three are particularly important in the mat weaving industry. The common Tamil name for these is korai. Two of these *Cyperus corymbosus* Rottb. (syn *C. tegetiformis* Roxb.) and *C. pangorei* Rottb. (syn *C. tegetum* Roxb.), are commonly referred to as *pangorai*[6] and are used for producing fine mats. The third variety *C. exaltatus* Retz. is commonly known as *padupai* korai and is used for producing coarse mats (Amalraj, 1990). While wild korai can be found in wet and boggy areas throughout Tamilnadu, the cultivation of korai has gained popularity within the last decade with the widespread introduction of powerlooms for weaving coarse mats and the increased demand for the plant in the growing mat weaving industry.

4 As the word korai occurs throughout the book, to make for ease of reading, I will not italicise it after the first time.

5 'Sedge Research at Kew', Royal Botanical Gardens, Kew, England. http://www.rbgkew.org.uk/herbarium/sedges/sedges.html

6 There seemed to be considerable confusion about the botanical name and properties of korai used in Pattamadai mat weaving. Korai is variously identified as *Cyperus pongaris* (Mehta, 1960: 142), *Cyperus ponganis* (Nambiar, 1964: 1). However, it appears that *Cyperus pongaris* and *C. ponganis* do not actually exist and are a result of faulty nomenclature. It is reasonable to assume that the misnomers C. *pongaris* and C. *ponganis* arose from the corruption of *pangorai* or C. *pangorei*. I am grateful to Dr Simpson of the sedge research section at Kew gardens for his help in clarifying my doubts and for sending me the article by Amalraj.

The korai species under discussion are all perennial sedges. Most weavers of high quality mats say they prefer wild korai, but weavers also use cultivated korai, which is becoming increasingly popular with farmers as a cash crop. Korai crops require low maintenance and give high cash returns.[7] Cultivated korai is ready for its first harvest ten months after planting when the plants are approximately four-and-a-half-feet tall. Subsequent harvesting is done at six-month intervals. Once established, the crop yields for ten to fifteen years with the minimum of maintenance and negligible pest or disease problems (Amalraj, 1990: 169). So low are the effort and inputs and so high the returns, that in Karur district in Tamilnadu, korai cultivation is supplanting rice cultivation. The demand for korai is very high and merchants from the mat industry pay farmers in advance for the korai and arrange for its cutting and transportation (Geetha Raghuraman, 'Making hay in the sunshine', *The Hindu*, 09/02/1998).[8] Coarse korai mats woven on powerlooms are particularly popular for their use in the packing and transporting of perishable commodities such as fish and flowers as the texture and material of the mat allows the circulation of air and water and keeps the products fresh for a longer period of time. According to the clerk of the Fine Mat Weavers' Cooperative Society in Pattamadai, coarse mats are also bought in large quantities by government hospitals and similar institutions for use as bedding and seating

Korai mats, then, can be of different textures. How fine a mat is depends on the intentions and skill of the weaver, the quality and preparation of korai, and the type of loom used. Korai mats are divided into different qualities based on the number of warp threads and on the thinness of the weft strands. The finest quality mats referred to as superfine mats have extremely fine weft strands and between 102 and 142 warp threads for every nine inches of

7 Compared to an income of Rs 4,000 per acre from paddy cultivation, farmers claim that they can get, with much less care and investment, a net profit of about Rs 15,000 per acre from korai cultivation (Ganapathy, 'Useful work of art', *The Hindu*, 09/10/1995).

8 According to *The Hindu* (ibid.), the korai mat industry in 1995 provided jobs (both full and part-time) to over 20,000 people in the Karur region of Tamilnadu from where most cultivated korai comes.

the total warp width.[9] 'Superfine' mats of this quality are woven only in Pattamadai. They are almost always woven using wild korai. Also woven in Pattamadai are 'fine mats' of 52 counts, i.e. there are 52 warp threads for every nine inches of total warp width.[10] These take less time to weave and less preparation of the korai which may be cultivated. They are consequently less expensive in comparison to the 'superfine' quality.

The green stems cut from the korai plant are split lengthwise into two halves. These are dried in the sun until they turn a dull yellow. They are then sold either directly to mat weavers or more commonly to wholesale buyers who sell them on. These korai stems can be used in weaving without any further preparation although, like the korai itself at this stage, the mats will be coarse and thick and not very durable. This type of korai is primarily used in the powerloom mat industry.[11] In order to weave mats of finer texture, the korai needs to be processed further.

The fibres used in fine mat weaving are found in the stem within the outer layer which needs to be allowed to rot away before the fibres can be extracted. In Pattamadai, the korai bought from the supplier is first allowed to dry completely in the sun after which it is retted—this is the process of inducing the rotting of the outer layer. Bundles of the plant matter are immersed in water until fermentation starts at which point they are lifted out to drain. Bundles of korai are carried by the weaver, or a household member, to the Kanadiyan canal which cuts across the northern part of the town. Each bundle is weighted with a heavy stone and immersed

[9] There are three specific qualities of superfine mats: 100-, 120- and 140-count mats. All of these will be referred to by the term 'superfine mat'.

[10] Fifty count mats, are referred to by traders in Pattamadai and by Craft Enterprises as 'fine mats'. I will be using the terms 'fine mat' and 50-count mats interchangeably.

[11] Powerlooms use mechanised technology to speed up the weaving process. Due to the fast beating action of the reed, the korai has to be thick and able to withstand force. This makes the mats less durable in the long run. According to informants, 125 mats of coarse count can be woven on one powerloom in a day.

in the water in the direction of the current. This allows the stems to move gently in the water and offer minimal resistance to the current. The bundles are untied and rinsed every day to prevent the settling of soil and other water-borne dirt, and the position of the stone is changed from one end of the bundle to the other in order to ensure that the fermentation process is uniform. Fermentation of the korai occurs between three and seven days and when the weaver judges that the korai is ready, the bundles are removed from the water. In general the finer the desired mat, the longer the bundle is allowed to remain in the water though this period rarely exceeds a week.

Weavers stress the importance of immersing the korai in running water, particularly in the case of korai used in superfine mats. The waters of the Tamaraparani river which runs in the Kanadiyan canal is particularly prized for the coppery golden hue it is said to impart to the korai. When preparing korai for the lower-quality fine mats, some weavers use rain water collected in tanks in their houses both because it is more convenient and because of fear of theft of korai bundles. One weaver who has no facilities in her house to soak korai complained that she had had korai stolen from the canal on one occasion.[12]

Making Mats

In 2000, an informant placed the total number of looms in Pattamadai at between 300 and 400.[13] Not all of these looms

[12] This seems to have been a problem since 1961, 'An unwritten rule that korai grass should not be stolen exists, yet its safety depends more on the goodwill of people around rather than on any sanction imposed' (Nambiar, 1964: 10). While it appears that weavers in 1961 soaked korai in the canal for up to ten days, today most superfine mat weavers say that they rarely soak the korai for more than seven days.

[13] Shahul Hameed, former secretary of the cooperative society. An informant in her fifties claimed that there were seven looms in her father's house when she was growing up. Very few households in Pattamadai today can lay claim to quite so many looms or people able to use them.

have all the parts required for weaving—they may comprise some key components with the remainder made by local carpenters and others when required. From an informal survey of people weaving at the time of the study,[14] I estimate that there are around 50 fine and superfine looms operating on a more or less regular basis in Pattamadai. However, this number oscillates as people stop weaving for a few years and take it up again later. There are only two households whose entire income comes from mat weaving.

January 2000. My friend Vipul Sangoi—graphic designer and photographer—is in Pattamadai for the express purpose of filming the mat weaving process so that we can make a short film for display in the exhibition, Crafting culture: Pattamadai mats from South India, which opened at the Cambridge University Museum of Archaeology and Anthropology in 2002. Filming was done over two days in the houses of different weavers so that we could get a full picture of the making of a mat from start to finish. Here, I am going to retrace Vipul's and my movements as we filmed to describe not just the processes involved in mat-making but also the spaces, collaborations and work rhythms. The purpose of this is to give the reader a sense of the work of weaving.

As Vipul and I leave my house in the Brahmin section of Pattamadai early on the first morning we encounter two Labbai women who had come to the canal in order to wash themselves, and to pick up their korai bundles that had been soaking in the waters of the canal. The combining of different chores is fairly common, and it is not rare to see women walking to or from the canal carrying a bucket of washing in one hand while the other hand balances on the head a bundle of korai.

We walk on to Abdul Wahab's house. Abdul and his wife Peer Fathima both weave superfine mats. Their daughter used to weave but has now left the house to go to her marital home in a neighbouring town. She does not weave anymore. Abdul's fourteen-year-old son

[14] Almost all the fine and superfine weavers' houses were covered in this informal survey. In addition I also met many coarse mat weavers (i.e. those who wove mats under 50 count) by spending a morning with a trader who visited weaver's house regularly, collecting finished mats and selling raw materials. I later revisited some of the houses on my own.

also does not weave, going to school instead. The previous day Abdul had told us that, having just finished weaving one mat, he was going to be laying the warp for another mat. His brother Saad Ali who, with his wife Noorjahan, also weaves superfine mats was going to be helping Abdul lay the warp for the new mat.

Abdul and Peer Fathima's house is not very large and of a fairly standard pattern. The house is approached by a yard. Like many other Labbai houses, Abdul's yard is surrounded by a compound wall to separate it from the lane, though it has no gate. Some households with more than one loom might reserve a part of the yard for the second loom. In such cases the area over the loom is thatched or covered in some way to protect loom, and mat and weaver from the sun.

On crossing the yard the visitor climbs a few steps to enter the verandah. In Abdul's house the verandah is partially open with plaited dried leaves forming the front wall. The verandah is roofed. Beyond the verandah is the main room of the house where the loom is placed. This is where the members of the household weave and sleep. In order to be able to lay out a loom, this room has to be at least 12' × 6', and indeed Abdul and Fathima's main room is not much larger than this. The loom dominates the room when a mat is in progress. It is dismantled and put away during periods when there is no weaving. The room is lit by one bulb hanging from the ceiling. Some natural light comes in through a window on the wall between the verandah and the main room. Beyond the main room is the kitchen, this is the same sort of size and shape as the verandah. The kitchen wall forms the back wall of the entire compound. A door allows independent access onto the small lane that runs behind the house.

Saad Ali and Abdul are seated on their haunches at either end of the loom passing the warp thread from one end of the loom to the other. This is a good moment to describe the loom.

The Pattamadai loom, like other mat weaving looms, is fairly simple.[15] The basic function of any loom is to secure the warp

[15] Hecht (1989: 9) surmises that weaving developed from mat and basket making. In both of these, relatively pliant plant materials are

threads and to provide a framework for the interlacing of the warp with the weft, and for the tightening of the construction of the fabric which results from this interweaving of weft with warp.

The area that the loom normally covers in a space is demarcated by the presence of four stakes (*mulai kambi,* corner rods) driven into the ground to form the four points of a rectangle of area 9' × 6'. These stakes hold the loom in position and it is imperative that they are strong. To this end, a foot and a half of each approximately three-foot-long stake is sunk into the ground. To these stakes, joining up the breadths of the rectangle formed by them, are tied two wooden beams—*suthu pirimaram* and *mun dhandu*—which define the spatial limits of the loom.

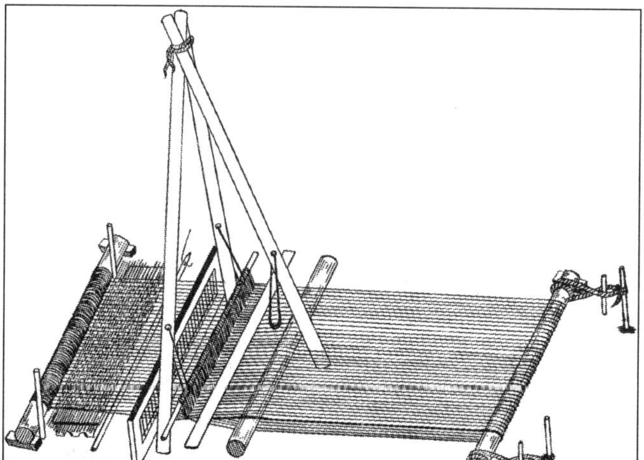

The mat weaving loom.[16]

interlaced, often without the use of any special apparatus. In the case of mat weaving however, where strips of plant material were laid out parallel to each other to facilitate even interlacing with the other strips which were to cross them, the first set of strips may well have been tied to two parallel bars to keep them in order and stop them from changing position. The beginnings of the loom may be linked to the securing of the *warp* strips to such bars.

[16] Image adapted from Nambiar, 1964: 48.

The warp threads are held parallel to each other under even tension. The device used to keep the warp threads evenly spaced is known in Tamil as the *achu*. The *achu* is made up of parallel slivers of wood or metal set into a wooden frame. These form openings ('eyes' or *kann*) at periodic intervals through which the warp threads are passed. In general, the greater the number of warp threads, the finer the textile produced. The achu is free to move along the entire warp and is also used to beat each weft row into place after it has been interlaced with the warp in order to tighten the construction of the fabric. The *achu* is a crucial tool and one of the more difficult ones to source for the superfine mat weaving loom. This will be discussed in Chapter 9.

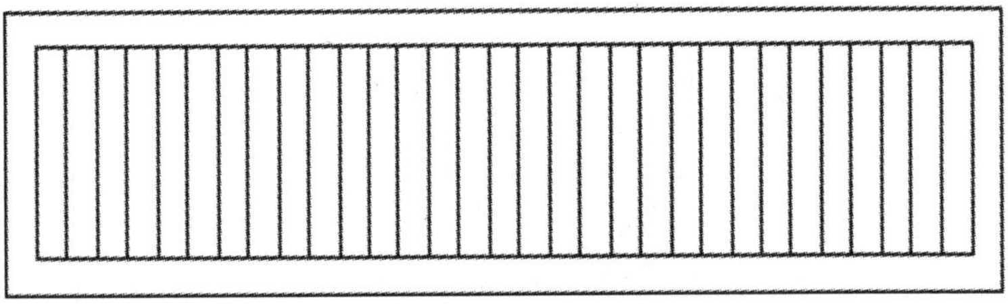

Indicative drawing of the reed/*achu*. For superfine mats the frame is made from wood and the 'eyes' from metal.

Abdul has already been to the market to buy the cotton/polycotton thread used for the warp.[17] The brothers begin the laborious albeit, for them, routine process of laying the warp. One loops the thread around the *mun dhandu* and passes it through the first eye of the reed, to the other who loops it around the *suthupirimaram* and passes it back so it can be passed through the next eye of the reed, looped around the *suthupirimaram* again, etc. This goes on until the warp is fully laid to the required width. The warp is composed of one continuous thread. Peer Fathima was busy in the kitchen though she would keep coming into the main room where the loom was being laid and look on as the two men worked.

[17] In 1961 (Nambiar, 1964), weavers purchased cotton yarn from the market and prepared it for weaving by starching it and winding it onto a spool. Weavers describe this as a laborious task and have since moved to buying spools of thread that can be warped without any preparatory work.

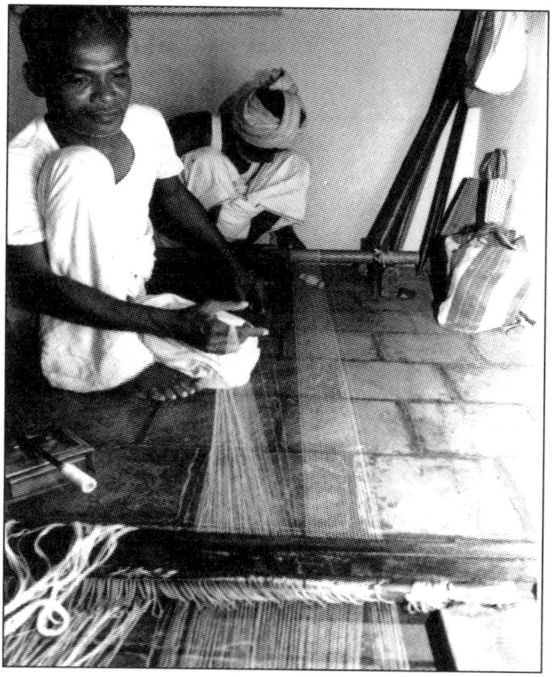

Abdul Wahab and Saad Ali lay the warp.
Photo courtesy: Vipul Sangoi.

The warp is finally laid, with a few breaks when Saad Ali leaves for a while, lunch is served and eaten, and a few other essential chores done. The tension of all the threads is evenly adjusted. It is time for the next step—the vertical separation of the odd and even warp threads so as to allow the easy passage of the shuttle or stick bearing the weft. In the mat weaving loom this is achieved through the use of a shed stick which is inserted through the warp so as to divide it vertically; the lower threads are then lifted up by means of little loops tied to each thread and the whole tied to a rod which is suspended above the warp on a tripod. The first weft strand will be inserted in the space created by the shed stick between the threads of the warp. Before the next one is inserted, the lowered warp strands will have to be raised and the upper ones lowered. The weaver will do this with her foot by pressing down firmly on the shed stick. This alternating pattern of warp and weft will be repeated throughout the mat.

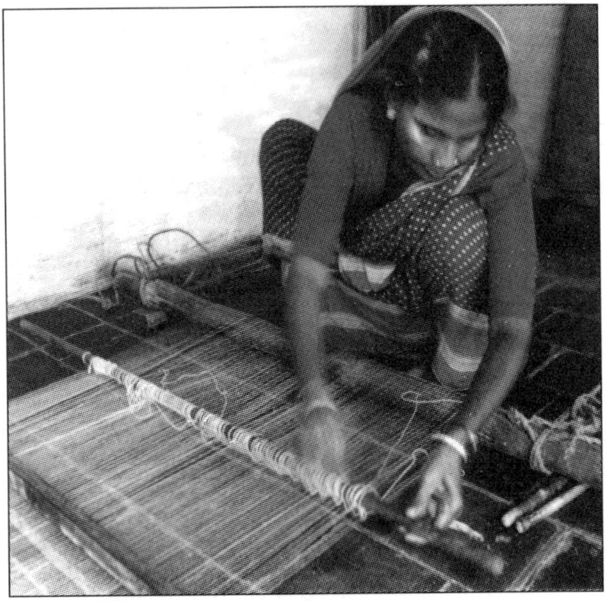

Separating the warp threads to create the shed.
Photo courtesy: Vipul Sangoi.

The next day, while Peer Fathima places by the loom weft strands of korai that Abdul and she have already prepared so that she can settle down to weaving, Abdul sits down on the verandah to prepare more weft strands from korai he has just brought back from the canal. Before we move on to Hasan Fathima and Peer Mohammad's house where a mat is well on the way and where we can follow the process of weaving, let us briefly stop and watch Abdul at this highly skilled task.

Abdul sits with the damp korai beside him, picks up a stem and, with the help of a sharp knife, removes the outer layer of the stem and the soft pith in the middle. The damp bundles are fragrant and the slightly fruity smell of the rotted reeds fills the air. As he works he talks to us. At one point he describes the transparent outer layer of the stem as glass-like (*kannadi pole*) and refer to the process of removing it as being akin to peeling off the layers of an onion.

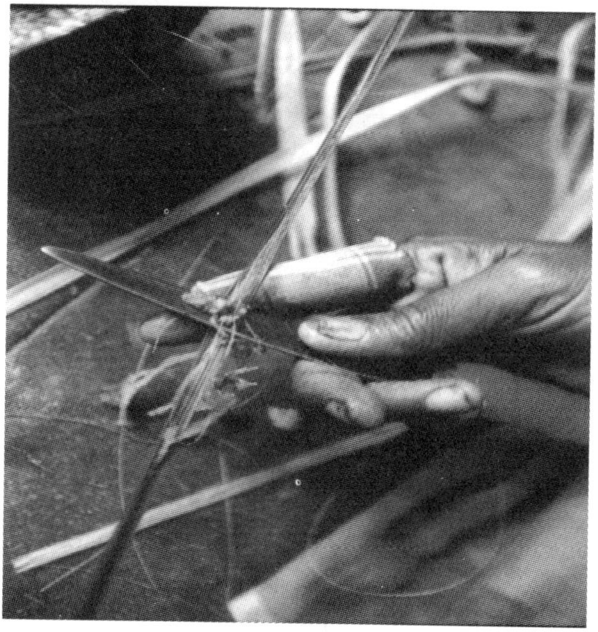

Removing the pith after retting. *Photo courtesy*: Vipul Sangoi.

Next, and with the help of a very sharp needle-like knife, the stem is split into several strands (varying from three to seven).[18] The strands thus separated will form the weft of the mat.[19]

[18] Descriptions of the above processes exist from as early as 1917 (Pate) and 1964 (Nambiar). These show that many processes have remained largely unchanged from the beginning of the twentieth century to its end when I observed them.

[19] According to Nambiar, in 1961, this process was carried on entirely by men (1964: 11). This is not the case today and both men and women perform this task.

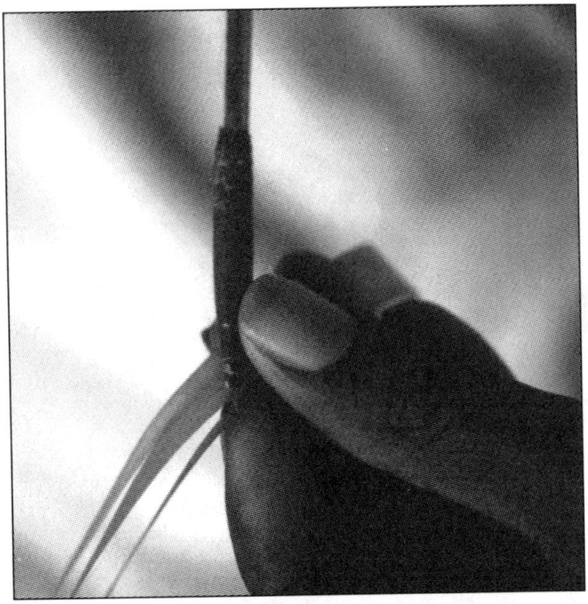

Splitting the korai into fine strands. *Photo courtesy*: Vipul Sangoi.

Once the bundle is done Abdul will spread out the damp split weft strands in the yard to dry in the sun until they take on a golden hue. This process is not without hazards as the korai is considered a delicacy by the goats which frequent the lanes and open areas of Pattamadai. Leaving Abdul and Fathima, Vipul and I move on to Hasan Fathima's house a few lanes away.

Hasan Fathima's house is larger than Abdul's. High compound walls—which form the external walls of some of the rooms—enclose the entire house and yard. Two platforms that open into the yard adjoin the kitchen and the main room respectively. These are raised to a height of about 3 feet of the ground. These platforms are roofed but the rest of the yard is partly open to the sky with some roughly thatched roofed areas. On one of these platforms the loom is laid out—the other has korai standing up in bundles or spread out to dry. There is also a sewing machine that one of Hasan Fathima's daughters uses. The young children of her two daughters and son play in the yard. The kitchen is separated from the rest of the house by the yard. This means that, unlike in Abdul's house, smoke from cooking on a clay stove with firewood does not make seeing and breathing difficult. The relatively open position of the platform also means the light is better for weaving.[20]

There are more people here involved in weaving or in weaving related tasks than there are in Abdul's house. Hasan Fathima's daughter helps with preparing the korai as does her elderly mother-in-law. Hasan Fathima's husband too can weave, though he is away at the time and anyway, prefers not to weave although he enjoys 'designing' mats for his wife to weave. He creates interesting combinations of patterns and sometimes even incorporates new designs he has seen on other textiles or baskets into mats.

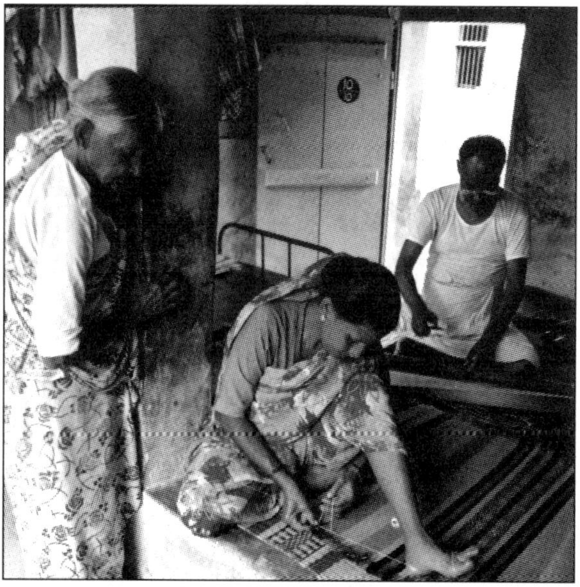

January 2002. Hasan Fathima and Peer Mohammad finish two mats while Nanni looks on. They are seated on one of the two partly open platforms in their house. Both mats were sold at the Museum of Archaeology and Anthropology in Cambridge. Peer Mohammad was very excited about designing mats 'the likes of which were not woven before.' *Photo courtesy*: Jonathan Woolf.

[20] On the land he was given by the government to build a house, Abdul could have had a house like Hasan Fathima's but chose to

Hasan Fathima is in the kitchen when we arrive but moves to her loom and sits on a low stool that is placed under the warp closest to the *achu*. This stool is for the weaver to sit on as she weaves. When a section of the mat is completed, the stool is slid forward so the weaver can work on the next section.

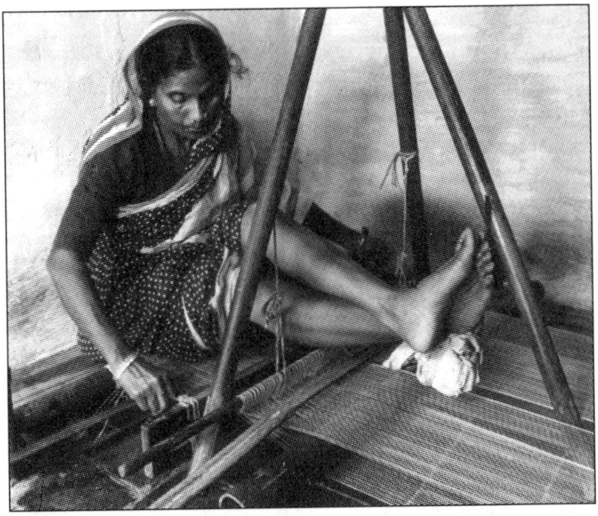

Hasan Fathima at her loom. This is difficult to see, but she is sitting on the section of mat that she has just finished weaving. *Photo courtesy*: Vipul Sangoi.

The actual process of weaving is not complicated, though the demands it makes on the body of the weaver are high. The weaver sits on the stool, beside her, on the floor where she can easily reach them, are strands of korai, a small bowl of water with which to dampen the korai, and a *kuchaali* or long split bamboo stick which acts as a needle/shuttle. The weaver places her feet into a cotton pad suspended from the tripod. In the first instance, the wet korai is threaded onto the *kuchaali* and passed through the warp, the weaver pushes the reed firmly back against the newly inserted

only construct on half the land, selling the other half to raise money for his daughter's marriage.

korai strand to move it as close as possible to the previous weft strand. Before inserting the next weft strand, she presses one foot firmly down on a flat piece of bamboo placed on the warp—this requires considerable strength and body balance and is among the hardest of skills to acquire (when I was learning to weave, I would frequently lose balance, only just keeping myself from falling sideways); when the pressure of her foot is removed by replacing it on the cotton pad, the depressed warp threads spring up again to create the counter shed.

The weaver then replaces her foot on the cotton pad, and having rethreaded the *kuchaali* with a new korai strand, passes it through the warp again, and so on till the mat is completely woven. In the case of superfine mats, after the korai has been inserted into the warp, it is twisted several times by the weaver before being beaten into position with the reed. This makes for a tighter construction and finer texture as the twisting makes the korai even thinner.

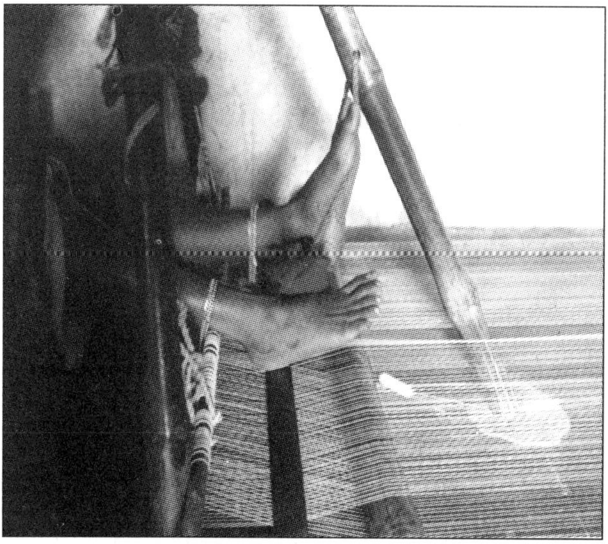

A weaver's feet on the bar. Note how she presses on the flat bamboo stick with her foot to change the warp configuration.
Photo: Soumhya Venkatesan.

At no stage is any part of the mat or warp hidden from the weaver's or observer's eye. This is an important aspect of the Pattamadai mat loom and a point in which it differs significantly from cloth looms where, in most cases, woven sections are rolled up under the loom so that the unwoven warp moves towards the weaver. The mat weaver travels the length of the mat as she weaves it. This is discussed in more detail in Chapter 9.

Abdul comes to tell us that Khadeeja Beevi has just finished weaving a mat and has asked if he could help her with packing it. We go with him to Khadeeja Beevi's house, passing Saad Ali's house on the way where he is working on a mat too. Saad Ali is widely acknowledged to be a very fine weaver and also to have a very good way with splitting the korai. His mats are soft as butter, and given that he favours plain undyed rather than highly patterned mats, this analogy is very fitting.

One of the most crucial aspects of mat-making is the process of packing (*kadathal*). As the damp korai weft strands dry, they shrink. To avoid any gaps in the fabric, the weft has to be tightened manually. The fingers of each of the packer's hands are curled into the palm. One hand is placed below the mat and the other on its surface. Moving her hands in unison, the packer pushes, firmly but very gently, the weft strands together. Packing is considered one of the most skilled tasks in the weaving process and is particularly important in superfine mats where a very tight weave is desired. Weavers describe the difficulty of compacting superfine mats by likening the process to working with flowers (*poopole kadathannum*). One false move and the whole mat can be damaged. Packing is done both while the mat is being woven with every foot being compacted down to around six inches. It is also done right at the very end just before the mat is cut off the loom. This final packing is crucial as no more adjustments are possible once the mat is off the loom. The packer has to ensure that the fabric is as tight as possible, also that patterns especially borders are symmetrical.

When the mat has been compacted and the requirements of symmetry satisfied, the weaver trims the rough korai edges along the length of the mat and finally cuts the mat off the loom with a sharp knife. The whole process, in the case of a superfine mat takes

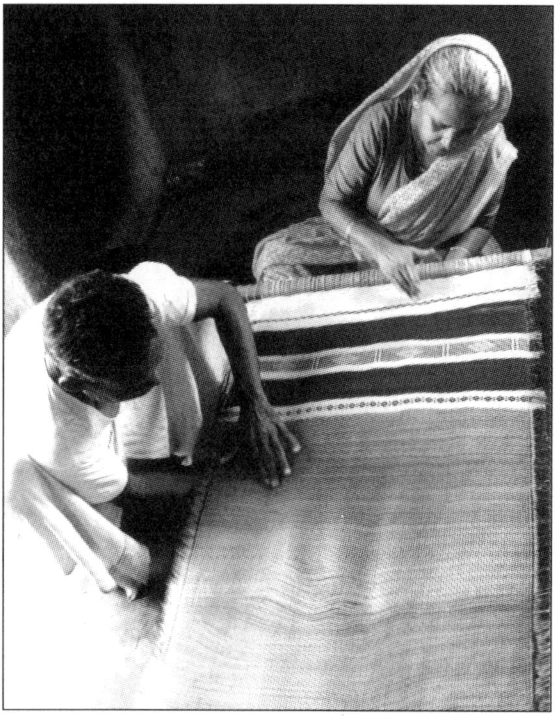

Abdul Wahab and Khadeeja Beevi pack a mat.
Photo courtesy: Vipul Sangoi.

anything between fifteen and 22 days, and in the case of a fine mat, between four days and a week, depending on the intricacy of the designs. Khadeeja Beevi's, Abdul Wahab's and Hasan Fathima's mats will all be bought by Craft Enterprises. Saad Ali, having fought with the NGO because they would not give him advances on mats, now sells his mats to Mohammad, a mat trader with a shop at the entrance to the town. At that time, in 2000 Saad Ali was one of the only weavers of superfine mats selling mats to Mohammad.

After the mat has been cut off the loom, the weaver uses a smooth stone to 'polish' it—he gently rubs the stone on the surface of the mat to break any bits of korai that might be sticking out, and finally either binds the edges of the mat by hand or runs up a cloth border on all four sides with a sewing machine.

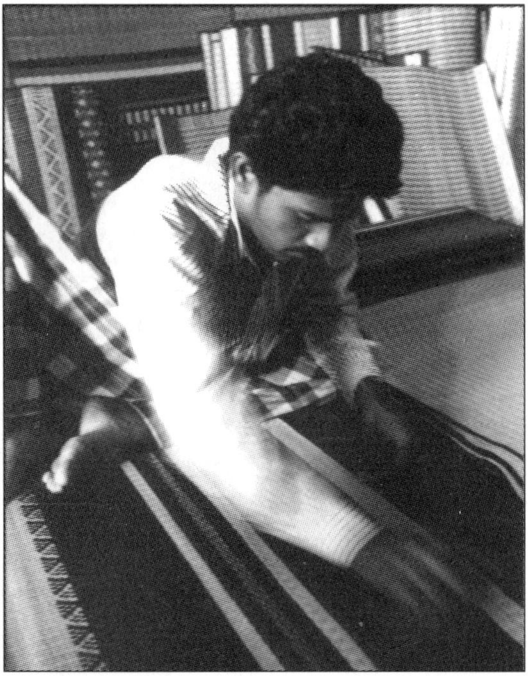

Sultan burnishes a mat with a smooth stone.
Photo courtesy: Vipul Sangoi.

By using korai of different colours, weavers can give mats simple borders of different coloured stripes. However, it is also possible to weave complex geometrical designs onto mats or to write letters of the alphabet.[21] This is done by counting individual warp threads and inserting weft strands accordingly. For more complicated designs, weavers draw the pattern onto graph sheets and use these as guides. Sometimes silk threads are used instead of korai to change the texture of the mat and allow for more intricate designs. The conversion of words in different languages into graphic designs allows weavers to 'write-weave' even languages with which they are unfamiliar.

[21] The main languages seen on Pattamadai mats are English, Tamil and Arabic.

Not everyone can 'write-weave' and the few people who can do it are in demand especially for mats that, like the Queen's, are used in gifting and where the person who is commissioning the mat wants a specific message woven on it. Ayesha, a weaver in her twenties taught herself how to write-weave and it is common to see her in different homes sitting on someone's loom and working. She gets paid for this at a rate that is agreed beforehand. Similarly, Chinna Peer, a young man who attends catering college nearby but spends his breaks at his parents' house in Pattamadai can also Write-weave and does so on occasion when someone asks. Chinna Peer's mother weaves fine mats regularly and he sometimes helps her. When he is in town the mats they weave together tend to the flamboyant with elaborate borders and, sometimes, large flower patterns in the centre. Graph sheets on which these patterns are drawn lie on the floor beside the loom.

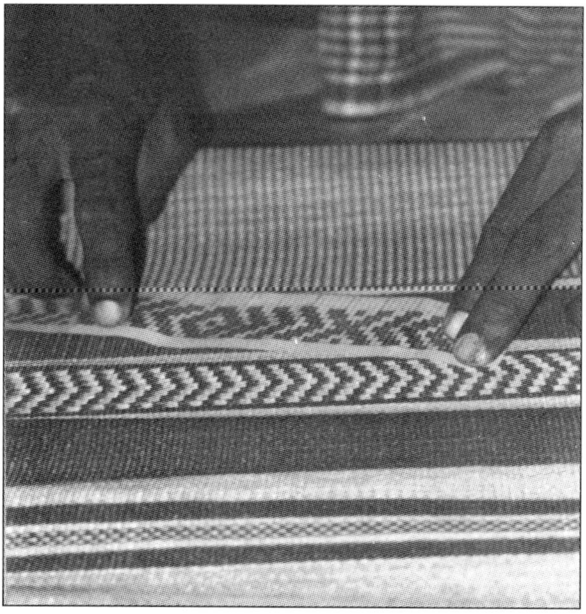

Abdul Wahab compares a paper design with the finished mat. This mat was sold to Craft Enterprises. *Photo*: Soumhya Venkatesan.

Two days, four houses, an NGO, and a shop. It should be clear from the above description that different people, usually from the same household, work together though on occasion they might collaborate with others as well—sometimes in return for immediate payment or on the basis that the service will be reciprocated at some later time. Within a single household some members might weave all the time—that is their way of earning a regular livelihood—while others may do other things returning to weaving or 'designing' on occasion. This latter is more usual in the case of men. Abdul's household is, in fact, the only one where mat weaving forms the sole means of income. Ownership over mats is often difficult to establish although difficult tasks like packing are generally the province of the most skilled member of a household.

Few weavers sell their mats directly to consumers. Almost every finished mat is sold either to a local Labbai trader or to an NGO—at the time of research Craft Enterprises was the main NGO to which most superfine weavers were allied. Traders and NGO sell these mats on usually at specialist craft bazaars held in Indian cities. Craft Enterprises only worked with the superfine quality of mats leaving fine mats to the Labbai traders. Fine mats, being cheaper and more useful in everyday life, are sold not only in craft bazaars but also find markets in less elite spaces and are sold both as craft objects and as ritual objects. This will be discussed in Chapter 8.

The Politics of Space for Weaving

As was seen in the previous section, most weavers work in their homes. Few weavers prefer to work in the communal weaving sheds (of which there are three—one owned by a trader, and the other two on the grounds of the cooperative society). The preference for domestic spaces for weaving should be seen in the light of organisational types for handicraft production throughout India. Cable *et al* (1986) identify four major types of organisation in the Indian handicrafts sector. Simple commodity production is characterised by family members who work in their homes and where goods are sold in local markets without the mediation of traders. In household production some wage labour may be found but the artisanal family remains in control of production and marketing decisions. In household production under a putting-out system, an outside agent is responsible for providing raw materials and credit and for marketing, but production is carried on within the household. This is most common when the cost of raw materials is high, e.g. in silk/metal thread weaving. Factory production is characterised by extensive specialisation and wage labour, high volume production for mass consumption in both domestic and foreign markets. This form of production is comparatively rare in the artisan sector. However, putting-out with specialisation could form what is known as an invisible factory where different stages in production are carried out in different houses which specialise in specific tasks.[22]

The Pattamadai mat weaving industry can most closely be identified with simple commodity production where the artisan is responsible for production within the household (though some specialised tasks such as 'name-writing' may be done by someone outside the home who will be paid). The price of the raw materials is low and value addition by the mat weaver (including in the preparation of korai) constitutes the significant proportion of the price of the finished product. The artisan might buy raw materials from a trader to whom the final product may also be sold but these are usually two separate transactions. The trader does not have any hold on the artisan by supplying him/her with raw materials. The finished mat is most commonly sold to a trader in Pattamadai or an NGO who then circulates it in distant markets. The artisan is also, by and large, able to control the sale of the finished product at least within Pattamadai unless he or she has taken an advance or loan from a specific trader to whom the mat must then be sold. The above factors inform the choice of space for weaving. It is,

[22] For a detailed account of artisanal production in the domestic sphere, see Meis (1982). For accounts detailing the organisation of production and distribution of cloth and other artisanal products in colonial and independent India where the above organisational types exist, see Haynes (1993; 1996a; 1996b); Ludden (1996b); Roy (1993; 1996); Specker (1996); Swallow (1992).

in part, to avoid control over their final product by traders that weavers prefer domestic spaces for production even though there are some non-domestic spaces for weaving, including two sheds in the cooperative society.[23] Any mat woven in the cooperative society has, by prior understanding, to be sold to it.[24] Similarly, Mohammad, who is the most prominent trader of 50-count mats in Pattamadai, and also deals in superfine mats, constructed a 'training and weaving' shed. Any mat woven within these premises was be sold to Mohammad.

No weaver who has the choice uses Mohammad's training shed—indeed the main users are Mohammad's daughters who sell their mats to their father anyway. Saad Ali, who, at the time sold his mats exclusively to Mohammad, had just finished telling me that he found his house very small and inadequate for weaving. I asked him and his wife if they would work in Mohammad's shed. The reply was forceful and used a common Tamil expression: '*Tchah*, who will work there! We will ride our horses in our own small pot! (*yenga gundu chattilla naanga kudhirai ottuvom*).' This expression, roughly translated, means we will be lords in our own spaces.

Not unusually, gender roles also affect choice of weaving sites. In Pattamadai, women are closely associated with the physical limits of their homes and much of their everyday work revolves around the home or is conducted in its vicinity. This includes weaving and other household industries such as *beedi* rolling. A female weaver at home may be required (alone, or with other women in the house) to collect firewood, buy daily provisions, prepare meals,

[23] The shed was constructed in 1999–2000 using a grant meant for improving infrastructure sanctioned by the district collector of Tirunelveli. Though the cooperative society has a serious working capital crisis, the grant could not be put to any other use according to the terms of the scheme under which it was given. The weaving sheds in the cooperative society are long rectangular rooms with looms arranged in a row. A few 50-count weavers work there, though more commonly the room is deserted. One Labbai said, 'At least the second shed can be used as a space to hold marriage feasts.'

[24] If a mat woven in the cooperative is sold elsewhere, the weaver has to pay a percentage of the sale price to the Cooperative Society.

collect water from a municipal collective tap, look after children, etc. It is, therefore, more convenient, when possible, to locate the loom within the house so that all these activities can be combined more easily than if the weaver worked elsewhere and kept having to return to the house. The fact that weaving is seen as one more household task (one in which men might join) is demonstrated by the fact that there is often no individual ownership of mats in Pattamadai. If a weaver is called away to deal with some household task, another member of the house who can, might work at the loom instead.

In the next section I will try and unpack the ways in which weavers feel and talk about their work. Through a discussion of how people learn to weave and what that involves, I will seek to show that most Labbais in Pattamadai, especially those who weave, have deeply ambivalent feelings about this work. This in part stems from the physical work involved in weaving, and in part from the way in which weaving is viewed more generally as old-fashioned work to which only people with few other choices are wholly committed. At the same time, there is also pride. This comes both from weaving well and more generally from hailing from the town and group where the 'finest mats in India' are woven.

Learning to Weave, Learning to be a Weaver

Many Labbais in Pattamadai, even ones who do not weave, describe weaving as their 'traditional occupation' (*paramaparai thozhil*). Good discusses the difference between the two Tamil terms *velai* and *thozhil*. According to him, *velai* refers to job in the normal sense, i.e. one's actual current paid employment. *Thozhil*, on the other hand, refers to hereditary (often caste-specific) speciality. Thus, one's *velai* may not be one's *thozhil* (Good, 1982: 26). This distinction seems to apply in Pattamadai as well. It is revealing that most people refer to mat weaving as *pai* (mat) *thozhil* and to *beedi* rolling as *beedi velai*. In fact, mat weaving is the only occupation which is commonly referred to as *thozhil* by members of the group. Trading, in which many men are engaged is referred to *vyaabaaram*, salaried jobs are termed *udyogam* and other kinds of jobs are termed *velai*.

Most people learn how to weave in their homes especially when other members of the household weave, and both loom and raw materials are around. Teenagers, especially girls, are encouraged by adults in the house to gradually start picking up weaving related tasks until they are able to do pretty much every thing related to making a mat. There is little systematic teaching. The cost of the raw material is low and, therefore, not a deterrent to this kind of learning. It is, in fact, seen as important within the home that girls especially learn how to weave and/or how to roll beedies or leaf cigarettes. It is worth reiterating what the mother of a teenage daughter said to me: 'we teach girls how to weave and to roll *beedi*s as a way of giving them a choice. A boy can always go out and work, but a girl cannot and she may need to have some way of making money after her marriage.' More than one person has said similar things. To this end, girls are also sent outside the home to apprenticeship training schemes that are occasionally organised by the government and run by weavers recognised by the state as 'master craft producers' (discussed in Chapter 6). Weaving here is a resource—something that you do not necessarily want your daughter to have to call on as it is hoped that her husband when she is married will earn enough to support the household, but is useful to have just in case it is required. Few households are able to get by on the income of just one person as the previous chapter showed.

By 1999 I had started to learn how to weave. I felt that if I had to go beyond the craft discourses to see how weavers felt about their work, I had to try and experience this work myself. I asked a household of weavers to whom I was close if they would teach me. I also attended, whenever possible, an apprentice training session wherein Kadher was appointed by the government to teach weaving to students who would be paid a small stipend to attend the six-week-long course.

In the apprentice training space, teenage girls gathered day after day and seemed to spend most of the day desultorily working on weaving related tasks. Korai was being prepared and mats were being produced, but there was a lot of chat and a lot of giggling. There were not enough looms for all of them. Anyway, most already knew how to weave—having watched mothers and others in their homes weave and having sat at looms themselves with someone telling them what to do as and when necessary. Several could also roll *beedis* or leaf cigarettes. Their main reason for attending the apprentice training scheme seemed to be the stipend they were given. Another reason was the opportunity to leave the house for a few hours a day and spend time in congenial company. Normally unmarried sexually mature females are confined to their homes until their marriages.

As far as Kadher was concerned, having trainees who already knew how to weave was a good thing as, under the terms of the trainee scheme, all the mats made during the training period were his to sell. He was rarely in the house that had been hired for this purpose, but was busy with his own projects. All the trainees were female—this too was no coincidence. Even though both men and women can and do weave, weaving in Pattamadai is by and large seen as women's work for the reasons outlined above. Also, few parents would have allowed their daughters to attend the weaving course if there had been young men present.

Furthermore, for Kadher who was keen to be a successful mat trader, female trainees posed less competition to his ambitions–their structural position and the restrictions placed on girls and young women makes it harder for most of them to engage in the craft worlds and travel to craft bazaars, etc. Larger notions of how Muslim women are constrained also makes it less likely that they would be approached by members of the media or by others outside Pattamadai interested in the craft.

Needless to say, my weaving skills are nothing to write home about but what I did learn from the experience of learning around people who were also learning was how weaving is viewed as a resource and one which requires low capital input. In both spaces where I tried to learn weaving two things struck me. The first was the lack of any systematic teaching. The second was the ways in which along with learning the physical tasks of weaving, people were also learning ways of thinking about weaving—as a resource, as something they would do if they needed to earn money, as difficult work with few returns, as one thing they might do alongside other, more socially valued things—marrying, having children, etc. In short, they were learning to be *weavers*. This is a gendered role.

There is less pressure on boys to weave or learn other household-based income-generation tasks. Indeed, as we saw in the previous section, many men can weave, though only a few describe themselves as weavers. Even Saad Ali who is exceedingly proud of his skills as a weaver emphasises that he can do, and has done other things in the past. Saad Ali left Pattamadai once in the 1980s in the company of his brother Abdul. Both men lived in a nearby city and sold sweets they made or bought in the main bus station and on buses.[25] Their reminiscences of these times did not seem to give them pleasure and they recounted tales of hardship where they had to pay bribes to police and bus-stand officials to be allowed to sell their wares. They added that vendors would often be blamed for any theft or crime in the bus station and on occasion had to pay extra bribes to the police to avoid harassment.

Disillusioned by these experiences the brothers returned to Pattamadai. Abdul did not leave again—both he and his wife now weave mats. This is their sole source of income. Despite his commitment to the mat weaving industry however, Abdul sometimes laments his lack of education and skills to work elsewhere and to get a government job. He does not describe mat weaving as his preferred livelihood; nor does he see living in Pattamadai as his preferred life choice. Rather, both seem things to which Abdul has resigned himself and he often compares himself with one of his brothers who lives in Madras and has a government job. At the same time, Abdul is proud of his skills as a weaver and often talks about the 'special mats' he has woven. The warring elements of pride in, and resignation towards, mat weaving appear to be a common theme that runs through the self-narratives of several weavers.

Isakki Muthu, clerk of the Pattamadai Labbai Fine Mat Weavers' Cooperative Society, claimed that the reason for the decline in mat weaving lay in lack of contentment: 'They go to Tirunelveli and to other places, they see other people and want to send their children to school. They are not happy to sit in their houses and weave.'

[25] Abdul once taught me how to make ginger fudge—potent and sweet/hot, it was delicious.

Others explain why they do not weave, or did not learn mat weaving as children, by saying that they 'had no need to do so' (*thevai illai*) or 'we (or our parents were) are people of means' (*vasadhi ullavanga*) or 'my father or husband is in government service so I was never taught or needed to know any work including weaving.' One young female weaver's brother has a diploma in automobile mechanics. When I asked her if he could weave, the answer was unequivocal, 'No, he is educated (*illai, avanga padichavanga*).' Even an eleven-year-old girl whose mother, grandmothers and two aunts (mother's sister and father's sister) weave, voiced the opinion that if it were at all financially possible, most people would abandon mat weaving. Mat weaving is almost universally seen as drudgery and as difficult work (*kashtamaana velai*).

What then does the social role of weaver imply? The answer to this question depends in part on whom one asks. It also depends on people's relationships to the mats that they weave. I suggest that there is a difference between a weaver—a social role, usually denoting helplessness and lack of success in other spheres; and knowing how to weave which can become a way of achieving other aims—most Labbai traders can weave even if they rarely do so. Apart from a few exceptions, men weave when they want to achieve something other than just money—fame, the opportunity to meet a powerful person or join an important network. For this they do not need to weave day after day as do weavers who earn their livelihood from their mats and who are tied to their looms and to their homes.

Both men and women emphasise the hard physical labour that weaving involves. 'It causes back pain and stomach problems, it weakens the eyesight, it can affect the reproductive health of young women' are common complaints. The body on the loom goes through a huge amount of physical stress. Having the feet up on the foot pad leaving the back unsupported, having to constantly move one foot down to press hard on the bamboo stick to create the shed, bending low over the mat when picking out designs. All of these are difficult, especially if one has to do them for several hours, day after day. And yet, 'what choice do we have?' they ask. 'We need the money.' When there is money, people often stop weaving only to take it up when money becomes tight again. Writing about the *Patta* painters of Raghurajpur in Orissa, Bundgaard recognises that: 'To these people, the crafts they produce are first of all a source of livelihood. Their engagement in craft production is…a matter of economic necessity…the importance of economics in the lives of craftsmen cannot be stressed too much…' (1999: 81).

But, there is pride and excitement too for some people in producing innovative, interesting and, to them, beautiful objects. One can over-determine the importance of money—for some weavers the desire for fame and recognition as well as the opportunities afforded by these are also valuable. However, money is important.

Production and Re-production

An exclusive focus on physical production elides the ways in which the mats are doubly produced—discursively as craft objects (this was discussed in Chapter 1) and physically.[26] Indeed the former is crucial for the continued production of superfine mats as the weavers have little use for them. This is discussed below. However, it is important to think about the physical work that goes into making a mat, as this affects how weavers think about their work—as difficult, old-fashioned, high in opportunity cost, and lacking in mobility or advancement. Within Pattamadai, to be a weaver is to be identified in a particular way—as someone who is

[26] Haku Shah writes about encouraging a woman to take up applique work when her husband whom Shah knew was out of work: 'Although she was not making [appliqué pieces], but I thought being a mochi caste [Cobbler] she may be able to do so…in earlier times the mochis decorated saddles with chain stitch embroidery…The illiterate often possess an unspoiled creativity' (Shah, 1999: 52–3). Here, Shah justifies his encouraging a woman to take up a physical skill on the basis of an inherent disposition of which *he* is aware and she not. Indeed she demurs at first and then tries her hand at applique at his insistence. Needless to say, he writes that she becomes good at it. Such is the relationship between skill and knowledge. The point is not that Haku Shah's help did not manage to turn around the life of this poor family, rather it is how he arrived at a solution for her.

poor, who has few choices. It is a feminised position even if both men and women weave. Outside Pattamadai and within the craft worlds, weavers are romanticised, their work seen as creative and materialising the essence of the nation and its rich heritage. This positions the weavers and their objects within a national narrative. It also affects expectations about how a mat ought to look as I will show.

The re-production of Pattamadai mats as craft objects takes place outside the home; often outside Pattamadai town as well—in the offices of non-governmental and governmental agencies, museums, English and other language newspapers and magazines and other media, specialist craft shops and bazaars. It is development agents and other members of the craft worlds who actively engage in the word images of craft and who shape the object and the image of the particular craft to fit in with idealised perceptions originating elsewhere. Traders too participate in this re-production. The most successful of the traders speak about the mats as examples of India's ancient craft tradition, invoke the mat gifted to the Queen and urge representatives of governmental and other development agencies to ensure the mat's (and, by extension, their own) presence in various fora. They speak of the dying craft tradition and the urgent requirement of marketing and other support to ensure that the craft survives—this despite the fact that mats readily find markets today. The traders also utilise the media in their efforts and arrange to give mats as gifts to important politicians and other famous people. Few weavers concern themselves with these processes—merely ensuring that they can sell what they make and allowing themselves to be spoken for, even objectified in certain spheres. Furthermore, for most weavers, especially females, this knowledge or form of production is harder to learn. Some do not want to learn it, others who might want to do so find it difficult to access the spaces where this knowledge is reproduced and circulated. The Labbai traders jealously guard their access to the craft worlds and only weavers who are closely associated with traders—usually their sons or daughters are encouraged to go to craft bazaars and engage with the craft markets. Sons especially, though they might know how to weave, are taught not to be weavers but to be traders.

Thus, few weavers participate in re-production of the mats yet it is crucial if the mats are to find a market. Superfine mats, especially, are expensive, reflecting the amount of time taken to produce them. Costing up to Rs 4,000 or £50 each, they are produced for sale—weavers cannot afford not to sell them; even if they could afford to hold on to their mats, they would have no use for them. One weaver said to me: What do people do with our superfine mats once they have bought them? She was quite serious in her question. The mats are too fine and slippery to spread on the floor to sit or sleep on. Most weavers use mats all the time in their homes to sit or sleep on, but they prefer the coarser thicker machine-made varieties that are readily and cheaply available in the market. A few have fine mats, but hardly any Labbai household in the town has or uses superfine mats.

Aesthetics and Authenticity

People who buy craft mats display them on their walls or place them on floors like rugs. They buy these mats in specialist craft bazaars organised by NGOs and governmental agencies, or from craft shops in cities like Madras and Delhi where the mats are displayed alongside other Indian craft objects. In the words of one craft developer, 'crafts are traditional yet contemporary.' This vision of craft is a way of ensuring that modern India can march hand in hand with ancient India. Craft mats sold in these spaces have to conform to a stringent set of visual criteria. Ideally they would be dyed with vegetable colours and decorated with geometric patterns and stripes. These are considered 'traditional' and, therefore, authentic. The authentic mat is identified on the basis of museum samples and from older mats that may be found in the homes of urban elites and, therefore, already reflect their taste. There will be no writing on the craft mat, nor will it have any representational images.

By and large most mats that weavers make are not dissimilar to those they have woven in the past. While weaving these mats does not generate huge excitement among weavers, it is a rare weaver who will not take great care in the making of the mat and in ensuring that the key aesthetic criteria of finely textured fabric and symmetrical patterns are satisfied to the best of his or her ability. Even in a household where different people's work has gone into the mat, the most skilled among them will take charge of the weaving of designs and the final packing. Weavers frequently judge their own work and that of others, and they do this on the basis of the texture of the fabric and the neatness of the work—something that is a product of skill in splitting the korai, laying the warp, and in the tightness of the weave and the packing. There is, then, pride in doing a job well, and in producing an object that is acceptable and unexceptionable. Not doing this has financial repercussions. Money from weaving translates into food and subsistence.

The point I want to emphasise here is that by and large weaving is seen as something that brings money. This is the bottom line and dictates the forms that mats take—colours, patterns, sizes have to conform to what traders—NGOs, local Labbai traders or wholesalers—want and can sell.

It is the month of Ramadan in 2002, two days before one of the most important festivals of the Muslim calendar—Eid ul Fitr. I am in Jeenat's house. Jeenat is furious. A mat she has woven for a wholesale buyer is in the process of being rejected by the buyer who commissioned a number of mats from her. The reason for the rejection? The colour of the mat Jeenat has woven does not correspond to the woman's request for a 'coffee-coloured mat'. Rather than the purplish black that the woman meant by this name, Jeenat has woven a dark blue-green mat. Both women are obstinate—the buyer will not take the mat, and Jeenat, who needs the money to buy special foods for the Eid festival, will not back down from her claim that the mat has been made and cannot be rejected. She is not arguing about the qualities of the mat—rather her initial point is a technical one about the name of a colour and what is meant by it, and later, and more insistently, a financial one—'it is Eid, I spent so much time weaving this mat, I need the money, what am I going to do with it if it is not sold.'

In the end, I buy the mat—to my eyes it is beautiful. It is now spread out on my office floor where I see it everyday.

There is a very real fear that a mat on which time, money and effort have been expended will be rejected. Most weavers are content to weave mats that will sell—altercations like the one detailed above do occur but not very frequently. There are, however, a few weavers who seek individual recognition, and to innovate and display their technical skills and taste. For most weavers, a memorable mat that indexes the taste and technical virtuosity of its maker is one that has bright colours, has writing woven into it and also perhaps a representational design. The mat may have silk threads interwoven with the korai. This permits both textural variation and finer designs. The avenues for a weaver to weave such a mat without having to bear the considerable opportunity costs on their own and then to successfully make a mark with it in the craft worlds are extremely limited.

In 1999 Fathima decided to weave what she called a 'special mat'. She wanted to enter this mat for a prestigious craft awards competition—the national awards for craft producers (discussed in Chapter 6). Fathima spent time and effort on the design of her mat. In addition to incorporating silk threads into the mat, she also decided she wanted to weave a complicated central design into it and chose a picture of the Taj Mahal. This needed to be rendered into a weavable format. She did this by plotting the entire design onto a graph sheet. The colours she chose were bright and vibrant—pinks, greens, blues. The mat took time to weave, and unlike most mats woven by weavers, was not commissioned by anyone nor was there a buyer for it. Fathima submitted the mat to the awards competition. It did not win an award nor was the mat returned to her for well over a year. Hearing that I was on my way to Delhi Fathima asked me if I would track down her mat for her. Accordingly I went to the Government of India Handicrafts Office and was redirected to the Tamilnadu State Handicrafts Emporium in the city. The mat had been there until recently, I was told, but had just been sent back to Fathima. The head of the emporium was disdainful about it—'who would pay money for that!' she exclaimed. 'It is too modern and bright, not like an *authentic* Pattamadai mat.'

Having seen photographs of this mat and watched the making of another 'special' mat woven by Khadeeja Beevi for a national award that also incorporated silk threads, bright colours, writing and an image of a peacock (this too did not win an award), and having listened to people in Pattamadai as well as Khadeeja and Fathima talk about their mats, it was quite clear to me that both women were weaving mats that they (and others in Pattamadai) found both beautiful and technically highly skilled. Nevertheless, at the national level, both mats were completely disregarded as 'inauthentic' and deviating too much from the accepted aesthetic. The craft weaver it seems must only produce 'craft objects' recognised as such by the craft worlds. Their own aesthetic is disregarded when it does not conform to this larger vision of what the craft object ought to look like.

In this chapter, I have shown both how the mat is made, and how the weaver is made. I suggested that we cannot know why weaving occupies a negotiated status in Pattamadai without knowing what the work involves and how it is learnt, and alongside this, what other things are learned. The chapter questions assumptions about the non-alienability of 'craft objects' from their makers—a common way in which craft is opposed to industrial production—and shows how, notwithstanding weaver's involvement with the object from 'sedge to silk', the value of the work is nevertheless caught up in the dynamics of the market and is subject to combining with *skill* in making the *knowledge* of how to make things that will sell. This is not always vested in the same person. Rather, weavers are seen as skilled, and craft experts, a category which might include some traders who can but do not weave, as knowledgeable in how a mat ought to look, what it stands for, how it should be spoken about. Craft objects in India are, both in terms of their physical forms and the descriptions that surround them, the product of collaborations between artisans and interested others. The objects are not separate from their descriptions. They are outcomes. This will emerge time and again in other chapters of the book. The next chapter focuses on relationships within the craft industry between weavers, traders, the fine mat cooperative society and NGOs.

5 Uneasy Balances

In Chapters 3 and 4 we entered weavers' homes to explore the ways in which households and individuals strategise within the limits of their larger constraints. The discussions showed that weaving has a negotiated value in Pattamadai. I suggested that the Labbais of Pattamadai 'own' mat weaving in three separate ways. First, the technical knowledge of weaving is relatively easily accessible, either within the household or within the larger kin group, to any Labbai in Pattamadai who wishes to learn the skill. This makes every Labbai in Pattamadai potentially a mat weaver. Second, mat weaving is an important aspect of the self-identification of the Labbais of Pattamadai and is identified by many as the 'traditional occupation' of the Labbais. Third, the fine and superfine mat weaving industry of Pattamadai has been classified as a craft activity within the larger craft discourses, and the Labbais of Pattamadai have been deemed a 'craft community'. The mat weaving industry and the Labbais of Pattamadai are both targets of specific kinds of developmental activity and are eligible for participation in the various schemes of the central and state governments and other agencies working with crafts in India. These include training programmes, marketing opportunities and micro-credit schemes. Weavers only form one part of the mat weaving industry in Pattamadai. Other actors include traders, the cooperative society, and the non-governmental organisation, Craft Enterprises.

I suggest that, for the Labbai group, the existence of the mat weaving industry represents a resource through which they can not only earn a livelihood, but also collectively and/or individually tap into government funds and loans from the formal sectors of the economy. Thus, individuals may profess a commitment to the mat weaving industry, whether they actually weave or not, so that they can benefit from craft development schemes. Most people are aware that non-weavers often access governmental and other funds meant for weavers. Even those who weave, rarely invest these funds into weaving.[1] This too is common knowledge. There is, thus, a certain amount of cooperation and complicity within the larger Labbai group. At the same time, the presence of conflicting interests between different individuals and groups can lead to tensions. The simultaneous existence of both—complicity/cooperation and competition—mean that the weaving industry is characterised by uneasy balances and short-term alliances. Furthermore, there is also a tendency to avoid closure of relations. By unpacking the various relationships within the mat weaving industry, I show in this chapter

[1] As has already been discussed in Chapter 3, in the section 'fluctuating fortunes', under a 'loan to artisans scheme' the local bank initiated a group loan scheme whereby specially constituted groups of twenty female weavers would be given low interest loans of Rs 10,000 each to be used for production purposes. Two such groups were formed; not every woman who joined the groups was a weaver, nor, to my knowledge, did any of the women use the loan amount for production purposes, i.e. as working capital or to acquire capital assets. Most households used the amount to pay off debts; some used it to acquire jewellery. One weaver household said that they would have built a weaving shed but, as the loan amount was too small for that purpose, a gold necklace was bought instead. The weaver described this as a form of saving. For a discussion of problems and issues relating to group micro-credit schemes in India, see Kaladhar (1996).

how they are in a constant state of negotiation and managed by local actors who strive to benefit, at least in the short term, from as many opportunities as possible, whatever their source. 'Creative opportunism' is thus an important organising principle.[2]

In this chapter I move out of the home to the spaces where mats are bought by different kinds of wholesaler and focus on the interplay between weavers, traders, cooperative society and NGOs. Through a processual examination of local organising practices within the mat weaving industry, I argue that while craft developers (state agencies or NGOs) see the Labbai group as a community that is based around production, consumption is equally, if not more, important to the group and may be seen as coterminous with the boundaries of the community. This affects the ways in which members interact within the group and with various development agents and schemes.

Weavers and Traders

As was suggested in the previous chapter, the successful trader transcends the relatively powerless role of object producer, becoming instead a producer of images. I suggest that the trader is not merely someone who buys cheap and sells dear. He actively adds value of an intangible but nevertheless crucial kind by engaging with, managing, and shaping (this last to a very small extent) images of the mat weaving industry as a 'traditional craft industry'. We can think of the trader as a source of value in two ways. First, as someone who buys objects produced by weavers, he makes the mat valuable to the weaver in monetary terms. Second, in selling the mat on, he makes it valuable through positioning it as a traditional craft object. The trader's engagement with the craft worlds is also directly valuable to him. It enables him to build up networks and become more visible outside Pattamadai. As a consequence he becomes the focus of intervention programmes and schemes. This in turn increases the influence he has over the mat weaving industry.

2 Dore and Mars (1981: 39) use the term to refer to the mobilising of motivational resources which the local culture and social structure make available as the fuel for collective effort.

Thus influence within the mat weaving industry can result from recognition outside Pattamadai.

To both weavers and traders, the mat represents an income. However, for the trader to realise an income from the mat (especially in the case of relatively highly priced fine and superfine mats), he has to refashion the mat and make it more than an object for sale. It has also to represent an ideal. To this end, traders engage with prevailing images of craft outside Pattamadai in ways that differentiate them from weavers. In fact, 'sweet speech' (*inimaiyana pecchu*) is identified by actors in Pattamadai as one of the most important assets of powerful and persuasive men.[3]

The most successful local traders are influential in more arenas of Pattamadai Labbai life than just weaving. They are concerned not merely with the productive capabilities of the group as mat weavers, but also with social reproduction, which includes consumption. Mohammad, for example, is the head of the Labbai Association and a member of the Pattamadai mosque committee.[4] The president of the cooperative society is one of the group's main moneylenders and has key political connections.

3 The phrase was used by a weaver while talking about a trader. This term, sweet speech, is used more generally to explain how persuasive people get their way. It is not necessarily a compliment.

4 Caste or group alliance is an important organising factor in Pattamadai as in other parts of Tamilnadu (see Mines, 1984, 1994) and different caste groups have formed associations. Individuals join craft groups to protect both individual and collective interests. The Labbai Association is one such organisation. Mohammad, the trader and also president of the Labbai Association told me that the association exists to resolve disputes between different groups in the town and within the Labbai group. From what I could gather, the association has few powers and can only be effective when actors are willing to accede to the recommendations of the board of elected officials. Male heads of households pay a monthly subscription of two rupees to the association. This allows them and their households to participate in the association and also, importantly, to borrow the large vessels used for cooking during feasts. These vessels are owned by the association and stored in the second important Labbai organisation in Pattamadai, The Labbai Fine Mat Weavers' Cooperative Society. This latter will be introduced soon.

In this section I describe one of the fundamental inequalities existing between weavers and traders. This can broadly be characterised as follows. Traders, for reasons that stem from their personal attributes and/or connections and relative wealth, have more access to resources and to larger networks than weavers. It is they, rather than weavers, who have a voice in the craft worlds. As crucial intermediaries in the conversion of mats to money, weavers are dependent on traders. However this implies another type of dependency. Traders are dependent on weavers for their stocks of mats. This recalls Giddens's insight that 'all forms of dependence offer some resources whereby those who are subordinate can influence the activities of their superiors' (Giddens, 1984: 16).

This affects the balance of relationships between traders and weavers. Weavers, by not weaving, or by choosing to sell elsewhere when possible, can and do affect traders adversely. Additionally, the categories of weaver and trader are fluid. Weavers sell their own mats to end-users if the occasion arises. Some traders are weavers themselves while others are closely linked with weavers, often their wives or daughters weave. Office bearers and members of the cooperative society also trade on their own account, a few weave. The lifestyles of traders and weavers are often very similar; to meet various expenditures weavers and traders frequently draw from the same pool of strategies including, among others, migration of household members to the Middle East, loans from moneylenders and ROSCAs.

Kinship is a normative factor in the mat weaving industry, but although some weavers speak in terms of selling their mats to a particular trader because he is a close relative, it does not necessarily prevent them from moving to other traders if they are dissatisfied with the existing situation.[5] To this end, traders often have to coax and coerce weavers into selling them their mats. They do this through what can be termed a mixture of patronage and

[5] For discussions relating to kinship as an organising practice in artisanal production in India, see Mehta (1997) and Meis (1982). Outside India, see Long and Richardson (1978) and White (2000). In Pattamadai, the closest parallels can be drawn with the groups described by Meis and Long.

exploitation. A trader may lend a weaver money which is to be repaid in mats over a period of time. A trader may also sponsor weavers for awards or send selected individuals to sell mats on their behalf at craft bazaars. For both of these latter the trader needs to have contacts outside Pattamadai.

While many networks in Pattamadai, particularly among the Labbais are 'closed networks' based primarily around kinship groups, some Labbais are participants in 'open networks' (Beteille, 1996). Open networks comprise individuals from many walks of life. They have the potential to keep growing and to encompass other networks. Traders, because of the nature of their work, which takes them outside Pattamadai and allows them to interact with members of craft worlds and buyers from diverse backgrounds, often participate in open networks. People in Pattamadai do recognise, as Simmel did, that: 'In trade, which alone makes possible unlimited combinations, intelligence always finds expansions and new territories, an achievement which is very difficult to achieve for the original producer with his lesser mobility...' (Simmel, 1950: 403).

The negotiated value of weaving, especially observed in the narratives of men who weave, is closely linked to Simmel's insights about the distinction between the producer and the trader. The weaver cannot be mobile. The very nature of his occupation requires his physical presence at the loom, which is firmly fixed in space. Men who take up trading (of mats or of other kinds of articles) or become migrant workers, on the other hand, sample new experiences, difficult though their lives may be. Their narratives reveal distaste for certain aspects of migration and pleasure in others. Some weavers, therefore, want to take up trading. They see this as a better choice than the drudgery of weaving. One such weaver was especially eager to relate his experiences in Delhi and Hyderabad where he went to sell mats. Other weavers, usually female, while not necessarily content with weaving, have fewer options.

As representatives of weavers and the weaving industry to the world outside Pattamadai, traders are very visible. But they occupy an ambiguous moral position. While they can be cast in a paternalistic role because their activities create markets for products made by weavers who cannot, for various reasons, sell their own products, they are more often depicted as exploitative because they buy mats from weavers and sell them on at higher prices. Certain kinds of traders/trading organisations are, however, less vulnerable in this regard than others. These include cooperative societies and non-governmental organisations whose motives are seen as essentially disinterested and which are seen as existing to 'empower' the weavers through various means.

Some weavers supply their mats only to specific traders. The strongest weaver-trader alliances reflect very close kinship ties and the trader may be the weaver's father or husband. However, weavers also ally themselves to specific traders for other reasons. These include kinship ties, the security that the trader will always buy the weaver's mats and give advances when needed, though this may also, as weavers point out, be a form of exploitation. Within the same household, one weaver may sell her mats exclusively to one trader, while another weaver may sell hers to another. Some weavers sell mats to whoever is willing to pay for them. They resist an exclusive relationship with any one trader. Most weaver-trader relationships are fluid and it is not uncommon to see a weaver who was selling mats exclusively to one trader, shift her entire business to another. Weavers and traders also collaborate in order to gain access to opportunities emanating from the craft development mechanism.

I will now focus on two prominent Labbais who own mat shops in Pattamadai. One of them, Meeran,[6] concentrates on the wholesale mat trade, supplying mats to shops throughout India. He is himself a weaver who makes superfine mats. His wife weaves 50-count mats and his son works with him in the mat shop. The other trader, Mohammad, who was introduced in the previous chapter, concentrates on retail sales especially on mats as 'craft' and ritual objects. Neither of the two men trades exclusively in Pattamadai mats, though the latter specialises in the retail sale of

[6] Between the completion of fieldwork and the publication of this book, S M Meeran has passed away. He is sorely missed.

50-count Pattamadai mats while the former sells mats of different qualities to shops and to handicraft emporiums.

Mohammad and Meeran can be described as rivals, yet because they have carved out specific spheres within which they operate, they are able to work in Pattamadai in relative harmony. This is true even though there have been instances where they have competed directly against each other to gain control over weavers or weaving equipment. The competition over weavers, particularly, can be intense. One weaver who sells her mats solely to one of the two men, spoke of how the other was always asking her to sell him mats too. Information is also jealously guarded. Both traders knew, for instance, that I was on speaking terms with the other. This led one of them to make a point of always asking me what the other had said or was doing. I tried to be guarded, but am sure did nevertheless pass on some information.

Despite the simmering rivalry, these 'mat-shop men' (*pai-kadai kaarar*) as they are referred to in Pattamadai, can and do make common cause on occasion especially when there is any perceived threat from outside. They are also first cousins—sons of sisters. At the marriage of the daughter of one of them, I was told that the wife of the other played an important role as the aunt (father's brother's wife) of the bride. It is thus difficult to characterise the exact nature of the relationship between Mohammad and Meeran and their families. Like many relationships it is marked with elements of cooperation and rivalry.

Both Mohammad and Meeran set up their mat shops in Pattamadai in the late 1970s. Before that, they were sales agents for the cooperative society and used to buy mats from the Society to sell elsewhere. Indeed the history of the cooperative movement in the Pattamadai mat weaving industry is punctuated by the struggle between private enterprise and community endeavour.

In the next section I trace the Pattamadai Labbai Fine Mat Weavers' Cooperative Society from its inception to the present day. This serves to provide the background for the emergence of the cooperative society and private traders in Pattamadai, to analyse the relationship between the society and traders, and to discuss weavers' perceptions of both traders and the society.

The Cooperative Society

The Pattamadai Labbai Fine Mat Weavers' Cooperative Society was founded in 1954 following a visit to Pattamadai by Kamaladevi Chattopadhyay. The cooperative was not the first association of weavers formed in Pattamadai. In 1937 a group of forty weavers came together to alleviate two of their most pressing needs—the development of a steady market and access to raw materials. The impetus seems to have come from outside the group:

> Though fine mats were produced for a long time, the Lubbais never thought of organising themselves into any association or society to present an organised front...Mats were produced individually and sold to wholesale merchants...It was in the interests of the wholesale merchants to prevent any organised effort towards forming an association or a society...Some philanthropic customers...saw the woeful state in which the weavers existed and advised them to unite together to form some sort of economic organisation to improve their economic condition. (Nambiar, 1964: 5–6)

However, despite increasing membership numbers, the association of 1937 was, according to Nambiar (ibid.), marked by inefficiency and corruption. This led to its ultimate dissolution in 1950. Soon after that a fresh association was formed and re-registered. This new association, however, was unable to resolve the problems that had beset the earlier one.

The main issue facing both the associations of 1937 and 1950 was the assumption of control by private traders and the promotion of vested interests. Thus Nambiar writes of the 1937 association, '...the Secretary of the Association who was himself a wholesale merchant used to purchase the finished product at a low price and make a profit by selling at a high price.' Similarly, of the 1950 association he says, 'It was every man for himself...no one worked for the benefit of the Association' (ibid.: 6). In 1953, as was discussed earlier, following the public display of a mat specially commissioned by an individual for presentation to Queen Elizabeth II on her coronation, the Pattamadai Labbai Fine Mat Weavers' Cooperative Society was formed with the encouragement and financial support of the erstwhile All India Handicrafts Board.[7] For a time, at least from the somewhat nostalgic recollections of weavers, the Cooperative seems to have had the support of every mat weaver and trader in Pattamadai.

In 1961, when Nambiar and his associates studied the mat weaving industry, they reported that 173 persons were employed in the production of fine mats; all of them belonged to the Labbai community. Further, 'no mat weaver is outside the control of the Society. There are no independent workers. This is a unique feature of the craft' (ibid.: 6). Weavers, in their narratives regarding 'those days', corroborate this. According to one weaver, twenty or thirty years ago, if a van drove into Pattamadai, there would be no doubt in anyone's mind that it was headed for the society, as they refer to it, to pick up mats. Another weaver described how, when she was young, every time a mat was begun on a loom, officials from the cooperative would show up and mark the mat to indicate that it was claimed by the society. No one was allowed to sell mats privately. This 'control', according to weavers, was a good thing as there was no space for private traders who might exploit the weavers. [8]

There is little doubt that for a time the cooperative society was able to win concessions for weavers from the state and central governments, both for individuals and for the industry as a whole. Thus, in 1974, on the representations of the cooperative society and with the support of the speaker of the Tamilnadu legislative assembly,[9] weavers who did not own their houses were given land for housing by the Tamilnadu state government. A photograph on display in the society building in Pattamadai shows smiling weavers

[7] This has since become the Office of the Development Commissioner (Handicrafts).

[8] The word 'control' is one used commonly by the weavers and traders in Pattamadai. It refers to the ability of an individual or institution to curb and direct the actions of others. Control can be a negative or a positive thing. Here, it is clearly seen as positive that the cooperative society controlled weavers.

[9] He was also the first secretary of the cooperative society.

being presented with deeds to land. Similarly, in the 1960s the cooperative was able to win concessions from the state government giving it exclusive rights over korai growing in certain areas.[10]

Today, few weavers sell mats to the cooperative, which is faced with a working capital crisis and, therefore, unable to pay them. Most weavers in Pattamadai prefer to sell to private traders or to Craft Enterprises and, after the NGO ceased to be, to other kinds of trader. Of the 250 or so members of the cooperative, less than twenty weave. Stories about corruption among office bearers abound. Weavers and traders also claim that office bearers favour their close associates over others in most matters. Both weavers and the president, vice-president and secretary of the cooperative link the decline in the society with the re-emergence of private traders in the Pattamadai mat weaving industry in the late 1970s and the early 1980s. On the other hand, traders claim that they broke away from the cooperative because of its corrupt and inefficient workings. For weavers the decline of the cooperative has meant the loss of an important means of representation and organisation. This is something that many of them recognise and lament. As one weaver said, 'The existence of private traders who compete with the Society is like pouring the water of one river into four rivers.' But, of course, four rivers can go to three more places than just the one river. This too is recognised.

The most prominent office bearers of the cooperative society do not weave nor do immediate members of their families. This distances them from weavers' concerns. More significantly, two of its five directors (including the man who was vice-president at the time of fieldwork) are prominent moneylenders within the Labbai group. The high interest rates that they charge on loans cause considerable distress and anxiety. This adds to the common perception that the cooperative (as represented by these office bearers) has no incentive to help weavers get out of the cycle of poverty and debt. Despite this, few weavers seriously question the

[10] This, however, had lapsed for a number of years until Craft Enterprises made an attempt to revive it in 1999–2000. See Venkatesan, 2002b, Chapter 7.

continued existence of the cooperative society. According to one man, the society is the only registered organisation of the Labbai community. It represents the Labbais of Pattamadai. He argued that, for this reason, it should not be dissolved, whether or not it worked to help weavers, because it still served a function for the Labbais of Pattamadai. His is not an uncommon position. In part, his comment indicates how mat weaving is tied up with the identity of the Labbais of Pattamadai despite the fact that many Labbais do not weave. It also shows how the society is identified by local actors as an organisation through which government funds and aid for craft development can be channelled and utilised by the larger Labbai group.

Private Traders and the Cooperative Society

The private traders and the office bearers of the society are Labbais.[11] They act as middlemen between the weavers and the craft worlds. In that sense their presence is crucial to the mat industry. Both traders and the cooperative deal in various kinds of mats (including powerloom mats and plastic mats). Their stock is not confined to Pattamadai fine and superfine mats. They are thus less dependent on the weavers than the weavers are on them. However, cooperative societies, as I discussed earlier, have one advantage over traders. The governmental emphasis on the formation and support of cooperatives as a way of empowering artisans has meant that many government schemes are only available through the cooperative structure. If they want to benefit from these, the cooperative society must not only exist, the traders must also be on friendly terms with its office bearers. Even though traders compete with the cooperative for markets and weavers, they do not stand to gain from its dissolution. In this, traders' attitudes are very close to that of the weavers. The difference is that traders and the cooperative can and do come together to counter developments which they perceive as inimical to their control over the mat weaving industry.

[11] The exception to this is one society director who is a member of a scheduled caste as per state government requirements. The current secretary, who is a salaried employee, is not Labbai.

The traders have constructed a sophisticated discourse around the cooperative. At different times and depending on the situation, traders decry the cooperative or uphold it as an ideal institution. When they show visitors around Pattamadai or speak to reporters about the mat weaving industry, traders are at pains to point out the shortcomings of the society and to present themselves as reasonable alternatives. In an article in *The Hindu*, Mohammad said: 'The people in one voice complain that [the] price offered by the society [sic.] is low compared to the hard work put by them. Further the private businessmen provide the cash on hand for the finished products' (20/10/1994).

Mohammad and Meeran also make veiled allegations of corruption (*oozhal*) against the cooperative. Yet both are members and emphasise this fact when it is expedient to be so.

The cooperative society and the private traders have, in effect, forged an uneasy alliance. Office bearers of the cooperative and several weavers blame the traders for the decline of the society. The traders claim that weavers do not want to supply their mats to the society because they are not paid promptly. The fact that traders rarely pay weavers promptly for their mats is, of course, not considered worthy of mention. Traders also point out that according to its own rules, the cooperative can only pay standard prices based on the size and count of mats sold to it. According to them, this discourages good weavers from supplying mats to the cooperative as they are paid the same amount as weavers who are less skilled. It is certainly true that the cooperative is permanently short of rolling stock. When a large order is placed with the cooperative or when it receives invitations to exhibitions it has to buy mats from the traders and is, therefore, dependent on them.

The dynamic nature of the mat weaving industry and the compromised nature of the cooperative society is made clear by the fact that the newest mat shop in Pattamadai opened in the last few months of 2000. The shop was opened by the brother of the president of the society. Many Labbais in Pattamadai claim, however, that the real owner of the shop is the 'president'.[12]

[12] He is commonly referred to by this term throughout the Labbai group.

Weavers, Traders and the 'Society'

'He [the trader] does not pay me on time. But I do not quarrel with him. He has his own problems and he is also a relative.' These words of a mat weaver show some of the issues which affect the relationship between weavers and traders in Pattamadai. Weavers not only interact with traders within the context of the mat weaving industry. As members of the same marriage group, mosque and community association,[13] weavers and traders interact on many levels. Other considerations, therefore, impinge on, and affect relationships.

Notwithstanding weavers' complaints about traders' practices (especially delayed payments for mats), weavers see the traders as being 'like us', i.e. from a similar background and facing similar constraints. As many Labbai men are traders by profession, they and their families are aware of the vicissitudes of the trading profession. One weaver summed it up: 'A trader takes so many risks. Traders...have to cope with slack seasons. This is why they do not pay us on time and buy mats from us for far less than they can sell them.'

The weavers of Pattamadai can be described as 'cottage-craftsmen' (Goody, 1982) or as 'own-account household production units' (Cable *et al*, 1986: 43). Both these terms refer to the fact that the processes of manufacture and sale are controlled by members of the domestic group itself. Most weavers work in their own homes and are not part of an 'invisible factory' or 'putting out system'. This does not mean to imply that there are no factors which limit or seek to limit the household's control over the products of its labour. What it does mean in Pattamadai is that theoretically at least, mat weavers are able to sell their mats to anyone who wishes to buy them.

Traders, especially those who live and work in Pattamadai, constantly seek to control, through various means, this freedom of the weavers. The main purpose of this is to ensure a steady supply of mats for the trader. To this end, a trader might encourage weavers

[13] The Pattamadai Labbai Association.

to be dependent on him through the giving of loans and advances.[14] Not all weavers take loans from traders, however, and such weavers are able to sell their mats to whomsoever they choose. Traders also delay payments for mats, thus creating and sustaining a relationship based on the money owed to the weaver. One weaver remarked, 'They take four or five days to pay you for a mat and you have to keep going to them to collect your money. They also know when you have a new mat on the loom.[15] So when you go to collect your money, they ask about your mat and you cannot say "no, I will not sell it to you", as this will further delay payment.'

Saad Ali, widely acknowledged as a very skilled weaver, agreed with this analysis but felt that traders could get away with this kind of behaviour only with mediocre weavers: 'My mats are good so he [the trader] knows that he has to pay me or I will take the mat back. I can easily find another buyer for it. Those who weave bad or ordinary mats are stuck because they cannot demand their mat back; they may not find other buyers.'

This, in fact, is an important pointer to the way in which traders handle different weavers. Unlike the cooperative society, which is obliged to pay the same price to all weavers, traders (as they frequently point out) are free to vary the price according to the quality of each mat. If a weaver makes a mat, the merchant does not have to accept it, yet often does for strategic reasons (also see Roy, 1993: 21). Sitting in the mat shops I observed on many occasions the ways in which traders withheld payment from weavers despite taking the mats which the weavers brought in. A partial payment might be made. When the weaver protested and said (s)he needed money and required the full payment, the trader would prevaricate pleading his own constraints and lack of

[14] Arterburn discusses similar practices among silk weavers in Kanchipuram (1982: 113–4).

[15] Mohammad, for instance, employs a man who rides around Pattamadai on a bicycle, collecting finished mats and keeping an eye on mats on looms in various houses. Meeran's household produces part of his stock. He also buys mats from a Labbai woman whose son goes to weavers' houses every other day both to collect mats for her and to collect 42- and lower-count mats in which he trades.

cash. Sometimes, a little more would be given. At other times, the trader would persuade the weaver to wait a few days or until (s)he brought in the next mat.

Some weavers do not face these kinds of problems, however. A very skilled weaver who can weave intricately patterned mats said that she rarely had any problem with the trader to whom she sold her mats. On the contrary, payments were prompt and were raised when the prices of raw materials went up. She added that, while she only supplied her mats to one of the private traders, the others were always asking her to sell him her mats. She did not want to do this, as she was happy with her situation. At the same time, a weaver who does not get on with traders might find it impossible to sell his mats, however good.

The fact that weavers and traders are linked by many ties also means that judgement about actions takes place on several levels. One weaver suggested that while he could do what the traders did, he would not as he feared divine judgement: 'I can sell a mat for far more than it costs to someone who does not know better. But if I do that, and someone in my family falls ill, I would feel that this is Allah's judgement on me and his way of taking away the extra money I made on the mat by making me spend it on medicines.'

Another weaver discussed the amount of money spent on medication for his ailing wife by an office bearer of the society, whom he described as extremely corrupt, in very similar terms. Perhaps to stave off such criticisms, traders affect clothing that is noticeably different from most weavers. The president of the society, as well as the two most prominent private traders in Pattamadai, is completely dressed in white. This garb, described by a man as 'a devout Muslim's uniform', is usually worn by the well off. Some weavers however are cynical. One weaver said, 'These people want to look respectable to divert attention from the things they do.'[16]

[16] This kind of criticism is common and levelled at people who are seen to be acting in morally dubious ways yet, or perhaps, therefore, affecting clothing that indicates their piety. Traders are not the only targets of this kind of criticism.

The above words show the extent to which this weaver felt that the traders wore masks to gain their own ends. He drew an interesting parallel between the face they showed the world, through their clothing and their 'honeyed speech' (*thén mozhi*), and the real situation as he saw it. This weaver does not supply his mats to any of the traders in Pattamadai. He sells all his mats to Craft Enterprises. In fact, it is the weavers who supply all their mats to the NGO, who are most critical of the traders and of the cooperative society. I discuss this in more detail in the next section.

Another weaver described the traders as being successful at trapping weavers. Referring to the fact that traders give loans and advances to weavers and, therefore, control their production, she said, 'They trap us like fish in a net. They strew money [for bait].'[17]

It gradually became clear to me as I listened to different weavers tell of their interactions (or often more appositely, tussles) with traders that the situation was complex and fluid, with constantly shifting alliances and interests. For instance, kinship structures form a normative framework in the mat weaving industry in Pattamadai. There is, however, room for negotiation as the idiom of kinship is emphasised or disregarded depending on circumstances, and as individuals see fit.[18] Nissa, who had supplied mats exclusively to

[17] Khadeeja Beevi, November 1997. Khadeeja Beevi, at the time used to supply her mats exclusively to Craft Enterprises. In early 2001, she was supplying mats to traders and to Craft Enterprises. By 2003 she was supplying mats to a private trader, though occasionally also to the new cooperative organised by Crafts Enterprises weavers. She and her husband (who occasionally weaves) were also weaving on their own account, seeking, like Fathima in the previous chapter, to get an award from the national government.

[18] This ties in with findings from other parts of the world. For instance, in artisan workshops in Peru, articulation of kinship ties are a way of emphasising the client status of artisans vis-à-vis the master-artisan; on the other hand, the same discourse is used by artisans to stress the cooperative or egalitarian nature of their relationship with the master (Long and Richardson, 1978: 197). While the kind of artisan workshop described by Long and Richardson does not exist in Pattamadai, the articulation of kinship ties to serve certain ends is very much a feature. Also see de Neve (2007).

one trader in January 2000 because, she claimed, he was closely related to her husband, had, in January 2001 completely stopped selling him her mats. The fact of the close relationship, it seemed, had ceased to exert its hold upon her. The reason she gave was that Mohammad had refused to give her a large advance when she was desperately in need of money. Another weaver who was extremely critical of the traders three years before and sold his mats to Craft Enterprises, now sells his mats mainly to Mohammad, whom he acclaims as a wise man with great knowledge of the weaving industry. However, he refuses to countenance the thought of working in the weaving shed which Mohammad is having constructed, therefore, indicating his desire remain free of the trader's control.

It seems as if the traders and weavers in Pattamadai are seated on a see-saw. Neither side in its endeavours to maintain the upper hand is unwilling to enlist support where it may be found. For superfine weavers of Pattamadai, the NGO is one such source of support.

The next section focuses on Craft Enterprises as a trader of superfine mats. I will discuss how trading became a part of Craft Enterprises' agenda in Pattamadai. It will be seen that even though they have what could be described as opposing aims in Pattamadai, the NGO, the private traders and the 'society' have, to a certain extent, come to a somewhat stable division of roles in the mat weaving industry. Again, I argue that this fits into the general pattern of organising practices.

The NGO as a Trader

Craft Enterprises started work in Pattamadai in 1995. At the end of 2001, the NGO had its funding terminated and has now ceased to exist, although some individual members of the NGO continue to retain ties with, and on occasion work with, Pattamadai weavers.[19] Simmel's words seem appropriate to think about this NGO: 'The wanderer who comes today and stays tomorrow'(Simmel, 1950:

[19] The bulk of my research was carried out when Craft Enterprises was active in Pattamadai, though I have also conducted research in the town after the NGO ceased to exist at the end of 2001.

402). As the stranger/wanderer who nevertheless remains, Craft Enterprises 'is not radically committed to the unique ingredients and peculiar tendencies of the group', but can be 'objective'. The objectivity is, in this case, 'a particular structure composed of distance and nearness, indifference and involvement...objectivity is by no means non-participation...[it is] a positive and specific kind of participation' (Simmel, 1950: 404).

In keeping with its aims of revitalising crafts and enabling crafts producers to earn a viable livelihood through craft production, the NGO's agenda included the development of stable markets for Pattamadai mats through the purchase of mats in Pattamadai and their sale elsewhere. Indeed, the nature of the mat weaving industry and the centrality of money in weavers' concerns meant that the intervention had to be market-led from almost the very beginning and Craft Enterprises soon became 'an alternative trader' (Craft Enterprises, 1998).

In Pattamadai, Craft Enterprises decided to work with weavers of superfine mats rather than with weavers of 50-count or coarser mats. The NGO made this decision on the grounds that traders in Pattamadai were able to access and establish regular markets for 50-count mats which 'have a greater functional relevance in the contemporary home' (Craft Enterprises, 1998: 50). The higher cost of superfine mats, and the fact that they were considered to be of limited utility in the markets to which traders had access, meant that these mats were relatively neglected. Weavers of superfine mats were, therefore, taking up 50-count mat weaving or moving to other occupations.[20] The decision to work with superfine mats also had the secondary effect of allowing Craft Enterprises to work in Pattamadai without challenging the traders' monopoly over the circulation of 50- and lower-count mats. In fact, initially Craft Enterprises actively worked with the traders and the cooperative, buying superfine mats from them rather than from weavers. This situation changed.

[20] Nambiar indicates a similar movement from fine mat to medium-count mat weaving (1964).

> [We issued] a guarantee to buy all the superfine mats woven, so that the weavers would not give up their craft, and would weave regularly. This we put in place in the first few months, followed up from Bangalore with almost monthly visits, and kept buying up all the stocks with [Mohammad] and the Society...After about a year, the weavers decided to jump the chain and come to us directly, which we were neutral to, saying that they would decide to handle their affairs with the traders and the Society in the light of this. We began to get two mats a month, which slowly rose to eight, and now averages to about twelve. They [weavers] watched us stock and then sell these in exhibitions and sales for a while. They began taking our marketing more seriously and joined our efforts completely only when a selling capability was demonstrated by us. (pers. comm., Sastry, Craft Enterprises, 2000)

This decision of weavers reveals the lack of any centralised control in the mat weaving industry. Traders and the cooperative have no means of imposing sanctions on weavers who refuse to sell their mats to them. At the most they can bind weavers to them through advances or loans, threaten their expulsion from the cooperative society or, in some relatively rare cases, refuse to buy mats from certain weavers. According to weavers, even though traders and officials of the society frequently utter such threats as 'Wait till Craft Enterprises leaves Pattamadai and then see what becomes of you,' there is nothing concrete that they can do.

The work of Craft Enterprises not only represented a loss in income for the traders but also a weakening of their control over the weavers and their manufacture. In 2000, some 50-count mat weavers wanted Craft Enterprises to buy their mats and sell them outside Pattamadai. Traders were, not unnaturally, tense about such a development. Mohammad told me that he had discussed this issue with the Craft Enterprises representative, 'I told them that they could work with the superfine mats industry but that they should not touch 50-count mats.' It is, however, unclear what he can actually do if Craft Enterprises starts working with 50-count mats. However, the NGO decided against branching into 50-count mats as they felt that that segment of the mat weaving industry did not require assistance.

When traders did want to buy superfine mats from weavers (usually because they have a large order for this kind of mat),[21] they foundd that few weavers who sold their mats to Craft Enterprises wanted to sell mats to them. This caused a certain amount of resentment. Sulaiman, a trader, said in 2000: 'Craft Enterprises is good for the weavers but [its activities mean that] there are never any superfine mats available for us when our customers want them...Craft Enterprises is not willing to sell superfine mats to us at their cost price but expect us to buy the mats at the sale price. They tell us to pay their sale price of Rs 2,000 for a mat which costs Rs 1,000 in Pattamadai.'

Sulaiman's father, Meeran, elaborated: 'Before Craft Enterprises came to Pattamadai, everybody would help everyone else. If a trader had a big order for superfine mats, he could count on all the superfine weavers to sell him their mats. Now, however, some superfine weavers only sell their mats to Craft Enterprises and the united, helpful practices (orrumaiyaana *pazhakkangall*) are gone' (Meeran, Pattamadai, 2000).[22]

Ironically, among the NGO's main aims were the revitalisation of the craft community:

> In 1946, a superfine mat collectively woven by the community was gifted to the then Governor of Madras Presidency with an appeal for korai growing land for the society, and a maternity hospital for the village. In 1993, the first national award for mat weaving was given to Beevi, which improved her father's business and drew a lot of attention to Pathamadai. Both events benefitted the community and its craft. However, while the 1946 event represented a community's collective lobby for its craft with a vision for the future, the 1993 award symbolised a trend towards individual recognition and publicity. Insights into this transition are essential for designing the

[21] Or because they want to give a superfine mat as a gift to a politician or celebrity. This is discussed in Chapter 7.

[22] Sulaiman, unlike his father, can be said to have had a good relationship with the NGO. When a large export order for place-mats made of 50-count mat fabric was brought to Craft Enterprises by a shop in Bangalore, they passed it on to Sulaiman who executed it successfully.

intervention to have a profound positive impact on the community. (Craft Enterprises, 1998: 49)

I could find no evidence for the claims made about the 1946 mats though it seems clear that a mat was indeed presented to Sir Archibald Nye in that year. The Census Gazetteer on the fine mat weaving industry comments that it was a case of 'every man for himself' between 1937 and 1954 (1964: 6). But Craft Enterprises continued to look to the past for inspiration: 'In former days, the occupational division by caste, the guild system, etc., created a strong sense of community that protected the craft. Today...the craft is largely practiced individually or in family groups and hence issues of common interest are not protected. We have to recreate organisations around the craft' (1998: 24).[23]

Based on its understanding of the past, the NGO thus identified the re-creation of the craft community as one of its goals, however, it faced considerable opposition from traders and the cooperative society. In line with its emphasis on the 'craft community', in 1999 Craft Enterprises encouraged eight weavers who regularly sold mats to the NGO those weavers to form a 'core group'. The idea was that the core group would meet regularly and take collective decisions about the direction in which they wanted the project, and the mat weaving industry as a whole, to move. However, 'It is highly likely that members themselves do not perceive any other significance beyond the working capital...the group has settled well into a rhythmic pattern of buying, stocking and sending mats' (Report, July 1999).

By 1998 Craft Enterprises had established a steady market for superfine mats. This encouraged more weavers to resume or begin weaving superfine mats and raised income levels significantly. Unlike 'top-down' intervention programmes, the NGO did not distribute land or grants/loans of money. It did not give weavers advances against mats to be woven at a future date nor did it distribute awards. Weavers who worked with Craft Enterprises are aware of this. This

[23] Not all craft development agencies romanticise the past. Tyabji, for instance, points out that 'the traditional guild had too many hierarchies' (2003: 16).

influenced their relationship with the NGO and while they sold mats to it, few felt the need to manage their images in line with the picture of the idealised craftsperson. However, this does not mean that weavers who work with the NGO did not engage with the dominant images of crafts in other contexts. Thus, Khadeeja Beevi, who regularly sold her superfine mats to Craft Enterprises and who had a certain amount of visibility stemming from her position as Pattamadai panchayat president, used a newspaper interview to request that the government feed new life *to a dying industry* through grants to weavers (my emphasis, '*Nalividaindhu varum Pattamadai pai thozhilukku arasu maniyathudan kadan udhavi: thozhilallargal korikkai*' in *Dinakaran*, 01/12/1996).

The traders' growing resentment towards Craft Enterprises strangely, in some instances caused the cooperative society and the traders to make common cause. In May 1998, after Craft Enterprises had been working in Pattamadai for about three years, the society called for a meeting of all the superfine mat weavers and urged them to sell their mats exclusively to the Society. Both the prominent traders of Pattamadai were at this meeting. The Craft Enterprises facilitator wrote in her monthly report, 'Traders...were present as well, who become "members" [of the Society] when it suits them' (Pattamadai Project Report, April–July 1998).

At this meeting, the traders were appointed as sales agents for the society to sell superfine mats, i.e. control over superfine mat weavers and their manufactures would be divided between the Society and the private traders. Weavers who would not comply with the cooperative society's demand that they stop selling to Craft Enterprises were threatened with termination of their membership of the cooperative. On the other hand, traders, whose activities are more inimical to the well-being of the society, were not issued with this threat. Perhaps both traders and cooperative society felt that they have to unite to oppose Craft Enterprises' influence over the weavers, otherwise neither would be able to get superfine mats when they needed them.

However, even as traders ally themselves with the cooperative against Craft Enterprises, one trader, Mohammad, managed to find a way of working with Craft Enterprises. The relationship between

Mohammad and Craft Enterprises was complex. Mohammad, on occasion, helped conceptualise Craft Enterprises' intervention projects though he did not always supported these projects once they were underway. It would seem, and this is not unusual in the context of the dynamics of the mat weaving industry, that he was engaged in a constant process of negotiation with Craft Enterprises. Like the other relationships in Pattamadai that I discussed earlier in the chapter, this too was a complex one which is based on a mixture of opportunism, cooperation and tension.[24] Thus, on the one hand, Mohammad belittled Craft Enterprises' work by refusing to acknowledge their larger agenda: 'They are just traders too [*avanngallum vyabaari thaan*] but they speak English and know many rich people; they can also hire expensive halls to sell the mats. We cannot do all that.'

On the other hand, he was aware, and acted on this awareness, that cordial relations with Craft Enterprises could help him access new markets and new networks. In his turn, he mediated Craft Enterprises' interactions with the cooperative and with Pattamadai as a whole and used to frequently refer to Craft Enterprises representatives as his daughters towards whom he has a responsibility.[25] Craft Enterprises too acknowledged Mohammad as 'the most dynamic and successful trader...a spiritual leader of the community' and as having 'leadership potentials that could be tapped' (1998: 49).

Both Craft Enterprises and Mohammad were concerned with the creation of 'craft communities', but in very different ways. Craft Enterprises wanted to mobilise collective community action around mat weaving in Pattamadai. This, for them, was the way to ameliorate both the state of the craft and the lives of the weavers. Mohammad is engaged in constructing a 'craft community' for consumption primarily *outside* Pattamadai in his interactions with

[24] This is discussed in more detail in Chapter 9.

[25] As discussed in the Introduction, I too am included in this category and Mohammad has on occasion found me a place to live in Pattamadai. At the same time, he is deeply suspicious that I, like Craft Enterprises, will turn my hand to trade.

various NGOs and governmental agencies who look for community in craft. Within Pattamadai he runs a business, heads the Pattamadai Labbai association and sits on the mosque committee. He advises individuals on various issues, not only to do with weaving but also with other matters. He can be described as a broker, helping individuals interpret and negotiate their interactions with external agencies like banks and government officials. He also mediates in conflicts between different Labbais and maintains extensive networks with Labbais from Pattamadai who live in other places. Unlike Craft Enterprises his role is not restricted to weavers and the mat weaving industry, but reaches into every aspect of 'being Labbai'. But, as a private trader who competes with others kinds of trader, he is not interested in a 'craft community' that works. Even though the NGO saw Mohammad as a community leader, ironically Craft Enterprises's presence in Pattamadai undermined Mohammad's position within the Labbai group by providing weavers with a viable alternative to him at least in the sphere of weaving, though weavers and NGO did nevertheless go to him for other things.

Choices and Opportunities

In the period between October 1995, when Craft Enterprises started working in Pattamadai, and January 2001, traders managed to persuade at least a few of the superfine mat weavers to sell them their mats in addition to supplying mats to Craft Enterprises. One superfine mat weaver, Saad Ali, stopped selling his mats to Craft Enterprises and sells exclusively to Mohammad, who has since recommended him for an international award. Saad Ali claimed that he resumed selling mats to Mohammad because Mohammad was able to appreciate the fine quality of his weaving and paid him accordingly. Equally importantly, Mohammad was willing to give Saad Ali advances and loans. Other weavers, citing unbearable exploitation by traders as their main reason, stopped selling mats to traders and started working with Craft Enterprises. One weaver said, 'My daughter fell ill and had to go to hospital. The trader kept delaying the payment for my mats even though he knew of my need. He is my relative but he did not help me. I had to pawn some jewellery to pay for my daughter's treatment. I had to really struggle to get my money from him. I decided to stop weaving 50-count mats and take up superfine mat weaving so that I could sell my mats to Craft Enterprises. My co-sister [husband's brother's wife] has done the same.'

For this weaver, moving to Craft Enterprises involved a major change—from weaving 50-count mats to weaving superfine mats. Others who switched over to Craft Enterprises have similar narratives, delayed payments being the most common of themes. Some weavers sold mats to both to Craft Enterprises and to traders, even those who worked exclusively with the NGO tried to maintain (somewhat) cordial relations with the traders. It is my belief that they did so in order to keep their options open. One weaver's statement corroborates this: 'Sometimes things are done through the society, sometimes through other organisations or individuals. It is best to go to whoever can get things done for us.'

The superfine mat weaver who said the above words was, at the time, an important member of the Craft Enterprises core group in Pattamadai. This group, as was mentioned, was constituted of superfine weavers who sold to Craft Enterprises and who made production related decisions collectively with the support of the NGO. At one time, so great was her commitment to the NGO that when she wove a mat for the museum collection I was making, she wove both her name and that of Craft Enterprises on it. However, as her statement reveals, she was, at the same time, unwilling to sever relations in a way that would foreclose other opportunities. Thus she joined a group loan scheme that was coordinated by the president of the cooperative society.

The opportunity that this weaver was referring to involved a government scheme to issue occupation specific identity cards to craftspersons. In Pattamadai, the identity cards were being distributed both through the Society and through Craft Enterprises. The issue of the identity cards actually best sums up my argument that most Labbais in Pattamadai see mat weaving as a resource which they can use irrespective of whether they weave or not. When the scheme of distributing identity cards was announced early in 2001, the Society, which is normally deserted, was suddenly filled with people discussing the card, asking questions and making arrangements to get one for themselves. Labbais from all over Pattamadai went to the Society building to clarify doubts and to have their photographs taken for the cards. It did not matter that most of the Society's members do not weave. As some Labbais explained to me, 'The card is good. If you want a loan meant for a craftsperson, you just have to show your card and you can get the loan. There might also be other uses for it. It can only be a good thing to have a card.'

This is despite the fact that it cost money to get a card. The bearer of the card had to submit passport size photographs and have a blood test to determine his or her blood group.[26]

The end of Craft Enterprises came at the end of 2001 when the Confederation of Indian Industry which supported the NGO decided that it would no longer do so.[27] Earlier that year, the weavers who worked exclusively with the NGO had come together to form a new cooperative society. The idea was that the Craft Enterprises facilitator would work with this new cooperative society (let us call it the CE co-op) and gradually lead them into self-sufficiency through exposure to marketing, stock management, etc. The idea that the NGO should, if successful, write itself out of existence is a widely prevalent one in craft development. The untimely end of the NGO, however, came as a blow and the CE co-op suffered right at the outset from a lack of working capital and also access to markets—in both of these initial support from Craft Enterprises was crucial but the NGO did not exist as an entity anymore even though the NGO's former employees were still deeply committed to Pattamadai; two of them were elected to serve for three years on the board of the CE co-op. I was away writing up my doctoral thesis at this time, but when I returned it was with money from the sale of mats at the exhibition in Cambridge.[28] A proportion of this went, after much discussion, to the CE co-op to form working

[26] Neither I nor weavers with whom I talked could work out why the blood group was required!

[27] The reasons for this are complex and I am not able to discuss them in any detail here.

[28] Discussed in the Introduction.

capital. This amount although sufficient, could not resolve the larger question of markets as mats made needed to be sold. Weavers were unwilling to risk making mats that would not translate into money for them directly and indirectly to more working capital for the CE co-op. Some weavers then started to also supply mats to private traders and stopped exclusively working with the CE co-op as was originally envisaged. This, in part, has meant that traders are again able to use the blandishment of advances of mats to bind weavers to them and to undermine the newly formed cooperative. The CE co-op is still limping along most of the time though large orders in which Lila is often active do revitalise it for a while, but it is hard to predict what the long-term life of this organisation will be.

The Idea of Community

Jodhka (1999) points out that the notion of community is frequently invoked in India in the official discourses of development. Community, like civil society, is considered a good thing—a way of mobilising groups that are roughly egalitarian, and of helping them help themselves. However, 'in most of these discourses the internal structure of the supposed communities invariably gets elided in favour of a notion of moral bonds and cultural authenticity'(ibid.: np). Upadhya (2001) identifies two ways in which community has been conceptualised in studies of India. Within the 'primordialist' or what she calls the 'substantivist' model, communities are regarded as natural groupings based on ties of shared blood, language, history, territory and culture. She argues that the idea of community gained importance as the result of a long tradition of imagining India through categories that make it the oppositional other of the 'west'. 'Culturally' defined groups thus came to be identified as the authentic units of social organisation in India—hereditary artisanal groups are often characterised in this way. Constructivists, on the other hand, see communities not as anachronistic remainders of India's pre-colonial past but as invented by discursive processes, policies and actions of the state. This position, as Upadhya points out, is problematic. While bringing communities within the purview of history, it has

> A tendency to regard social identities as discursively constructed while ignoring the concrete political or economic structures within which such construction takes place...an absence of agency on the part of the colonised, an overemphasis on knowledge systems and discourses of the state and less attention to the ways in which such discourses get played out in actual social life. (Upadhya 2001: 41)

Both the primordialist and constructivist models tend to ignore the individual. In the former, all members of the community are seen as essentially alike, united by a common culture, which differentiates them from others and is the source of their social identity. In the latter, both individual and group are seen as acted upon rather than acting. Furthermore, the community as cultural group is seen as apolitical. This has been challenged. In his book *The warrior merchants* (1984), Mines shows how the organisation of the Kaikkoolar weavers changed in response to the roles played by leading individuals, who were in turn responding to changes in the political economy. Leaders created different kinds of organisations—*naadus*, cooperatives, caste associations, etc., which, when successful, attracted followers. Such associations were responses to the larger political climate. Mines' work shows that conceptualising 'the community' as a static entity based on primordial ties, unchanging except when buffeted by external forces is misleading, and in urgent need of critical questioning. At the same time, it is equally misleading to think about categories such as the craft community as purely coming from the outside and that are reified by particular relations of power. A more subtle analysis that incorporates questions of agency—both individual and collective—in craft producing groups is urgently required.

A number of academic studies on artisanal groups in India have revealed some of the enduring structures and practices underlying artisan's lives and work (among others, Brouwer, 1995, 1996, 1999; Dalmia, 1988; Mehta, 1997). However, this approach neglects processes of change in the micro- and macro-environment. In my analysis of local organising practices in Pattamadai, I have followed the actor-oriented framework advocated by Norman Long and others (Long and Richardson, 1978; Long, 1984; Long and Long (ed.), 1992a, 1992b). This is particularly pertinent to development research. The actor-oriented framework lays stress on the processual and emergent character of organisation. Nuijten in particular argues for a conception of organisation as a set of practices as, 'This implies that organising is not limited to formal institutions but can take the many forms in which... people are organised in their everyday life' (Nuijten, 1992: 204). Power is unequally distributed in the mat weaving industry and may stem from 'internal' and/or 'external' factors. This affects organising practices as actors ally themselves with other, more powerful or efficacious actors. However, because the mat weaving industry itself is dynamic with different opportunities emanating from the craft and development discourses and practices, channelled at different times through different actors or institutions such as the cooperative society, traders, weavers and NGOs, local organising practices are shifting and inclusive and relationships between different actors are subject to constant negotiation. Indeed, the relationship between the same actors may be marked by a mixture of cooperation and competition. This was something that the employees of Craft Enterprises were aware of and factored into their working practices notwithstanding their theoretical commitment to the notion of 'the craft community'. In this sense, the NGO's working practices were not unlike that identified by Quarles van Ufford as characteristic of the 'arena model' of development (1993).

The arena model does not conceptualise the policy process as an integrated whole, but as a series of multiple negotiations between different groups of participants. The model assumes that the linkages between different groups are problematic and the relations between them constitute an arena, a space in which the problems of differential interests and interpretations of what should be done must be settled. Initial goals and strategies may be accepted by members of different groups, yet these same participants may articulate different views and interests later on. There is no clear cut distinction between support and resistance, between implementation and the transformation of different intentions (van Ufford: 139–40).

Nevertheless, and has been discussed, one of the fundamental aspects of Craft Enterprises' public speech acts (at least in the early days) was the emphasis on the 'craft community' and the belief that the community once made decisions and acted jointly and should do so again in order to achieve and sustain development (1998: 16). In line with other community development programmes, there was a strong stress on the recovery of lost good practices.[29] The 'community' was seen as an agent. This, as Long points out, is a problematic assumption (1992b: 23).

In this chapter I have looked at local organising practices in relation to the mat weaving industry in Pattamadai. Through a detailed analysis of relationships and negotiations between different actors and groups in Pattamadai over a period of time, I showed that local organising practices are shifting and inclusive, and that the mat weaving industry is dynamic and complex. There is severe competition among the different trading bodies for control over weavers' production, for markets and for resources. This competition affects relationships. Weavers too make choices about whether or not to weave and to whom they sell their mats, though their choices are more restricted than those of traders. At the same time, actors, who on the face of it might have implacably opposing interests, may also cooperate with each other on specific projects. While it is possible to identify specific groups with shared interests, it is important to remember that membership of these groups is fluid and subject to constant negotiation. In relation to the mat weaving industry, people make opportunistic and strategic choices; these are informed and constrained by their habitus or structuring predispositions, but they are also a response to various factors including craft development. Furthermore, different individuals have different negotiating capabilities whether with other members of the group, or with NGOs like Craft Enterprises. This may be a result of structural factors—females are less able to do some things than males, a function of age; the resources to which one has access—people on whom one can depend to supply one

[29] See Mosse (1997: 257) for a discussion on the discourse of the community management of irrigation in Tamilnadu. The similarity between the two discourses, i.e. of Craft Enterprises and of the 'developers' in Mosse's study, is striking.

with money or mats, creditors, a house that one can pledge; and the demands placed on an individual or household—a daughter who needs to be married, a sick child, or a husband who is a reckless gambler. It may also boil down to the differences between individuals. The chapter challenges the existence of a romanticised and undifferentiated 'craft community' where all actors are seen as equally poor and powerless, and in need of development.

6 Production and Representation

This chapter focuses on the ways in which craft in India is not just about production but equally about performance. It does this through the examination of one of the most coveted of awards within the Indian craft worlds: the national awards for master craftspersons given by the Government of India every year. Out of approximately 1,500 entries every year, around 40 are chosen for national awards and merit certificates. These carry cash prizes, which are important, but far more important are the recognition and the opportunities that accompany an award. But, not every award winner is able to tap into the worlds that an award opens. Just being a good artisan is not necessarily enough. More is required. This is what this chapter explores.

Who identifies the master craftsperson? Is it the others in the producer group who recognise that one among them can throw better pots, weave finer cloth with more elaborate patterns, or do the most intricate embroideries? Or does this recognition and naming take place outside the producer groups?

The answer, of course, is that the concept of the skilled artisan exists both within and outside the producer group though the criterion for selection may vary in accordance with the scale within which comparisons are made. In Pattamadai, people refer to a few weavers and designers as extremely skilled either at specific processes such as the preparation of korai or in the whole weaving process. In 1993 and 1996, two mat weavers who submitted mats to the national awards competition, were awarded national awards and identified as 'master craftspersons' by the Offices of the Development Commissioner (Handicrafts) and Development Commissioner (Handlooms). Other weavers recognise the work of neither as exceptional. However, the pieces they submitted were deemed exceptional by the judges at the competition. The judges are influential members of the craft worlds including bureaucrats, museum staff and 'experts' from NGOs. They are expected to select around forty 'masterpieces' from among all the hundreds of objects submitted from different parts of the country; in other words, they are expected to have the knowledge and skills to select a number of 'masterpieces' from a vast variety of objects whose common feature is their identification as 'craft objects'.[1] The makers of these 'masterpieces' are then conferred the highest recognition given to any craft producer by the Indian government.

The master craftsperson is not selected solely on the basis of skill exhibited in the piece submitted to the awards competition. Other considerations impinge on this selection, including socio-political factors. In *India's craft tradition* (1980), Kamaladevi Chattopadhyay, who instituted the national award system in India, discusses the origins of what she terms 'master-craftsmanship' in India through a 'historicised' account of craft production and its context. Her account moves from a description of tribal manufactures through

[1] According to a Ministry of Textiles press release, 1,800 objects were submitted to the national awards competition in 1998–9 of which 49 were selected for awards (GOI, 22/05/1999). At the time of research, Ministry of Textiles press releases could be accessed on the world-wide-web through the official Government of India site (http://www.nic.in).

complex craft guilds and includes temple and court patronage of artisans. Defining master craftsmanship as 'mastery in the creation of crafts' (ibid.: 1), she lays stress throughout the book on the social significance of the person who has attained such mastery.

> In a craft oriented society, a master-craftsman was also a social leader and an important entity in the community, for craftsmanship was also a tribute to the high function of the human being who is endowed with attractive talents and is not just a physical frame... craftsmanship was a social activity which fulfilled a normal purposeful social function...the creative urges have to manifest themselves in visible and tangible forms through an integrated and disciplined organism. (ibid.: 12–6).

The conceptual difference between the artist and the craftsman is striking. Following the romantic idealist conception, the artist is seen as someone who functions outside the social milieu, producing art for its own sake.[2] The craftsman, according to Chattopadhyay's description, is bound to working within society, producing objects for general use. Innovation, creativity and skill are not enough, the master craftsperson has also to be a socially responsible leader. Chattopadhyay's characterisation of the master craftsperson as a leader of society continues to influence government policy and practice. The Office of the Development Commissioner (Handicrafts) offers the following advice to those involved in the process of selecting master craftspersons: 'It has been noticed in the past that the craftspersons/weavers of very young age have been selected purely on the basis of the quality of the entry received without considering the contribution of the person to the craft as a

[2] Coomaraswamy is cuttingly critical of the artist in the 'West': '"Art in India" and "Art in the Modern World" mean two very different things. In India it is the statement of a racial experience and serves the purpose of life like daily bread. Indian art has always been produced to a demand. The kind of idealism which would glorify the artists who pursues a personal idea of beauty and strives to express himself and suffers or perishes for lack of patronage, would appear to Indian thought ridiculous or pitiable' (cited in Chattopadhyay, 1980: 55).

whole.[3] This may be avoided' (*Compendium of Handicraft Schemes*, Government of India, 1998: 127).

Objects are also selected with 'special consideration...given to the languishing crafts and designs.' (Ministry of Textiles, press release, 22/05/1999). Craft forms identified as being most critically in need of support are thus given special consideration. Support takes the form of injection of resources, training, marketing opportunities and publicity all of which are channeled through the national award winner.

The master craftsperson is expected to teach craft skills to others in the producer group. To this end, (s)he can apply to the Office of the Development Commissioner (Handicrafts) to conduct an apprenticeship training scheme. These schemes provide opportunities for young people to learn crafts skills in a dedicated environment but, as discussed in Chapter 2, they also give them the opportunity to receive regular incomes for the duration of the course, as the master craftsperson is paid a monthly salary and the trainees, monthly stipends. For unmarried teenagers and young women, the course also provides a rare opportunity to be outside the confines of their homes. The master has a say (though constrained by the higher authority of the officials from the regional Handicrafts and Marketing Service Extension Centres) in who joins the scheme as a trainee, a certain amount of power is vested in him or her.[4] Furthermore, all objects produced by trainees become the property of the master and are usually sold by him or her, usually at craft bazaars and exhibitions to which (s)he, as a national award winner, is invited.

3 Such contributions include training others in the craft, and innovation and product diversification leading to increased market viability of the 'languishing craft'.

4 In the first training scheme run by the first national award winner in Pattamadai, the sisters of the award winner were signed on as trainees even though they could already weave. Similarly, the daughters of the second national award winner joined his training scheme as trainees though they do not weave, preferring instead to roll *beedi*s or leaf cigarettes.

National award winners as well as National Merit Certificate winners are given preference for participation in National Melas (Bazaars) and other international events (also see Bundgaard, 1996: 117). They become visible in the wider world that is interested in crafts and are given the opportunity to take up trading. It is, therefore advantageous in more ways than one to receive a national award.

The process of selection is lengthy. The object goes through a three-tier selection process. It is sent first by the craftsperson or sponsoring agency (often an NGO with whom the artisan has worked) to a state-level committee which examines all the objects submitted from throughout the state and selects some to be sent on to the next level, the headquarters-level selection committee. From there, if selected, the object is sent to the final stage, the central-level committee. At every stage, the committee consists of 'eminent experts in the field of Handloom and Handicrafts'.[5] It is noteworthy that craft producers do not make up any part of these committees. A former member of the central-level committee described the process of selecting the award winning objects:

> All of us are in this room where the objects are displayed. Everyone is just walking around. We want to finish and go home. Someone who knows [about a particular object] says something about it—what it is about, how long it would have taken to make. We look at the piece more closely. (interview, March 9, 2000)

It is clear that the process by which a select few win awards is highly problematic and reveals how fully power is vested outside the craftsperson, not only in the application process but also in matters of aesthetic taste and judgement and by the developmental discourses.[6] As Wilkinson Weber points out in the context of chikan embroidery of Lucknow,

[5] Ministry of Textiles, press release, 22/05/1999. See Compendium of Handicraft Schemes, Government of India, 1998 for a detailed breakdown of the constituents of the various committees.

[6] The fact that some artisans actively seek recognition by sending objects to awards competition can itself become a source of tension. Gurappa Shetty, a *kalamkari* painter from Kalahasti in Andhra Pradesh who was given a national award (1976) after Pupul Jayakar saw some of

> Ironically, defining and rewarding what best represents the finest Lucknow chikan is kept out of the hands of the women who make it. A select few have their work, their skills, and their knowledge legitimized by receiving an award. Once they are so recognised, what these women profess to know about chikan becomes privileged through being repeated to non-embroiderers by word of mouth, or through published documents, as the 'truth' about chikan...only the government provides a woman with the opportunity to express the full range of her knowledge and skill. (Wilkinson-Weber, 1999: 174)

Despite the large number of national awardees and the subsequent opportunities given to them in disseminating the craft through training schemes and market exposure, few academic studies have looked at national awards and their significance. Fisher's work, 'The All India Handicrafts Board and the development of handicrafts in India' (1972), the work of Wilkinson-Weber (1999) and Bundgaard's study, 'Handicrafts awards and their changing significance' (1996), provide significant exceptions.

In the following sections, I focus on the experiences of two national award winners in Pattamadai. The discussion focuses on two main points. First, the mediation and transformation of intervention programmes by weaver and traders. Second, I tease out the complex biographies of awards and argue that awards, despite the claims made about them, are only effective in the hands of effective agents.

The First Award: 1993

The first national award made to a mat weaver from Pattamadai was won by Beevi in 1993. Beevi is the daughter of Mohammad, the most prominent trader of mats in Pattamadai. An active member of the Crafts Council of India (CCI) and the Madras Craft Foundation (MCF) who was responsible for sending the

---

his pieces displayed in a public space, was at pains to emphasise to me that he did not actively seek an award, and furthermore that: 'A real craftsperson will not approach [anyone] for any national award.' He was thus fully aware of the contradictions between the crafts discourses and development practices (interview, Madras, March 10, 2000).

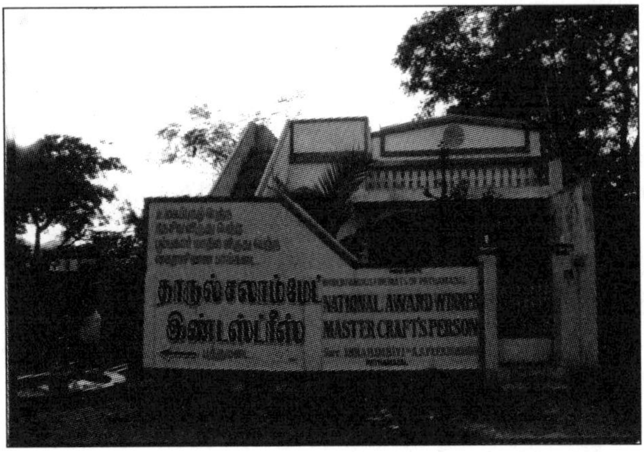

A national award made very visible. *Photo courtesy*: Vipul Sangoi.

award-winning mat to the national awards competitions discussed the circumstances surrounding the submission of Beevi's mat to the national awards competition:[7]

> One person from Pattamadai, Mohammad, was well known to the Crafts Council in Madras. He had worked with the Crafts Council before 1992 and we used to invite him to bazaars and exhibitions held by the Crafts Council. Sometimes, Mohammad would be accompanied to these events by his daughter, Beevi. He always described her as a very good weaver and said that she was the only person working in superfine mat weaving.[8] When the NGO decided to sponsor a Pattamadai mat at the national awards

[7] Under the rules of the national award competition, governmental and non-governmental agencies are encouraged to sponsor artisans' entries to the awards' competitions. The reason given for this is that, 'An artisan may not wish to block the time or resources in the making of a fine piece to submit for an award. In the light of this, the Handicrafts Board recommends that the piece be sponsored, i.e. bought by an NGO which would submit it for the award' (Compendium of Handicraft Schemes, op. cit., 127–8). However, see Bundgaard, 1996: 13, for a critique of this practice).

[8] At the time there were at least four weavers of superfine mats in Pattamadai.

> competition, I asked Beevi to weave a superfine mat. [I] specified the designs and colours to be used in this mat. However, when the mat arrived, it was far from perfect and there was no time to get her to weave another mat [because the deadline for submissions was approaching]. In the end, 'I just picked up a Pattamadai mat that was in my house and sent it to the competition attributing it to Beevi. She had probably also woven that mat. (Anamika [pseudonym], interviewed December 1999)

It was this mat that won Beevi the national award. Two things stand out in this description. First, while Beevi was the person chosen to weave the mat, she was not expected to make any choices about colours or designs, the representative of the NGO being deemed better at this than her. Second, when the mat arrived, it was judged as sub-standard. Another mat—one more accurately reflecting the aesthetic concerns of the development agent and, as was subsequently made clear, the competition judges—was substituted for it. The substituted mat was also almost certainly made by Beevi, but it was *not* the mat that she herself chose to submit. We come up here against the separation of knowledge and skill: while the weaver is skilled at making mats, members of the craft worlds claim knowledge about what objects that form part of the national craft tradition ought to look like. This is partly because the frames of comparison are enormously different—within the craft producer group where only one kind of product is made, and in the national awards competition where different kinds of object, skill and technique compete against each other and are evaluated on the grounds of authenticity, 'craft aesthetic' and need.

A remarkable feature of my conversation with Anamika was the almost casual way in which she told me about the submission of the mat and gave me permission to write about it. She did not seem to think that her decision to substitute mats was strange or wrong. Of course, in some ways it was the right decision. After all, the mat did win a national award! It is also equally significant that neither Mohammad not Beevi ever told me that the mat they had submitted was not the one that had won the award (nor could I find the words to bring it up with them). One could speculate that the mat itself was not of the utmost importance, it was the outcomes that its success brought that were important.

Submitting an incorrectly attributed mat for a national award reveals two things. First, despite the fact that the master craftsperson is a named individual, it shows a tacit acceptance of the idea that crafts come from an anonymous tradition where there is no single maker even if one individual is credited.[9] Second, it reiterates the fact that awards are meant not for individual skill but for the larger good of the craft community. In fact, the award can be seen as recognition of Mohammad's role in making the mat weaving industry viable and visible to a wide audience, including the Crafts Council of India. Indeed, according to Anamika, many members of Crafts Council of India believe that it was Mohammad who won the award. Newspaper reports too seem unconcerned about the actual identity of the award winner, some attribute it to Beevi, some to her father.

A shrewd businessman of 'sweet speech' as one weaver characterised him, Mohammad worked as a sales agent for the cooperative society before becoming a private trader. He first came to the attention of the Crafts Council of India some time in the mid-1980s and became synonymous with the mat weaving industry in Pattamadai. One Crafts Council of India member described him to me as the head of the whole Labbai family, i.e. of all the weavers in Pattamadai (Madras, December 1999). Furthermore, she believed that he was the national award winner and his position as family head would mean that all the weavers would reap the benefits of the award.

Within Pattamadai too, people refer to the award as Mohammad's. His role in its procurement seems to be in little doubt and many weavers claimed that the award was due to 'influence in the right quarters in Delhi', thereby implying that Mohammad had access to powerful people. Mohammad does not contest this. Indeed it adds

[9] Pupul Jayakar, for instance, wrote: 'The rural craft expression...by its very nature demanded a total anonymity of name. It reflected the familiar unchanging forms of rural life, its simple needs, its links with archaic magic and ritual' (1989: 5). This is a somewhat sweeping generalisation, as is clear from the situated analysis of the 'rural craft expression' that is Pattamadai mat weaving.

to his aura of success. It shows that people see him as powerful and efficacious. He, along with the president of the Panchayat and the president of the mat weavers' cooperative society, is one of three people within the Labbai group commonly addressed as *thalaivar* (leader).

The national award brought visibility to the mat weaving industry in the form of write-ups in the press. It brought the patronage of important personages in the craft worlds, and led to the establishment of Mohammad, who always accompanied his daughter to events to which she as a national award winner was invited, as the representative of the mat weaving industry. This both reveals gendered expectations about leadership,[10] and serves to indicate Mohammad's ability to engage with the discourses about crafts. Mohammad also translates the needs and priorities of local actors to bureaucrats, development agents and other members of the craft worlds and is thus able to enrol both sets of actors in his projects.

For example, after one of the two training schemes run by his daughter, Mohammad tried to get loans for all the participants in the training programme. The loan application was made jointly by the entire group to the Khadi Village Industries Commission. Each applicant requested a loan of Rs 38,000 which, she claimed, would be used to build weaving sheds in the yards of her house.[11] In order to secure the loans, the group prepared cost estimates, had building plans for weaving sheds made, paid bribes and made trips to the Khadi Village Industries Commission offices in Madurai and Tirunelveli. Some women who were involved in this loan application estimated that they spent between Rs 3,000 and Rs 5,000 on the above. Despite all these efforts, the loans were not sanctioned,

[10] He is, in fact, consistent in propagating the view that Beevi is incapable of attending bazaars or fairs alone due to her 'female shyness' (*penn pillai, vekkapadugirall*), though when I have been with her and Mohammad at bazaars, she has not displayed any discernible fear at being in a strange situation.

[11] This amount is substantially higher than the annual salary of many Labbai households where mat weaving takes place. It is not clear that the loans would have been used to build sheds.

though Mohammad himself was offered an individual loan by the manager of the local bank (through whom the application was being processed). Mohammad declined this offer because, he told me later, it would look bad if he took a loan that was denied to the rest of the group. Here, even though the project was not achieved, Mohammad was able to demonstrate both his personal power and his commitment to the group.

The national award thus served to increase Mohammad's stature within and outside Pattamadai. It brought visibility and publicity to Beevi, to Mohammad and to the mat weaving industry; it also reinforced Mohammad's position as a local leader. The opportunity to attend craft bazaars and exhibitions were used by Mohammad to enlarge his mat trading business and also served to provide, through him, markets for mats woven in Pattamadai.

Through his engagement with the various ways in which craft is imaged, Mohammad is engaged in constructing a 'craft community' for consumption primarily *outside* Pattamadai. As has already been mentioned, Mohammad plays an important role both within the Labbai group (weavers and non-weavers) and in the interface between the craft worlds and the mat weaving industry. As a prominent trader, he is a source of livelihood, even while he is described by some as exploitative. His role in Pattamadai may be described as ubiquitous. It is not restricted to weavers and the mat weaving industry, but reaches into every aspect of 'being Labbai' in Pattamadai.

The Second Award: 1996

A second national award for mat weaving was won by a superfine mat weaver, Kadher, in 1996 for a mat he submitted to the awards competition. This award came in part because of Craft Enterprise's work in Pattamadai.

The world of crafts development is a small one. In 1994, when a prominent member of the Confederation of Indian Industry (CII) decided that CII should initiate and fund a project which would help revitalise rural industries, he consulted Gita Ram, a very active and prominent member of the Madras Craft Foundation, and a member of a prominent industrial family. From this was born a new voluntary organisation—Craft Enterprises—which began work in October 1995 with three crafts in south India, one of which was Pattamadai fine mat weaving.[12] The choice of the mat weaving industry as a development target in this case can be linked to the publicity brought by the first national award, the Crafts Council of India's interest in Pattamadai and Mohammad's successful popularisation of the mat weaving industry following his daughter's national award.

Craft Enterprises's early experiences in Pattamadai in 1994–5 were significantly mediated by Mohammad whom they identified as a 'guide'. At the inception of the Craft Enterprises project, Mohammad suggested that Craft Enterprises adopt two main courses of action. The first concerned the reintroduction of natural dyes (Tamil: *iyarkai sayam*; Craft Enterprises, 1998: 50).[13] In January 1996, the NGO held a three-day workshop in Pattamadai to demonstrate the techniques of natural dyeing.[14] Lila had her own reasons:

> My real reasons were—to get to know the community I chose natural dyeing over 'design documentation' as the first activity as the latter did not have 'action'. We knew that we would be getting into marketing to ensure fair wages and regular production, but we had to create mats that were different. Vegetable dyeing was more of a preparatory phase. The subsequent standardisation of dyeing at individual homes in the next few weeks got me close to [weavers]. (pers. comm. 2006)

[12] A study to select craft villages in south India was conducted between November 1994 and March 1995. Thirty-one villages were considered of which eleven were short-listed and finally four were selected of which Pattamadai was one (Craft Enterprises, 1998).

[13] The second suggestion concerned the development of an improved loom which would reduce the physical difficulties experienced in the existing loom. This was discussed in Chapter 8.

[14] I was not in Pattamadai at the time of the workshop but was told about it by weavers and traders in Pattamadai and by the Craft Enterprises representative. I also read Craft Enterprises reports on the workshop.

The workshop was open to any weaver who was interested. Craft Enterprises reports discuss in detail the lukewarm response that the workshop evoked. Only one weaver, Kadher, actively participated in the workshop. Later that year and with the active support of the NGO, he submitted a vegetable dyed mat to the national awards competition. This mat won a national award. According to Craft Enterprises, 'There was a dramatic change in their [artisans'] attitude after Kadher won the award for his natural dyed 140 count mat…They [then] took to natural dyeing...with great enthusiasm' (ibid.: 50–1).[15]

It seems to me that by suggesting that Craft Enterprises encourage the reintroduction of vegetable dyes in Pattamadai, Mohammad was doing two things. First, he was trying to find a way to tap into the increasing demand for naturally dyed craft objects. Second, he was under the impression that like other intervention programmes in Pattamadai, Craft Enterprises would channel the intervention through him. The fact that Lila began to live in Pattamadai from October 1995 and soon established contacts with other weavers, meant that she did not look to Mohammad to mediate between them and the larger producer group. Furthermore, the natural dyes workshop, which the NGO opened to anyone who was interested, had the unexpected result of creating a second national award winner in Pattamadai. The rift between Craft Enterprises and Mohammad began to widen.

After winning the national award in 1996, Kadher received several invitations to attend craft bazaars. Some of these were at Beevi's cost as only one award winner from a particular craft group is invited to any exhibition. Part of the logic behind these invitations is that the craft bazaar promotes direct contact between producer and consumer thereby dispensing with exploitative traders. Ironically, Kadher decided to take up mat trading. He started buying mats from other weavers to sell at bazaars and also set up a mat shop in Pattamadai. Kadher's decision is not surprising. At craft fairs and bazaars to which he is invited by governmental and other organisation, the award winner is expected to sell what are ostensibly his manufactures. In fact, the timing of invitations to fairs (they

15 This underscores the appeal of awards.

usually arrive a week or two before the event), and the artisan's subsistence needs which force him to sell each piece as soon as it is made, mean that the award winner does not have the means to build up stock to sell at these bazaars. More often than not, the artisan buys, or takes on a consignment basis, other weavers' mats and sells them at a profit. The national award scheme can thus be seen as a way of transforming a producer into a trader.[16]

The receipt of the award, the setting up of his shop and the invitations to bazaars brought Kadher into direct competition with Mohammad. As a national award winner, Kadher, like Mohammad and Beevi, could enter the ranks of the authoritative figures in the craft worlds and represent the mat weaving industry and the larger producer group in the media and at craft events. However, despite the fact that Kadher is an enthusiastic and innovative weaver, has given some newspaper interviews and has attended most bazaars to which he received invitations, he has not been able to utilise the national award as effectively as Mohammad.

In January 2000, Kadher compared himself adversely with Mohammad and lamented to me that the national award had brought him nothing but difficulties. Indeed Kadher's case demonstrates the other side of awards where expectations are raised but left unfulfilled. Kadher's enterprise can be seen as an instance of one who achieved external recognition, but failed locally. Certainly his relations with other traders and some weavers in Pattamadai deteriorated after his becoming a national award winner: 'Before [the award], I would sell mats to Craft Enterprises and to private traders. Now, due to jealousy that his daughter is no longer the sole recipient of a National Award, Mohammad has stopped taking my mats. Others are also jealous and neither Craft Enterprises nor the other traders buy my mats.'

Mohammad rarely acknowledges Kadher's receipt of a national award. This seems to be a function of the fact that Kadher suddenly became a competitor for benefits from the craft worlds and craft

[16] Even in training schemes, as I discussed earlier, the national awardee retains the products made under the aegis of the training programme. These are usually sold by him/her at bazaars and exhibition to which (s)he is invited.

development. National awards are not new in Pattamadai, nor are they restricted to the mat weaving industry. Besides the two awards for mat weaving, three inhabitants of the town have received national awards in the fields of Sanskrit, education and physical education. In Mohammad's shop are displayed photographs of (what he claims are) all the national award winners in Pattamadai. Kadher's photograph is conspicuously absent. Photographs line the walls showing Mohammad and Beevi with various celebrities, the award plaque, which normally sits in a box along with a sample of 'the award winning mat' are displayed ceremoniously at appropriate moments. Mohammad thus uses his shop as a way of advertising the award and his own success. Indeed the large signboard outside the shop proclaims its connection with a national award winner. The shop itself, located opposite the main bus stand and directly off the highway, is immediately visible on entering Pattamadai and attracts visitors, including journalists looking for a story. Kadher's dwelling, on the other hand, is tucked away in one of the innumerable lanes which wind through Pattamadai and is less readily accessible.

Mohammad has successfully appropriated the significance of the award to advertise his own business and to make his mats 'craft objects'. Three of Mohammad's daughters weave, all of their mats are sold in Mohammad's shop. He is, therefore, assured of a steady supply of mats from his own home and can experiment with designs and colours. He also buys mats regularly from a number of other weavers in Pattamadai, some of whom do not sell to any other trader. Mohammad's son helps him manage the shop. This allows Mohammad to travel to bazaars and exhibitions. Beevi, when she is invited to bazaars, simply takes with her stock from Mohammad's mat shop. Kadher, on the other hand, until he opened a shop, had to go around Pattamadai trying to persuade people including the mat shop owners and the cooperative society to lend him mats on approval that he could sell.

Kadher's mat shop failed and had to be shut down. The debris from this attempt, including a large painted signboard with the name of the shop, occupied for a long time a corner of the room where Kadher used to weave. None of Kadher's children weave. His wife helps with weaving but does not produce any mats on her own. He did not have sole control over the manufactures of any weaver but himself. Kadher's output rarely exceeded a mat a month and he had to buy mats from other weavers to sell. But he found this difficult because he could compete neither in terms of financial nor in terms of personal resources with someone like Mohammad.

Though Kadher blames his difficulties on the jealousy engendered by his award, other factors also play a role. Unlike Mohammad, Kadher is not seen as a powerful man in Pattamadai. He is younger than Mohammad and less subtle in his dealings with others—both inside and outside Pattamadai. He rarely engages with the prevailing discourses on craft, and while he speaks with enthusiasm about weaving different kinds of mats, he commonly speaks of his award as a means of achieving prosperity and personal recognition instead of emphasising, like Mohammad, the more acceptable idealistic ways in which the award is conceptualised.

Mohammad is not a weaver, nor did he win the award for weaving. However, as a trader he is able to influence the production of innovatively designed mats. He is enthusiastic about commissioning new designs, buys mats from several weavers and, as the representative of the mat weaving industry also puts forward the names of selected weavers and designers for awards and external recognition. This not only gives credit to others but also enhances Mohammad's reputation. A superfine mat woven by a weaver, Saad Ali, was sold by Mohammad to the Crafts Council of India. This mat was submitted to an international crafts competition and won an award. A report in *The Hindu*, which Saad Ali says was not written on the basis of an interview with him, mentioned not only the award winner's name but also Mohammad's, 'Mr Shatali [Saad Ali] used to market the mats manufactured by him thorough his uncle Mr Mohammad...Winning awards is not a new thing for the family of Mr Mohammad. His daughter Mrs Beevi won the national best craftswoman award...a few years ago' (Reporter's Diary, *The Hindu*, 11/12/2000).[17]

[17] Saad Ali, it will be recalled from the previous chapter, has a stormy relationship with Mohammad, leaving him for Craft Enterprises and returning to him when he fell out with the NGO.

Within Pattamadai these factors enhance Mohammad's status and he is seen as someone who is able to access governmental and other patronage and get awards. Outside Pattamadai where he takes on the role of representing his daughter and the larger mat weaving industry, Mohammad is the face of the industry. Kadher, on the other hand, though invited to craft events, has not managed to achieve the same kind of recognition. According to Mohammad, 'When Kadher won a national award, he took to thinking that he too could do what I had done. Consequently he set up a mat shop, and started dressing like an important man. But he could not do it. What does he think of himself? He thinks he can wear white clothes and he will become like me.'[18]

Kadher also fell out with Craft Enterprises. Several reasons are cited for this. According to Kadher, his disagreement with the Craft Enterprises coordinator arose from his being unwilling to share his special knowledge of dyes with other weavers who worked with Craft Enterprises. The Craft Enterprises' weavers and Lila, in turn, allege that he lied to them about a dye he had used, claiming that it was a natural dye when in fact it was a chemical dye. When Kadher cites the community-orientated nature of the Craft Enterprises intervention as his reason for not working with the group, he is making (to my mind) a statement about his personal skills which he is unwilling to share with the others. This runs counter to the ideal view of crafts (including that accepted by Craft Enterprises), which stress the notion of the craft community such that a benefit extended to one selected artisan should reach the whole group. Mohammad, on the other hand, while emphasising the skills which won Beevi her award, is always quick to point out his eagerness to use this as a way of encouraging and teaching others in Pattamadai to weave.

[18] As has already been mentioned, white clothes indicate prosperity and respectability. Most weavers wear checked sarongs and vests over which they throw a towel or shirt when going out. Traders and other 'big men' are dressed entirely in white.

Active Helplessness

In 1996, Beevi, sent a letter in English to the chief minister of Tamilnadu requesting him to 'save the centuries old mat weaving industry of Pattamadai.'

The letter identifies the writer as belonging to a 'minority community', i.e. Muslim, and as coming from 'a very poor family of Lebbais' sustained by 'my father [who] is aged and...managing the family with his meagre income [from] a mat shop in the village.'

Mat weaving is described as 'our hereditary craft' but 'at present the industry is not prospering now only a few families are engaged in this craft with great difficulty.' The writer contrasts the demand for the mats from 'several distinguished visitors from all over India and abroad' with the position of the weavers who are 'poor Muslim Lebbais working hard day and night to earn their meagre livelihood and to preserve the industry for the future.'

Identifying herself, 'with humility and reasonable pride' as a national and state award winner for fine mat weaving the writer lists her personal contribution to 'the growth of the crafts' as an instructor in two apprenticeship training schemes. Finally, she makes two requests, based on the addressee's 'proverbial sympathy to people like me, who are in indigent circumstances.' The first request is for monetary assistance to build a house for herself on a plot of land allocated to her by the government and the second is for monetary assistance to set up a training institute '...so that the age-old cottage industry could be preserved.'

The language throughout is flowery, stressing the writer's humble position in relation to the addressee. It reiterates the state of helplessness of the writer and all the other craftspersons in the village for whom she speaks. Yet, it is only for herself that she requests a house, though the training institute would be used more generally.

Beevi's letter is a very good example of the exercise of agency through its disavowal. It reflects the structure of the development mechanism which places the craftsperson in the position of a supplicant vis-à-vis 'a benign' government. It also shows that the writer is fully engaging with the dominant ways of imagining craft in India. The writer presents herself as someone who is struggling to preserve an *age-old industry for the sake of future generations.* There is here an implication of selflessness in the face of the larger goal of preserving the mat weaving industry. This fits in with the way artisans are projected in the discourses about crafts as helpless individuals struggling to retain their identity and prevent the loss of an aspect of national heritage. The need for preserving and helping the mat weaving industry is strengthened by the claim that the craft has been appreciated by distinguished Indians and foreigners—it is not only the artisans who believe that the craft industry is important. Finally, the letter draws attention to the fact that Beevi is a national and state award winning craftsperson. In other words, her status as a craftsperson has been legitimised by awards which stem from the same discourses on craft to which she is appealing. The writer has thus already successfully engaged with the craft mechanism and, as a result, has gained not only a piece of land on which she wants to build a house, but also the right to speak for the larger producer group.

The authorship of the letter is interesting. Beevi, in whose name the letter was sent, had little to do with the project. Her father, Mohammad, was the driving force behind it.[19] Equally, the situation is not as simple as portrayed in the letter. As has already been discussed, Mohammad is the main person behind the revival of Pattamadai mats as 'craft objects' since the late 1980s and is the town's leading mat trader. Far from suffering from the 'extinction of the centuries old craft of mat weaving' Mohammad spends significant amounts of time ensuring that he has enough stock for the various exhibitions and bazaars to which he is invited. He can even afford to turn down orders on occasion. In fact, none of the teenagers in Mohammad's household was being taught to weave at the time. Yet, because they are primarily involved in the informal sectors of the economy, it is not easy for either him or his daughter to obtain a large enough bank loan to build a house and a training shed.

[19] Mohammad had to get someone to write the letter in English for him. The flowery and formulaic language of the petition is usual in missives sent to government officials especially when seeking favours.

The question of the training shed is in itself complex, as is the statement that artisans are struggling to keep the mat weaving industry alive. Within the framework of larger constraints faced by individuals and households, livelihood choices reflect, among other things, personal preferences and the negotiated value of weaving in Pattamadai. Furthermore, as I showed in Chapter 4, weavers if at all possible prefer to work in their own homes while traders seek to control the productive capacities of weavers. The existence of a training shed owned by a trader where looms are made available for weavers who then have to sell their mats to the trader, can be seen as one more round in this contest. Any weaver who used Mohammad's training shed would have to sell the mats made there to Mohammad. Few wish to tie themselves up in this way. Finally, through the ownership of a training shed a national award winner might ensure that more training schemes are routed to her rather than to the other national award winner, who has no such space.

The contrast with Kadher's attempt to secure a house cannot be more striking. Shortly after he won the national award, he got his daughter married and spent a large sum of money on the marriage. As a result of this, he, his wife and children moved into a rented house in the 'Harijan' section of Pattamadai.[20] He said to me, 'I wrote a letter to the government and said that it was not correct that a national award winner should live in this part of the town. I requested them to allocate land for a house.'[21]

When nothing came of this request, he spoke to a member of the Crafts Council of India and requested that she give him a loan of Rs 50,000 offering his national award plaque as security. Again this request met with no success. In both cases, Kadher was acting against the spirit of Indian craft. In the first instance, instead of stressing his position as a member of a marginalised social group, Kadher indicated that, as an award winner, he was entitled to

[20] This was the term he used to me. He was referring to the low-caste areas close to the main highway and also near the Labbai area.

[21] I did not get to see the letter, nor do I know to whom Kadher sent it. He told me about it rather bitterly.

better accommodation and should not have to live among low caste people. In the second case, he was equating his award with money. This is completely counter to the picture of the master craftsperson as being unmoved by financial gain.

In 2000–1, Kadher was living in a rented house. He was weaving and selling these, and mats that he would buy/commission from other weavers, to a few customers. When even this became difficult, he gave up weaving altogether and set up a small tea stall in a nearby town, giving up all work with mats. In the same period, Mohammad had secured money in the form of both loans and grants to build both the house and the training shed.

So far we have focused on the idea of craft and on the craft producer. But the craft producer is only a craft producer because he or she produces craft objects. The next two chapters concentrate on the Pattamadai mat as a craft object.

7 Talking About Mats

The study of things had its heyday at the beginning of anthropology's modern history, in the late-nineteenth/early-twentieth centuries, before being eclipsed by a focus on non-material aspects of human life. Things are again coming to form the focus of significant anthropological attention (for a survey of the changing fortune of things in anthropological analyses, see Henare, 2005: 1–9; also Chapter 8). To varying degrees, things in these analyses cease to be mere exemplars or illustrations, coming rather to be recognised as active in social life. It has now become commonplace in anthropology to say that things are crucial in the creation of social persons, and that relations between people and things, as much as between people, are legitimate objects of anthropological enquiry. My analysis in this chapter draws on the work of Appadurai and Gell to focus on the social life (Appadurai, 1986) of the Pattamadai mat and the ways in which it may be seen to have agency (Gell, 1998).

Breckenridge makes a case for the deeper analysis of objects in the context of South Asian studies:

> Things...have a social life in which they are circulated, exchanged, traded and variously valued...The etiquette of their movement, possession, production, circulation and use is a notable part of systems of rank and appropriateness in South Asian society...In Hindu South Asia, distinctions are drawn between people and groups through the prescribed and selective use of food, vessels, clothing, shelter and space. Ethnographic theories of caste take particular account of the system of etiquette associated with commensality and household consumption of food. Less attention, however, has been paid to the selective and prescribed use of domestic *durables* for generating and reproducing caste discriminations and distinctions. Yet, durables such as cloth, furnishings, metal vessels and shelter form an important aspect of drawing, centering and prejudicing social relations, particularly relations *between* social groups. Social distinctions...are nurtured, sustained, enclaved and reproduced from one generation to another through the manipulation of a system of durables as well as through the management of a system of perishables. (Breckenridge, 1986: 58)

I would add that the ways in which certain things become meaningful has important consequences for their producers and that this too should form a part of any thing-centred analysis. Chris Gregory (1997) suggests that the increasing focus in anthropology on things is accompanied by a tendency to concentrate on consumption. This, he suggests, detracts from a focus on production; we are increasingly moving away from a consideration of the conditions in which labour is extracted from people in the production of things to the ways in which things are used in the making of (consuming) social persons.[1] This is an important criticism in light of the ways in which *craft objects* (as opposed to just any mat, or piece of cloth or basket) are doubly produced—physically as well

[1] This approach is different to the one advocated by Carrier and Heyman (1997) who suggest that it is equally important to focus on the barriers to consumption and, therefore, to the ways in which people may effectively repackage themselves as desirable or strategise effectively and make the most of opportunities. There are some analogies to be drawn to the barriers that weavers face in availing opportunities and bettering their lives and how the category of craft then becomes an important strategising paradigm.

as discursively. The Pattamadai craft mat is a collaborative outcome of the embodied skills and knowledges of Labbai weavers/traders and the knowledge about craft that emanates from other sections of society that I have termed the craft worlds, including local and national governments and their employees, development agencies, museum curators, craft experts and patrons. This affects the markets for these objects, which mainly comprises elites who are also often physically, socially and politically distant from the weavers. For the weaver, who only participates in the production of things for sale, their re-production into meaningful objects of desire for consumption by others is crucial. But the doubly produced object does more than bring in money—it re-creates the Labbai of Pattamadai as a *craft producer* and, thus, as a certain kind of subject and object of attention.

Mats for Marriages

Where and how one sits is important for Tamils. In rural Tamilnadu, mats are extensively used in seating. The bare floor is considered dirty and unhealthy.[2] In some situations, even when available, chairs are rarely used, for instance in spaces and times set aside for worship. It is considered inappropriate to sit on an uncovered floor while reciting from sacred texts or performing religious rituals. While deerskin and bull-hide are ranked highly as seats for ritual purposes (Pandey, 1993), they are not easily obtained or practical and are substituted with other kinds of seating, usually wooden planks or mats. Mats thus play a part in rituals, including marriages. As Pattamadai fine and superfine mats are primarily marketed as 'marriage mats' (*kalyana pai*) for upper-caste and high-status Brahmins, I will be looking at the use of mats in Brahmin weddings in some detail.

The Hindu *samskaras* or 'rites that impart fitness' (Good, 1991; Pandey, 1993) do not specifically mention mats as important artefacts

[2] Some people claimed that korai had health-giving properties. One man proffered the opinion that as korai grass mats retained heat in winter, and remained cool in summer, they were good for the health and prevented piles (Narayanan, Pattamadai, February 2000).

used in marriages.[3] However, ethnographic accounts of marriages and other ceremonies from the latter part of the nineteenth century make incidental mention of mats.[4] These are revealing. Maclean, for instance, in his description of the marriage ritual of the Brahmins, describes how, after the bridegroom is welcomed and various rituals are performed, 'the bride...goes to the western side of the [sacrificial, *homam*] fire and sits down on a mat, while the bridegroom offers six oblations of clarified butter, some of which he pours over her hands...' (Maclean, 1987 (1885): 235). This preceded the seven steps, or *saptapadi,* which is the most important of all the marriage rites (Pandey, 1993).[5]

The 1917 *Gazetteer of the Tinnevelly district*, while devoting an entire section (pp 218–20) to the manufacture of Pattamadai mats, does not discuss their use in marriages in any detail. Similarly, Rao devotes a chapter to the mat industry of Madras Presidency (1929: 148–53) and has a section on Pattamadai mats, but makes no mention of their use in marriages. Both list the uses of coarse mats as packing material and describe how finer mats are spread

[3] Pandey mentions a few artefacts used as part of marriage ceremonies, though he does not go into the details. These include a couch of grass (a mat?), a brass vessel with a brass cover, and certain gold ornaments.

[4] Indeed, ethnographic writing from the late-nineteenth and early-twentieth centuries in India (in which category I include census gazetteers and reports) are rich in descriptions of things and processes that are deemed significant for the people being described or interesting to the writer. Pate's 1917 *Gazetteer of the Tinnevelly district*, for instance, has detailed descriptions of the Pattamadai mat and the processes of manufacture.

[5] Also see Thurston who writes that among the Holeyas of South Canara, the bridegroom sits on a mat specially made by the bride—the marriage ceremony lasts for four days, during which time none of the party should fail to sit on the mat. Among the leaf-wearing Koragas of South Canara, bride and bridegroom take a cold bath and sit on a mat with a handful of rice between them. Among the hill Urulis of Coimbatore, when the bridegroom's party come to the bride's house, their walking sticks are received on a mat as a sign of respect (Thurston, 1907).

on the ground and used for sitting or sleeping on. In 1934 specific mention is made of marriage mats: 'What are commonly known as 'marriage mats' have a profusion of red coloured strands of the grass (korai) and at least two of them have to be presented to the bridal pair. The Madras market gets a good part of its supply of mats from this [Tinnevelly] district' (*Tinnevelly district gazetteer*, 1934: 200).

The census gazetteer on the mat weaving industry of Pattamadai cites weavers to suggest that the demand for mats 'was high in the marriage and festival seasons and the main buyers of fine quality (50-count) mats were Hindus, particularly Brahmins' (Nambiar, 1964: 29). According to informants (weavers, traders and elderly Brahmins in Pattamadai and elsewhere), Brahmins of Pattamadai and neighbouring areas have bought Pattamadai fine mats at least since the 1960s for festive occasions. Certainly, the fact that only the highest quality artefacts are desired for use on auspicious occasions, must play a part in the selection of fine and superfine mats for marriages and similar functions. As ritual and economic elites in the region, Brahmins could afford to buy higher quality expensive mats (including those from Pattamadai) for festive use. This may have been the cause for the identification of Pattamadai mats as items of brahmin, and, therefore, elite, consumption, with especial focus on their use in marriage and other ceremonies. Today, Pattamadai mats are increasingly being marketed by both local traders and development agents as *the* marriage mats of Brahmin groups. As marriage mats, they are used in ritual contexts and are part of marriage prestations.

The importance of mats in ritual contexts should also be seen in the light of the identification of korai as a grass, and the importance of certain grasses in Hindu ritual. Grasses (Sanskrit: *yavasa*, Tamil: *pullu*) of several species were deemed sacred and played a prominent part in Vedic ritual, including rites of passage ceremonies. They were strewn upon the place of sacrifice, especially around the *vedi* or altar. The sacrificial seats for the priest and the sacrificer were also strewn with rushes and grasses. From rushes and grasses were made the cushioned pallet of Hindu ritual and the meditation mat of the brahmin (Walker, 1995). The best-known and most ritually efficacious variety of sacred grass is *darbha* (*Poa cynosuroides*, genus *borage*).[6] *Darbha* has long leaves tapering to needle-like sharp points and, like korai, the stem is triangular in cross-section. A circlet of specified number of stalks of darbha plaited and worn on the finger is called a *pavithram* and is worn by key participants in Hindu rituals (also see Ayyar, 1998: 151–3).[7]

In Pattamadai, Mohammad frequently claimed that korai (genus *cyperus*) was the same as *darbha* grass (genus *borage*) and, therefore, that korai mats were an integral part of any important ritual, including marriage. Once, while likening korai to *darbha*, he pointed to his finger and said, 'Korai is the same as the grass that is tied around the finger during ceremonies.' Another knowledgeable Brahmin informant, trustee of two temples and in charge of the Brahmin marriage hall in Pattamadai, emphasised that *darbha* and korai had similar wedge-shaped tips. This made 'korai and *darbha* one and the same'.[8] Korai mats, therefore, had great efficacy when used in rituals. The conflation of korai and *darbha* is used, particularly by Mohammad, to sacralise Pattamadai mats and to claim that they are suitable, even essential, in marriage and other ritual contexts.

'Silk Mats' and Marriages

In order to speculate how Pattamadai mats in particular (korai is, after all, the most common raw material in Tamil mats) may have come to be identified with mats used in marriages, I now look at some Tamil marriage and menarche songs translated by Duvvury

6 See Walker (1995: 106) for a description of the creation of *darbha* grass from the back of god Vishnu in his incarnation as a turtle (*Kurma avatar*). Vishnu is an important Hindu god and, along with Brahma and Shiva, forms the Hindu trinity. Also see *Ka* (Calasso and Parks, 1999: 16) for another story relating to *darbha* and the nectar of immortality.

7 It must be added that this is a curious book, composed partly of the writer's strong opinions on the greatness of Hinduism, and partly of a detailed rendering of Hindu rituals and beliefs.

8 The identification of korai with *darbha* was vehemently denied by a well-versed elderly Brahmin woman in Madras.

in her study of Tamil Brahmin women's rites of passage (Duvvury, 1991). Duvvury was not looking for or at references to specific objects, and the fact that mats appear in so many songs is testimony to their importance in the ritual landscape (emphases in the quotes below are all mine). Thus, in the *Shobhanam* or auspicious song sung for Iyer girls at the menarche ritual (*tirandukuli*), the menarche of the goddess Parvati is described as a joyous and lavish occasion,

> Parvati's mother spread ten measures of paddy on the floor, placed a *silken mat* on it and made Parvati Devi stand on it... (Duvvury, 1991: 113)

Similarly, in a swing song (*oonjal paattu*),[9] the swing on which the bridal couple are seated is described thus:

> The four cardinal points forming the four gold chains,
> On such a swing, Narayana swings with his radiant consort.
> Behold the marriage of Lakshmi!
> The world forming the gold plank, the shastras
> forming the *silken mat*,
> Your wonderful sight washes away people's sins... (ibid.: 149)

A *nalangu* song[10] makes prominent mention of mats as well,

[9] The swing or *unjal* ceremony is performed before the main marriage ceremony, i.e. the *saptapadi* or seven steps. In this ceremony, the bride and groom are seated on a swing (on which a mat is usually spread). The bridal couple is fed with bananas soaked in milk (*palum pazhamum*) by various female relatives, who also sing various songs referring to the marriages of gods, mainly Rama and Sita, Vishnu and Lakshmi, and Shiva and Parvathi. In such songs it is common practise to substitute the names of the bridal couple for the names of the gods. As the couple swing themselves gently, married (but not widowed) female relatives perform ceremonies to ward off the evil eye and placate any jealous spirits, which may have evil designs on the couple (Ayyar, 1982: 2; Duvvury, 1991: 154).

[10] Like the swing ceremony, the *nalangu* ceremony is a *laukik* rite which forms an important part of the marriage proceedings. In this ceremony, the bride and groom are encouraged to make each other's acquaintance through a series of light-hearted yet highly ritualised games while members of both parties sing songs and crack jokes. For a detailed description and analysis of *nalangu*, see Duvvury (1991: 155–61).

> Marutvadi, Saraswati, Lakshmi and Arundathi asked them both to sit facing each other on a *silken mat*... (ibid.: 157)

Songs pertaining to rituals in Brahmin marriages and other functions make references to silken mats (*pattu pai*) spread on the surface on which the bride and groom are seated. The reference to silk mats may be a product of poetic license; there are certainly many other extravagant allusions in these songs, including to golden planks and gold chains. The only certain fact is that, from contemporary observations and from informants' accounts, mats (of any count, often new, especially for the bride and groom) are almost always spread out as seating on these occasions.

The preference among Hindus, especially in ritual contexts, for finely and tightly woven fabrics is well noted (see for example, C A Bayly, 1986), as these are considered less permeable and, therefore, better able to repel polluting matter. Coarsely woven fabrics, conversely, attract and trap polluting materials in the environment as the weave is loose and penetrable. Finely woven silk is highly desirable for use in rituals. Because of their silk-like texture and tight weave, Pattamadai fine and superfine mats are often referred to as *pattu pai* (silk mats) by those who come in contact with them. The materiality of the mats makes them able to be treated like silk, especially in ritual contexts. This, as well as the advantages of being identified with elite consumption, might serve to explain the identification of Pattamadai mats as Brahmin marriage mats by both traders and users. In the urban context in particular, as the general use of mats has diminished, expenditure on marriages has increased, and as Pattamadai mats have become more well known as a result of craft development initiatives and shrewd marketing, the expensive and silk-like mats of Pattamadai (*pattu pai*) have increasingly come to be identified as *the* silken mats (*pattu pai*) of brahmin marriage rituals. As a Brahmin woman in Madras said to me, 'For my daughter's marriage, the priest suddenly said we had to have a *pattu pai*. Thank god I knew where to get a Pattamadai mat at short notice, otherwise what would we have done!' (Madras, February, 2000).[11]

[11] She phoned a well-known patron of craft in Madras, who had a stock of Pattamadai superfine mats and sent her one.

Traders, in particular, are eager to reinforce this identification through their shop signs, media interviews and at bazaars and exhibitions. Both the main traders in Pattamadai have signs outside their shops describing both the fine *and* superfine mats of Pattamadai as *pattu pai*. Similarly, Craft Enterprises refers to Pattamadai superfine mats as *pattu pai*. However, it is significant that weavers in Pattamadai do not refer to the mats as *pattu pai*. They refer to all mats of 50 counts and above as *ella pai*, from the Tamil verb *ella*, meaning to split after retting. This indicates that the korai for fine and superfine mats is split before weaving. To further distinguish between fine and superfine mats, weavers refer to the latter as *murukku pai*. This title originates from the Tamil verb *murukku*, to twist. This refers to the fact that the weaver twists each wet weft strand after inserting it through the warp. Thus, weavers describe mats in terms of processes of manufacture. It is the traders who, at least in the public domain, refer to the mats in the language used by the dominant Brahmanical discourse. Referring to my own caste-specific use of Tamil words, one female weaver said, 'We don't say *pattu pai*, only *you* say that' (Beevi in Delhi, December 1999).

Not every one who buys mats for marriages from Pattamadai believes that they are *the* marriage mats. Pattamadai mats are also bought for marriages as a matter of taste and because they are considered beautiful. Furthermore, as they are handwoven and use very fine weft strands and a high warp count, it is possible to weave words into the fabric of the mat. Brightly coloured mats, with the typical *kairasi* marriage pattern and with names of the bride and groom and other details woven on them, appeal in particular to the marriage market, for they look festive, have no trace of the inauspicious colour black, and can be custom-made for the wedding. During the Tamil marriage season, large numbers of orders are placed with mat traders in the town. With the names of the bride and groom and the date of the marriage woven into them, these mats will be used during the marriage ceremony and then form part of the married couple's souvenirs of the wedding. Several of these orders come from marriage brokers who are hired by the bride's parents to organise the wedding. Marriage brokers find a marriage hall, organise the catering, and buy or rent various articles used in the rituals. They are powerful people; a successful marriage broker is hired to organise over a hundred weddings in the course of a year and sources many thousands of things used in the various rituals. The mat traders in Pattamadai are therefore keen to establish and maintain cordial relations with as many marriage brokers as possible.

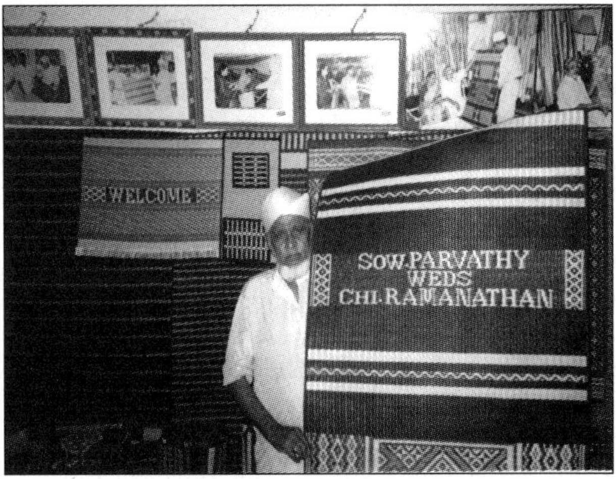

A S Peer Mohammad holds up a marriage mat in his shop.
Photo: Soumhya Venkatesan.

Mr Ananthakrishnan, who regularly buys mats for marriages and 'other religious purposes' from Mohammad in Pattamadai, in a letter to me discussed the growing taste for Pattamadai marriage mats in Coimbatore town where he lives. He wrote that he saw his first Pattamadai marriage mat in 1997 when he obtained one for his daughter's marriage from Lila (of Craft Enterprises), with whose family he was acquainted. Shortly after the marriage, spurred on by the number of people who found the mat beautiful and wanted one for use in their own homes and on ritual occasions, he started ordering mats from Mohammad (whose contact details he acquired from Lila). He has since ordered around 20–25 mats of different types each month. These include marriage mats, small mats used for seating during the daily *puja* (worship) and *pandhi* mats used for seating guests at feasts. He takes a commission on each mat that he orders from Mohammad.

> Before the introduction of Pattamadai mats for weddings in Coimbatore, people were going for Karur mats (coarse variety) and Chittur-Palghat mats (medium quality)...Pattamadai mats got a good name in Coimbatore since 1997 when I introduced them. I got steady orders from marriage contractors of good standing. I feel that my efforts in this regard will in a small way preserve the custom and heritage of India by giving patronage to the Pattamadai mat industry. (A Ananthakrishnan, in a letter, 02/03/2000)

It is interesting to note in Mr Ananthakrishnan's narrative how the mat from being something beautiful and suitable for ritual purposes, and therefore desired, becomes an exemplar of India's heritage and custom in a way that the mats of Karur and Palghat (also handmade, through coarser in weave) do not. Here is a good example of the effects that words (Mohammad's and Lila's) as well as the objects themselves have on actions.

Another regular marriage mat buyer, Mr Narayanan, who lives in Tirunelveli but whom I met in Pattamadai, reiterated the importance of buying new things for use in marriages. Though he agreed that there was no ritual requirement that *Pattamadai mats* be used in marriage ceremonies, he felt that these mats with the names of the bride and groom woven on them were so beautiful and uniquely able to commemorate the event that they were perfect for weddings. He added that as Pattamadai mats were expensive compared to mats from other places, people were only willing to buy them for marriages. Mr Narayanan's analysis is congruent with the general practice of treating the wedding as an arena for showcasing the wealth and status of the marriage parties.[12]

[12] Though, as Good points out (1991: 1), it is a mistake to see marriage expenditure as only involving wasteful ostentation, for they serve social as well as ritual purposes, reinforcing and reproducing the social order.

In January 2000, within the first week of the Tamil month of *Thai*,[13] Mohammad's shop had orders for about twenty marriage mats. All over Pattamadai, in January, weavers were engaged in making *kairasi*-pattern marriage mats and those who could weave-write names on mats were in high demand. So important is the marriage mat market that, for 'urgent mats' (*avasara pai*), traders were getting more than one weaver to weave identical mats with the names of the bride and groom so as to make the order in time. The extra mat would later have the korai strands, which made up the names and other specific information, pulled out in a painstaking process and sold at a diminished price reflecting its reduced length. This practice, which cuts down on profits (as the 'name writers' have to be paid regardless of whether the name is retained or removed), indicates the importance of the marriage mat trade.

The importance of the Brahmin custom, both in economic terms and as a marker of status can be discerned from Mohammad's emphasis on this market. While sitting in his shop, I observed how quick Mohammad was to realise that a visitor was a Brahmin and to greet them with a *namaskaram* (an unusual mode of address for a Muslim man—most others, and not just Muslims, in Pattamadai, say *vanga* or please come) and with a certain amount of deference and knowledge of their needs and customs. Perhaps as a result of this, he has a large Brahmin clientele for his wedding mats. The same clientele also comes to him when they require other kinds of mats, i.e. prayer mats, *pandhi* mats and mats for secular uses, including craft mats. In fact, Mohammad frequently makes the claim that he knows as much about Brahmin marriage practices and taboos as Brahmins themselves.

Objects or classes of objects are important not only as a way of maintaining boundaries between classes, castes and other groups, they may also be used, often self-consciously, to transcend boundaries where individuals or groups seek upward mobility. Emulation of

[13] Tamil months are based on the lunar cycle. Some months such as *Thai* (mid-January to mid-February) are considered very auspicious for marriages.

elite consumption practices includes the process of Sanskritisation (Srinivas, 1966) where lower caste groups (or sections of them) seek upward mobility through the adoption of higher caste, especially brahmin, practices, including consumption (Harriss-White *et al*, n.d.: 24–25; Yanagisawa, 1996). Here, objects can be instrumental in altering perceptions about their users and are signifiers of social divisions and aspirations. Mohammad's desire to interact with brahmin elites reflects the high status of Brahmins despite the larger environment of anti-Brahmin sentiment in Tamilnadu, and highlights the influence of elite consumption on aspirational groups.

Through his talk, visitors to his mat shop are made aware of Mohammad's links with eminent Brahmin families from the area and in other parts of the country. Mohammad's 'designers' in Pattamadai are encouraged to, and often, make mats that appeal to Hindus, including woven representations of the god Ganesha and *kuthu villakku*.[14] Innovative products made in Mohammad's shop include small hand fans (*visiri*) created by cutting 50-count mats into circles, surrounding these circles with tinsel paper and attaching handles, also made with small bits of mat. These are sold for use in the *Kasi Yatra*, one of the ceremonies in a Tamil Brahmin marriage.[15] A Brahmin woman at a crafts bazaar once suggested to Mohammad that the mat on which one sat to pray should only seat one person. Otherwise the benefit (*payan*) of the prayer would also go to anyone else who happened to be sitting on the mat. Mohammad started cutting up large mats and selling these as prayer mats. He also tells prospective buyers why they should buy these small mats.

Mohammad is not only engaged in the continuing 'invention of tradition' (Hobsbawm and Ranger, 1993) by emphasising the

[14] These are tall standing brass/bronze/silver oil lamps often used for ritual purposes in Hindu temples and homes, though some are also used as decorative objects in the more public areas of houses.

[15] The *Kasi Yatra* is a playful ceremony wherein the bridegroom pretends to renounce the world, not go through with the marriage and sets off for Banaras (Kasi) and become an ascetic. To prevent this, the bride's father tempts him to enter the world of a householder with the offer of his daughter in marriage, fine slippers, a fan and other comforts.

Brahmanical consumption of Pattamadai marriage mats. He is also enlarging the existing galaxy of artefacts made using Pattamadai mats specifically for use in Brahmin marriage and other ritual contexts. Other local traders are quick to pick up these innovations, just as Mohammad is quick to pick up theirs.

When a Hindu customer comes to buy a marriage mat from him, Mohammad takes the mat, places it in a yellow artificial-silk bag especially made for the purpose, asks the customer to stand in front of him facing east, raises the mat to head height before lowering it to his eyes and, only then, hands it over to the buyer.[16] This is an impressive ceremony and, through its performance, the mat is partially decommoditised as Mohammad prays for the success of the marriage over it. The mat becomes *the marriage mat* and its purchase becomes an integral part of marriage prestations.

> Hindu South Asians do two things with household durables which appear to distinguish them. One, they construct their relations with objects based on principles similar to those used to construct relations with human beings. That is to say, objects are *systematically* ranked precisely because they belong to a system of objects, just as people are ranked because they belong to a social system...Two, social relations are conducted largely through the manipulation of this system of objects. And that may be illustrative of the extent to which gift (rather than market) exchange has remained the primary means by which to furnish a residence and clothe a family, on the one hand, and to establish, nourish and maintain social relations, on the other.[17] (Breckenridge, 1986: 60)

The gifting of objects, clothing and ornaments is strongly linked to life-crisis ceremonies in Tamilnadu, and also to religious festivals. The gifting often takes place in ritual contexts.[18] These

[16] Yellow is considered an auspicious colour by Tamil Hindus. See Hanchett (1988) for a study of colour symbolism in Hindu rituals.

[17] Breckenridge limits her observations to Hindus. In practice, other groups in India too accord objects significant places in social and ritual life.

[18] For instance, the parents of the groom give the bride, in the presence of the priests conducting the Brahmin marriage, the nine yards saree which she is to don for the crucial marriage ceremony: the taking of the seven steps.

gifts are almost always bought for the purpose. They start their social lives as commodities. The commodity can then move into other kinds of exchange, including gift exchange, especially as part of marriage and other prestations.[19] This is true not only of what are seen as luxury objects, including jewellery and fine cloth, but also of household durables such as pottery, mats, metal vessels and towels, all of which may constitute gifts at the time of marriage.[20] These objects may subsequently be used without reference to their original ritual purpose. The marriage mat becomes another household object and is used like all the other mats in the house, especially as it gets older.

Mats are not only an important component of Tamil Brahmin and other Tamil Hindu weddings. They are also used in Tamil Muslim marriages. Sitting in the town's mat shops, I observed that not only Hindus but also Muslims came from within and outside Pattamadai to buy mats for marriages. According to several Tamil Muslims in and beyond Pattamadai, it is necessary for the bride's side to buy two new mats for use in the *nikaah* (signing of the marriage contract) ceremony. This is rarely mentioned. This social fact does not produce effects (following Rorty, 1999: xxiv–vi), it does not accomplish anything to say that Muslims produce mats for Muslims whereas it does to say Muslims produce ritual objects for Hindus.

Craft and Ritual

The establishment of Pattamadai mats as *the marriage mats* for Brahmins brings them into new contexts of meaning and action.

[19] Commodities have formed part of anthropological analysis since Marx first noted their embeddedness in human relationships and put forward his ideas relating to commodity fetishism. For a review of the literature relating to commodities, see Appadurai (1986) and A Long (1992). Both Appadurai and Long emphasise the fact that its commodityhood is only one aspect of an object.

[20] In Pattamadai, after their *nikaah*, the newly wed Labbai couple go round to every Labbai house where they are seated, fed bananas and milk and given towels (*thundu*, thin woven cotton cloths) as part of marriage prestations.

It invigorates their circulation in contemporary urban contexts as ritually essential craft goods, both for Brahmins and for Sanskritising groups. The emphasis on Brahmin patronage of Pattamadai mats also highlights the role of craft in upholding the moral and social order by uniting what are normally perceived as opposites: low-caste producers and high-caste consumers; Muslims and Hindus; and, the village and the city.

The increasing tension between Hindus and Muslims has struck dismay into the hearts of many people who hold India's secular, pluralist democracy dear. For some, crafts are seen as a way of reinforcing the message that Hindus and Muslims can and have lived in harmony, and that they are embedded in exchanges that are mutually profitable and form an intrinsic part of social life. One of the ways craft development agencies working with Pattamadai mats explicitly do this is by emphasising the use of the mats in Hindu ritual. In such descriptions, found in newspaper articles, publicity and sale brochures and in public speech acts of development agents and traders, the mats embody the liberal ideal of harmony between Hindus and Muslims. The following extract from a card inviting potential buyers to a sale of Pattamadai mats in Bombay in 2000 is revealing: 'These exquisite grass mats known as Pattupais are traditionally given as a wedding gift by the Muslim weaver to the Tamil Hindu bride during her marriage and are considered prized heirlooms.'[21]

A journalist interviewing me (among others) at this sale asked me about my research. But his article confined itself to reporting two things: firstly, so famous are Pattamadai mats that a Cambridge PhD was being done on them; secondly, that I owned a Pattamadai mat, and had been recently married. Ergo, I had a Pattamadai marriage mat.[22] The article thus reinforced the idea that Pattamadai

[21] The exhibition was held between 2 and 8 January 2000. The invitation card was primarily written by the art gallery, Caché, based on materials provided by FACES.

[22] 'Such was the fame of the Pathamadai superfine mat that it became the subject for a PhD thesis by Ms Soumhya Venkatesan of the Cambridge University! Incidentally, both Soumhya and her mother received superfine mats as part of their trousseau!' V Gangadharan, 'Pocketful of

mats are *the* marriage mats for high-caste Tamil Hindus. In craft circles too, Pattamadai mats have, largely because of the publicity given to them by craft developers, come to be seen as the only authentic marriage mat used by high-caste Tamil Hindus from ancient times. This, despite weavers' and other accounts that mats of this silk-like quality have only been manufactured since the end of the nineteenth century.

Other important personalities in the craft worlds are instrumental in the growing perception of Pattamadai mats as *the* marriage mats of Tamil Hindus. The biggest buyer of superfine mats in Madras, Gita Ram, is a member of the Madras Crafts Foundation and of the Craft Enterprises steering group and an important supporter of craft development in India. A Brahmin, she is also a member of a large, culturally active, industrialist family of Madras—one of the most important industrial groups in south India. When I met her to discuss issues relating to crafts, she said that almost all the Pattamadai mats in Dakshinachitra were *bought by her to give as gifts to people at weddings.*[23] She is, therefore, active in propagating the identification of Pattamadai superfine mats as marriage mats in elite circles in Madras. The Madras Craft Foundation invites Mohammad to exhibitions and bazaars at its venue, Dakshinachitra, and has facilitated large orders for Pattamadai mats from industry.

Ram's involvement in, and support of, Pattamadai mats as craft and ritual objects and the consequent advantages, including visibility through awards, income due to large orders, and invitations to exhibitions show the importance of elite patronage in the context of the craft worlds.

But, and paradoxically, for craft developers, the mats used in

---

Business: new markets beckon grass mats of Tamilnadu', *Rediff Business Special*, 25/01/2000. (http://www.rediff.com/business/2000/jan/25mats.htm)

[23] Dakshinachitra describes itself as 'a center for the living traditions of art, folk performing arts, craft and architecture of India with an emphasis on the traditions of south India' (www.dakshinachitra.net/index.htm). A project of the Madras Craft Foundation, it also has a well-stocked craft shop. Artisans from different parts of south India are also invited to the centre to produce and sell craft objects.

marriages are aesthetically extremely problematic. The weaving of representational images and writing on the mat is what makes them popular as marriage mats; but these features are unacceptable in craft mats. The 'craft marriage mat' has no names, dates or representational images woven on it. It closely approximates the craft worlds' prescription of what an 'authentic' Pattamadai mat ought to look like. The only visual difference between the simply and geometrically patterned craft mat and the craft marriage mat is that the latter avoids the use of the inauspicious colour black. There are thus important divergences in the forms that mats take as ritual objects, craft objects and ritual craft objects. While considering the materiality of the mats (important in both craft and marriage markets), a distinction must be made between fabric and surface. While the fabric of the mat remains unchanged across these various contexts and is, in fact, an important component of its attraction (including the enchantment of reeds turned into 'silk'), the surface undergoes modifications in ways that reflect what people want to do with the mats, and their notions of beauty and suitability. As I suggested in Chapter 4, the tension between 'the traditional and authentic' and 'the popular and modern' has concerned those who seek to develop Indian handmade manufactures or traditional crafts since the colonial period. It stems from, and in turn reinforces the distinction between skill and knowledge that marks the workings of craft preservation and support in India. The artisan who, led by his own taste or by a lucrative market, deviates from the prescriptive model of the authentic craft object is, in his every interaction with the craft worlds, gently but firmly encouraged by elites interested in craft to 'return' to it.

Few weavers interest themselves in the performative recreation of Pattamadai mats as ritual and as craft objects. However, they do use 50-count mats for their own marriages. They say that this is a recent development. According to a mat weaver, increasingly, if the bride's side can afford the expense, both the mats bought for a marriage will be fine mats with the names of the bride and groom woven on them. If this is not possible, then at least the mat given to the groom to seat himself during the *nikaah* will be a fine one, with the names of the bride and groom and the date of the wedding woven upon it.

Another weaver said that for her marriage, over thirty years ago, she was only given coarse mats, not fine Pattamadai mats, and added that it was a modern practice (*naagarigamaana pazhakkam*) to give 'nice *pai*', i.e. 50-count mats. At the time of our conversation, she was weaving a marriage mat for the marriage of a close female relative (husband's brother's daughter). The mat, which was meant for the groom was to have the name of the bride and the groom and the date of the marriage woven on it. In this case, the weaver was not going to be paid for the mat but the woman who was 'writing' the names on the mat would be paid the standard rate of Rs 20 per line. Thus, even within Pattamadai, mats for marriages are partly, if not wholly, commoditised.

The use of 50-count mats for marriages within Pattamadai appears to be linked to the increased demand for them outside the town. The common assumption about rural craft objects, and indeed the idealisation of the inalienable nature of craft work, is that they move from being things made by producers for their own use, to serving a wider market. In Pattamadai this is reversed. Made by producers for the market, fine mats now also come to be used by their makers who pay for them either in cash or in opportunity cost.

I have traced here the interdependence between the ritual and craft markets for Pattamadai mats and shown how each builds on the other, thereby enlarging the market for Pattamadai mats, even extending this market to the producer group. The layers of meaning that the mats accumulate as ritual and craft objects informs their uses and continuing significance in both markets. However, I want to go beyond how objects come to mean things to think about how objects do things. I argue that while the process of signification is important in the social life of the mats, the mats are more than passive attractors of meaning, even if this attraction comes from their specificity and materiality. Rather, they are active in social life. Their materiality, their ability to enchant, attract and evoke certain kinds of comparison means that they influence people, causing some persons to act in particular ways, which in turn causes unanticipated events whose effects can last a long time. The next section focuses on the objects as acting rather than acted upon through a re-examination of Alfred Gell's theory of art and agency (1998).

The Agency of Objects

Nineteenth and twentieth century debates focused on whether India had a fine art tradition or not. Members of the nascent Indian art worlds of the early twentieth century actively set out to firmly position themselves within the category of art, claiming a voice in the larger world art tradition (see Guha-Thakurta, 1992). Artisans on the other hand, being of low status, based in village India, poor and marginalised, lost their voices, becoming spoken for, rather than speaking. Craft became a category that was taken over by grand visions of the nation and its heritage and, simultaneously, with pragmatic developmental concerns. The category of craft both enhances and constrains the agency of members. But, given that craft objects are crucial members of this category, what of their agency?

In Alfred Gell's ground-breaking work *Art and agency* (1998), an anthropological theory of art is defined as the study of 'social relations in the vicinity of objects mediating social agency'. His focus is not on a sociological analysis of art institutions, artists and art publics or 'the art worlds', and why they do not accept objects like the mats as art works, rather it is on the objects themselves, what they do and how they exercise agency.

Gell's is an action-oriented social theory of art that focuses on the specificity and efficacy of objects. Objects here are actors, not just acted upon. He actively resists semiotic analyses of objects (what they mean and signify) and symbolic analyses (art as a system of communication) focusing instead on what objects do in the social world. For Gell, art is 'a system of action, intended to change the world...This "action"-centred approach is...preoccupied with the practical mediatory role of art objects in the social process...The nature of the art object is a function of the social relational matrix in which it is imbedded. It has no "intrinsic" nature, independent of the relational context...' (Gell, 1998: 6–7). That is to say, an art object does not need to be recognised by an art world. It is recognised by its role as a social actor.

The notion of agency is crucial to Gell's theory of art. Agency, he suggests, is attributable to persons and objects that are seen as initiating causal sequences that are attributable to acts of mind, intention or will. The idea of agency is a culturally prescribed framework for thinking about causation. 'Whenever an event is believed to happen because of an "intention" lodged in the person or thing which initiates the causal sequence, that is an instance of agency' (1998: 17). Agents cause events to happen in their vicinity. So, we have two key elements in the definition of the agent. Firstly, the agent causes events. Second, the agent is seen to have intentionality (but it need not necessarily intend or anticipate all the events that it causes). But not everyone attributes intentionality to objects even if they do recognise that objects cause events.

The Muslim mat weavers I work with do not countenance this talk of intentionality, even though they fully recognise that their mats (in the absence of their makers) act on people, attract them, influence them and bring them to Pattamadai, whether to develop the industry or to write about it. This is where Gell's distinction between primary and secondary agents becomes critical. Before we go into this, it is well to reiterate that Gell's entire theory rests on the inherent sociality of agents, whether they are persons or objects. In the discussion of agency, all action is social—it is initiated in a social context and with social objectives in view. Furthermore, human agency is exercised in the material world vis-à-vis other persons and things, but the recognition of agency often comes after the fact. We only know after something has happened in the social world that there has been an exercise of agency, someone or something has acted as an agent. 'We cannot tell that someone is an agent until they act as an agent, before they disturb the causal milieu in such a way as can only be attributed to their agency' (1998: 20). The importance of this will be made clear soon, but first to return to the question of different kinds of agent.

A primary agent is an intentional being who exercises agency; a secondary agent causes events to happen but has no intention or will of its own. Objects (cars, landmines, paintings) are secondary agents. Primary agents distribute their agency in the causal milieu through secondary agents. They act through the action of secondary agents, or render their agency effective through secondary agents. It is only within the texture of relationality that objects can become (secondary) agents. But, and this is important, secondary agents are not passive or inert. In acting they may cause events that go beyond the intentions of, or are unanticipated by, primary agents. They generate the very possibilities of human action by virtue of what they are and do.

The reader will remember that it was the mat meant for Queen Elizabeth that drew the attention of the head of the All India Handicrafts Board and brought her to Pattamadai. Mr Rangan exercised his agency on the weavers who, in turn, produced the mat for the Queen. But the mat did not, in its turn, act for Mr Rangan as he hoped. Rejected as a coronation present, it nevertheless acted on Kamaladevi Chattopadhyay, who was moved by its texture and beauty. Years later, in 1975 Chattopadhyay was to write that 'the ivory-white mat, simple, with no trace or design is a superb piece, for its very simplicity has an allure, with its melting soft surface' (1995 (1975): 108). Perhaps the mat for the Queen, with its 'melting soft surface' interrupted by woven words that she saw in 1953, made her want to go to Pattamadai, find the weavers and encourage them to realise the potential, as she saw it, of the plain mat that did full justice to its texture. At any rate, Nambiar suggests that it was only on seeing this mat that Chattopadhyay and the All India Handicrafts Board 'became alive to the existence of this craft' (1964: 6). Chattopadhyay came to the Labbai group in Pattamadai. The Labbais of Pattamadai became identified as craft producers. The very term 'craft producer' is a composite, person+object. The naming of the mat as a craft object is what made its makers craft producers. This changed the group's status and raised their visibility within the nation. The mat here was an agent; it caused events, it effected changes in the social world and it created new possibilities and realities for the Labbai group in Patttamadai.

The agent is one who causes things to happen in his, her or its (causal) vicinity in the social milieu. The patient is the one on whom this agency is exercised. Agents need patients to exercise their agency. The same person or object may be an agent at one moment and a patient the next; indeed the theory is premised on the idea that any patient on which an agent acts is potentially an agent. Kamaladevi Chattopadhyay was a patient to the mat's agency; but quite quickly in her role as head of the national craft development board, she exercised her agency on the mats and the weavers, bringing both within the fold of craft, where they remain. The weaver, as the embodiment of an ideal that originated elsewhere, was remade as a craft producer and, therefore, an object of attention. The craft producer is able to act in the world in particular ways—but to do this successfully (as we saw in Chapter 6), he may have to embrace his own objectification. He has to be a patient to the agency of the disparate institutions and individuals who make up the craft worlds before he can acquire an effective voice within the craft worlds.

My emphasis on the craft worlds is not incidental. It is primarily within the craft worlds that the Pattamadai mat is agentive today, bringing development agencies, state officials, patrons and the benefits they bring in their wake to Pattamadai. The craft worlds, of course, are made up of a disparate and non-organised collection of people and institutions. Different members view crafts and craft producers through different lenses. Two strands are dominant in thinking about craft. The first emphasises the idea that crafts embody the nation's heritage and are intrinsically valuable. The second emphasises the poverty of craft producers and their need for help. Both often work together, but not always. When Ahmad was invited to sell mats at an elite craft bazaar which emphasised the former position, he struck a wrong note, persisting in talking about his poverty and need for financial assistance. This, said one of the organisers, put customers off him and his objects. They wanted beautiful things made by proud craft producers, not someone to pity. Ahmad's pleas would have struck a chord with certain kinds of newspaper journalists, not with wealthy consumers looking for beautiful traditional Indian craft objects. Ahmad, one could say, embraced the wrong kind of objectification of the craft producer in this context. So much so that his mats too were caught up in it and could not do anything.

Agency is not context-free; rather it is context-dependent and relational. This brings us to the art nexus within which Gell suggests art objects exercise their agency. Four terms make up Gell's art nexus: the index, the artist or maker, the recipient, and the prototype.

The index (or the art object) is a visible, material entity that permits a particular cognitive operation that Gell calls the abduction of agency. It is a kind of sign that allows the viewer to make a causal inference of some kind: the presence of smoke indicates a fire and, more pertinently for us, the presence of a mat indicates a weaver, the presence of a *craft* producer indicates a craft world. Any object by virtue of being a manufactured thing motivates an abduction which specifies the identity of the person(s) who made or originated it, the maker. It is to him (or them) that the causal responsibility for the existence and characteristics of the index is attributed.

The recipient or the one who receives the index may be of two kinds. The first is where the recipient acts as an agent in the manufacture of the index. An example of this is Mr Rangan, who commissioned a particular mat to be gifted to Queen Elizabeth II. Both maker and object here are patients to his agency. In the second instance, the recipient may be someone who encounters the index in a particular setting—a gallery or a museum, for example. Here the recipient is the patient to the index as agent. It acts on him in particular ways. It may cause him to want to own the object or a replica of it. It may even change the way he thinks about and acts in the world.

Finally, the prototype is an entity that the index represents or resembles, even if the resemblance is in the spirit rather than the letter. Not all indexes are based on prototypes.

Within the terms of Gell's anthropological theory of art, then, Pattamadai mats are 'art objects' as they can be inserted into the art nexus that is the Indian craft worlds. Every mat indexes its makers whether a particular weaver or the craft community or indeed India's craft heritage. Recipients include patrons who commission mats, developers, buyers and museum-goers. Every Pattamadai mat is a prototype of an 'authentic' Pattamadai mat—there is, of course, no inauthentic Pattamadai mat made in Pattamadai, but there is an ideal Pattamadai mat, especially in the minds of buyers and craft developers, and it is this that they emphasise as a prototype. Here the aesthetic concerns of members of the craft worlds come to the fore.

Gell's theory is revelatory because it shows how not only persons but also objects are active in social relations. We cannot only see how persons render themselves more effective by distributing their agency through objects, but also how the objects themselves are agentive in creating, mediating and maintaining social relations. Once appreciated as indexes of agency, objects can occupy positions in the networks of human social agency that are almost equivalent to the positions of humans themselves (Pinney and Thomas, 2001: 5).

I want to hold on to the qualifier in 'almost equivalent', but not because the proposition is too radical. Rather because, within the ideal of Indian craft, persons and objects cannot be separated. The craft producer, as person+object+idea is a synthetic amalgamation of persons and objects; and the craft object is object+person+idea. The components of the two terms are the same, but ordered differently. In some contexts the 'person' component of the composite comes to the fore as active, in others the 'object' component is dominant. Ahmad struck the wrong note at the bazaar discussed above precisely because he drew attention to 'person' when 'object' should have taken centre stage.

Gell's anthropological theory of art, though it shifts the anthropologist's focus to the objects as active in social relations, bypasses the political and economic contestations around the categorisation of objects. It does not let us see what the labels of 'art' and 'art object' do in particular contexts and why they may be contentious, even rejected. As I showed in the introductory chapter and in Chapter 1, the categories 'craft' and 'craft object' are products of specific historical, political, practical, ideological and aesthetic concerns. A thing's membership in the category of craft is contingent and subject to change; just as a 'rural manufacture' can become a 'traditional craft', so the 'craft object' of today may become an 'art object' tomorrow. While the materiality of the thing may, by and large, remain unchanged, its efficacy—what it can do, partly because of what is done to and with it—can undergo radical alterations if it is re-categorised.

In Pattamadai, weavers who care about these things and local traders actively resist the labels of art object and artist. In response to a member of a craft development NGO who suggested that Pattamadai mats were works of art and that each mat should bear the name of its maker, one weaver said she did not feel this would confer much benefit to individuals or to the mat weaving industry. The kinds of support available to craft producers and to craft communities are not available to artists whose work is less closely tied to the nation-building project. Furthermore, she felt that having names of weavers on mats would mark them clearly as produced by Muslims. This might make some Hindu buyers reluctant to buy them for ritual purposes. Here the category of craft is useful, that of art is not. But it is useful precisely because it is *as craft objects* that Pattamadai mats exercise agency in contemporary India, which is valued by those involved in the mat weaving industry.

Some weavers and traders are keen to go beyond the craft worlds and to use their mats to find new avenues wherein they can be visible and successful. In the next section I examine the use of mats as gifts as a way of activating specific kinds of patronage that draw on, but seek to go beyond, the craft worlds. I believe, based on the ways in which certain kinds of mats are spoken about, that the Labbais of Pattamadai actively seek opportunities to use their superfine mats as agents that can help them gain access to powerful people and places. The mats enhance and distribute the efficacy of not just the individual weavers and traders, but also of the entire Labbai group in the town and all the people who are involved in the gifting process.

Arguably the most important mat from Pattamadai to be given as a gift was the one commissioned as a gift to Queen Elizabeth II. Despite the mystery surrounding the whereabouts of the 'coronation mat', it forms part of the myth of Pattamadai mats: a report in *The Hindu* (27/10/1997) stated that the mat presented to the Queen on her coronation was on display in the Buckingham Palace Museum and claimed that it had been seen by a visiting politician.

The mat, of course, never did get to the Queen. No matter, the myth continues to grow.

The mat for the Queen not only put Pattamadai mat weaving on the craft map of India but also assured the mat weaving industry a place in the romantic imagination of the nation. People in Pattamadai are aware of the special place the royal mat occupies (they can hardly be unaware, given journalists' predilections for asking about it). Consequently, the mat given to the Queen is as widely spoken of within Pattamadai as without. The knowledge that I was studying in England brought with it a wake of questions about the mat presented to Queen Elizabeth. Had I seen the mat? What did it look like? Was it displayed on a wall?

No one anticipated the effect the mat for the Queen would have, and indeed its agentive qualities only become apparent in light of the enormous changes to the lives of the Labbais of Pattamadai caused by their identification as craft producers and, therefore, as objects of development. Superfine mats have since been presented to several important personages in the name of the Labbais of Pattamadai or of the Indian State (though they continue even here to index the agency of the makers) since the middle of the twentieth century. The prototype they draw on is the mat for the Queen. Few of these mats have come close to what the Queen's mat did, but gift mats build on and contribute to the identification of mats as craft and ritual objects. They draw attention to the mat weaving industry.

Gifting Mats, Opening Doors

The mat shops in Pattamadai are colourful and vibrant spaces. Mats are everywhere—some are hung up to display their colours and patterns, others are rolled up in big bundles and lean against the walls. Photographs line the walls—many show famous politicians and other important figures being presented with mats by traders and less frequently, by weavers. If asked, traders will open up folders which are stored in their desks to display press cuttings relating to the Pattamadai mat weaving industry. Almost every piece mentions the presentation of Pattamadai *pattu pai* as gifts to political leaders and celebrities, and their use in high-caste marriages. Some weavers also have similar folders with press cuttings and dog-eared photographs showing famous people with mats.

The census monograph on the fine mats of Pattamadai indicates that the main market at the time (in the 1960s) for the expensive superfine mats of Pattamadai was, in fact, a gift market. This was, in part, due to the 'State government's generous cooperation by way of presentation of [superfine] mats to foreign dignitaries whenever they visited Madras state' (Nambiar, 1964: 36). Appendix II of the census monograph lists 'some of the Very Important Personalities who were presented with Pattamadai [super]fine mats.'[24] These include Sir Archibald Nye, the last British governor of Madras, Queen Elizabeth II, President Khruschev, Marshal Tito, and the Dalai Lama among others (ibid.: 57). More recently mats have been gifted to the former Indian president, Abdul Kalam, and the former prime minister, Rajiv Gandhi (in both cases the gifts originated from within the Labbai group). A State gift of a mat was also made to President Gorbachev.

It is highly likely that the choice of Pattamadai mats as State gifts after 1953 was partly due to the positive publicity surrounding the mat meant for Queen Elizabeth II. Elite and powerful patronage, including that of Mr Chellapandian, the speaker of the Tamilnadu state legislative assembly from 1960, who had previously been the first president (1954–60) of the Pattamadai Fine Mat Weavers' Cooperative Society. As speaker, Mr Chellapandian continued to exercise an active interest in the mat weaving industry. According to weavers, he was responsible for the distribution by the state government in 1973 of common land in Pattamadai to weavers who did not own houses. A later speaker of the Tamilnadu legislative assembly, Mr P H Pandian, who hails from a town near Pattamadai, was also an important patron of the mat weaving industry and commissioned superfine mats for use as official gifts.

[24] Nambiar uses the term 'fine mat' to refer to mats of 100 and higher count. Today in Pattamadai and its markets and also in this book mats of 100 count or more are referred to as 'superfine mats'.

Mr Rangan's initial idea of giving a mat as a gift thus paved the way for many more 'mats-as-gifts', not only by the state but also by individuals and groups including the weavers. Indeed, the Queen's mat was the most important, visible precedent for the use of Pattamadai mats in state and other gifting, whether by Pattamadai Labbais, other individuals and collectives, and national and local governments. Unpacking the question of agency here, we get an interesting pattern of nesting. Rangan is the first agent, whose idea of giving the Queen a gift mat puts him in a relationship of patron to the weavers whose skill and knowledge of weaving cause the mat to come into existence. The weavers make the first part of Rangan's ambition a reality by weaving a mat that conforms to his requirements. Rangan's larger ambition of actually making a gift of a mat to the Queen is never realised. This is partly because of the physical form of the mat he commissioned—one which embodied his desire to make visible a connection with the Queen, and which in the end prevented the mat from being able to be presented to the intended recipient. The story does not end there. The materiality of the mat and the naming of the weavers on the mat brought Chattopadhyay to Pattamadai—in the end, the mat 'spoke' for the weavers in a space which they themselves could not enter.

Most gift mats are intended to create connections not only with the final recipient but also with other people or institutions that were crucial in either passing these gifts on, or publicising them. The gift mat thus creates or activates networks. More people claim ownership of gifts than are actually involved in making or commissioning them. In this context I will discuss two more gift mats: one given to the chief minister of Tamilnadu state, and the other to Prince Charles and Princess Diana of Britain on their marriage.

The first is a recent gift. In 2003 a specially made mat was gifted to the chief minister of Tamilnadu state by a newly formed 'self-help group' of ten female weavers. The Al-Bismi self-help group had come into existence to avail of loans from a government micro-finance scheme and was set up by the owner of a mat shop and his wife. The chief minister was visiting the nearby city of Tirunelveli. Self-help groups from all around the region were invited to set up stalls displaying their products. The chief minister would visit the space where the stalls were set up. The Al-Bismi self-help group was invited to attend this event. This invitation had required a lot of ground work. The owner of the mat shop in Pattamadai and his wife, who were crucial in setting up the group, manned the stall. They wanted to make sure the chief minister would not just walk past their stall but would spend some time there. A certain kind of mat could achieve what he wanted. A local artist was commissioned to paint the chief minister's face on a few mats and beneath that, a few lines praising her.

One of these mats was displayed prominently.[25] The chief minister stopped at the stall. The mat was gifted to her. Photographers were at hand. The next day the majority of Tamil newspapers and a national English language newspaper carried a photo of the chief minister holding up the mat with her likeness painted on it. Some of the newspaper reports carried the name of the self-help group, others did not. In some, the gift was reported as being from the fine mat weavers of Pattamadai. Here, to use Battaglia's term, agency was ambiguated (1997) in a way that extended the benefits of the gifting to more people than just the members of the self-help group or the mat trader who did all the work involved in the gifting.[26] Not everyone was unhappy with this ambiguation.

For the mat weavers, the gift was important in two respects. It brought publicity for the entire group and for their mats, which as commodities for sale would benefit hugely from the increased awareness of their existence. Part of its value was seen to be in the support shown to the chief minister by an ancient community of Muslim weavers—an important message in a religiously riven India.

[25] There were four mats in total. One was gifted to the chief minister. One was bought by a local party member. Two remained unsold, of which I later bought one.

[26] It seems apposite here to repeat Chari's words in *The Hindu* ('The wonder of the Pattamadai mat', 25/02/1996): '...Of course, no lore concerning the mat would be complete without its faery touch—way back in 1948 [sic.], out of the wealth of India's handicrafts, it was a finely textured Pattamadai mat which was chosen as India's wedding gift [sic.] to the then Princess Elizabeth.'

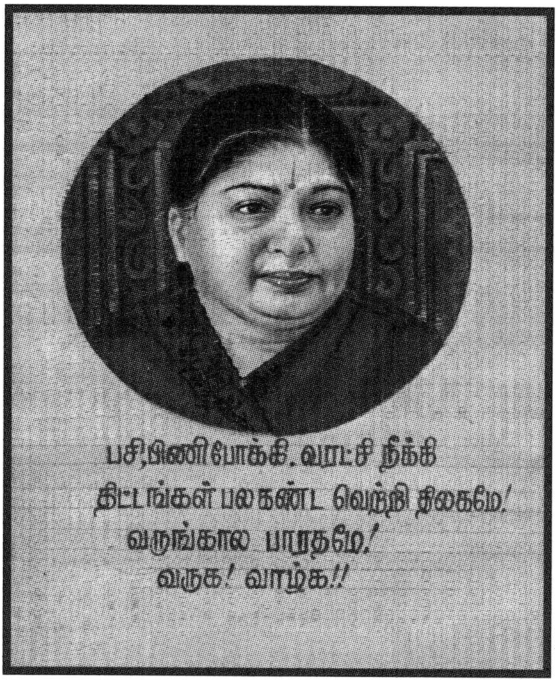

A mat for *selvi* Jayalalithaa.

In one newspaper the photograph of the chief minister holding the mat was placed next to another photo where she was serving food to a group of four people who were obviously identifiable as Muslim from their clothing.[27] The Tamil verses painted on the mat are especially interesting. They praise the chief minister as having ameliorated poverty and hunger and initiating many (development) schemes, of the kind that the weavers too hope to access. The chief minister showed her immediate support to the gift-givers by buying a superfine mat from them.

The day after the presentation to the chief minister, I was in Mohammad's mat shop. A local elite phoned to talk about placing

[27] In order to make visible their role as servants of the people, politicians frequently serve food to the poor, almost always in the presence of photographers.

a large order for a wedding with him. At the very outset, she asked him if he were responsible for the chief minister's gift. Mohammad, who had nothing to do with the gifting, and who, moreover, disapproved of the fact that the mat had the chief minister's face painted (rather than woven) on it by a local artist, said, 'We are all related. The gift-giver is my niece (mother's sister's son's daughter; so it is as if I gave it).'[28] Mohammad was here using the idea of the craft collective and, more specifically, the idiom of kinship to insert himself into an event that could give him publicity.

For the mat shop owner and the self-help group, the process of arranging to give the gift was in itself productive. They liaised with the press office of the political party to which the chief minister belonged,[29] party big men at the local level, and state government officials in charge of organising the chief minister's visit. These contacts are prized both in themselves and because of the benefits that may accrue from them in the future. Their poverty and low status mean that the Labbai group is by and large poor and marginalised within the state; contact with government and party officials who may provide patronage is very important. For this reason, the same man who gave the current chief minister the mat had also given her predecessor and bitter political rival another such mat when he was in power. Here, the ambiguation of his agency serves him well too, unpinning his specific role in the gifting and making the mat a gift from a larger group while nevertheless giving him access to important people.

Gifts may also be disowned or deliberately forgotten about as this next and final example shows. When Prince Charles and Princess Diana got married, an Englishman based in Bombay who knew a Brahmin who was originally from Pattamadai but lived in the

[28] Mohammad's disapproval did not prevent him from commissioning a local artist to paint on some mats once he saw how popular they were, Customers send photographs of themselves, their children or homes which the artist copies on to a mat.

[29] Ostensibly to get a picture they could reproduce; anyone who has been to Tamilnadu will know that it is impossible to avoid pictures of politicians. Whosoever wants to paint a politician's face has a million models from which to choose.

city, decided after hearing the story of the Queen's mat to gift a mat to the newly wed couple. He, therefore, commissioned a mat through his Pattamadai Brahmin friend. I assume the mat was sent to England, though my efforts to trace it have been unsuccessful. Today, pictures of this mat, unlike those of other mats gifted to celebrities, are never displayed in shops in Pattamadai. I had read about this gift in a newspaper article (again attributing it to the entire Labbai group rather than to the Englishman) and heard from someone in Pattamadai that Meeran had executed the order. Later, in Meeran's shop, when I asked him why he did not display this photograph in his shop, he explained: 'They are divorced now, what is the use of showing their wedding mat.'[30] Unlike the mat given to the Queen, this mat did not bring massive benefits to Pattamadai.

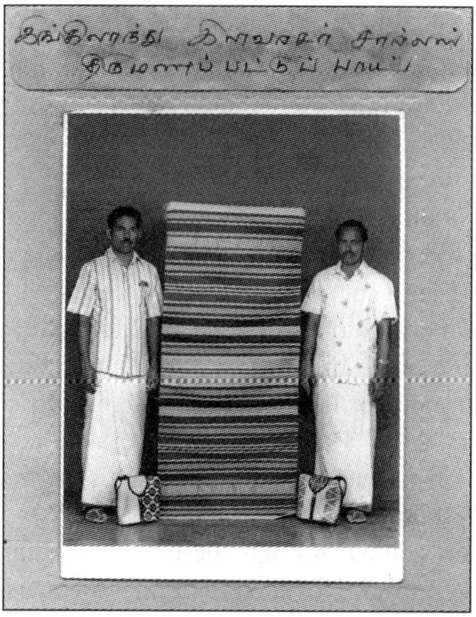

A mat for Prince Charles and Princess Diana.
Photo courtesy: S M Meeran.

[30] Meeran had also clearly read or heard on television or radio about the marital problems of the Prince and Princess of Wales. 'Her boyfriend [he used the English word] ordered the mat,' he told me, slightly slyly.

The gift was in that sense wasted, though the mat itself brought money to Meeran who oversaw the order and in whose house the mat was woven. However, as Meeran was quick to point out, the fact of its being commissioned at all was an example of the weaving industry's connections with high-caste Brahmin patronage. This, of course, was something that Rangan had initiated a few decades before.

The legend in Tamil on the top says: 'The silk marriage mat of England's crown prince Charles.' On the top of the mat are woven the words: 'Diana weds Charles.' On the bottom is the name of the man who commissioned the gift: 'Sir John King.' The man on the right is S M Meeran. The man on the left is a relative of S M Meeran's, though not a weaver.

Superfine Mats Lead, Fine Mats Follow

As we saw in Chapter 6, in addition to mats for marriages and mats as gifts, there is one more space where the superfine mats of Pattamadai become important in directing attention the industry as a whole and also to specific individuals. This is the national awards scheme for master craft producers, and allied support given by the national and local governments to award winners. Beevi won her national award for a superfine mat. However, the benefits accruing from the award were primarily used by Mohammad to widen the markets for fine mats. Indeed, until late 2000, Beevi herself wove only 50-count mats for her father's shop. That the superfine mat is seen by traders within Pattamadai as a tool and a resource is made evident by the fact that it has not been the superfine mat industry but rather the fine mat weaving industry that has benefited from any recognition gained through the use of superfine mats as gifts or competition entries. However, as agents, the mats go beyond the intentions of those who seek to distribute their agency through the objects. Thus Craft Enterprises came to Pattamadai, at the behest of the Crafts Council of India and the Confederation of Indian Industry, shortly after the first national award for a superfine mat was won by Beevi. Craft Enterprises' decision to concentrate on 'revitalising' the superfine mat weaving industry by establishing steady markets for superfine mats has had important consequences for superfine mat weaving in Pattamadai.

A certain number of superfine mats has always been sold in markets and shops but, from conversations with weavers and traders, it appears that before the arrival of Craft Enterprises, superfine mats were viewed primarily in the form of partial transactions in Pattamadai. They would create openings which would lead to further transactions in fine mats. By putting in place a mechanism for the regular purchase of superfine mats within Pattamadai and establishing markets for the mats outside Pattamadai, the NGO has made it possible for weavers of superfine mats to earn a regular income from their production. In doing so, it has fundamentally changed the way in which superfine mats are viewed in Pattamadai. They are now comparable to fine mats, and a significant number are produced and sold every month. Despite this, superfine mats continue to be used as agents, especially in the context of awards and in gifting.

Mats, particularly of lower counts, are also given to visiting officials from government offices, to policemen who stop off at the mat shops, and to others whose goodwill it is seen as important to achieve. These are described as necessary transactions, and as ways of influencing the course of events at a local level. Unlike the gifts given to celebrities, such gifts do not form part of a heroic narrative. Instead, they are construed as bribes. 'The official from the Handicrafts office came to my house, he wanted to see samples, I showed him some and he said pointing a small superfine mat, "My daughter could use something like this to place under her lunch-box." What could I do? I had to give it to him, after all he is an officer' (Kadher, January, 2000).

Ironies

In January 2001, I visited Abdul, a superfine mat weaver, in his house. He asked me to wait while he found a small news article about Pattamadai mats. I sat on a coarse mat in the verandah and he disappeared into the main room to fetch the article. Within a few moments, he returned with a thick plastic folder which had various press cuttings in Tamil relating to Pattamadai mats and documents confirming his participation in various workshops relating to mat weaving. He quickly rifled through these various bits of paper and found what he was seeking. Before handing it to me, he read the short paragraph softly to himself and started to laugh. 'You must photocopy this and put it in your report,' he urged, even before I had a chance to look.

The article was, in fact, a joke of the question and answer type submitted by a reader to the Tamil magazine *Kalkanndu*. Two people are discussing the visit of the speaker of the Tamilnadu legislative assembly to the British parliament in 1986. The speaker took with him a specially made Pattamadai superfine mat to present to the House of Lords. The joke is based around the suitability of this gift.

> Question: What was the reason for the presentation of a Pattamadai mat to the House of Lords by P H Pandian?
>
> Answer: Is it so that that gathering too can sleep? (*Kalkanndu*, 16/11/1986)

The humour comes from the gap between the domestic use of mats (objects which are unrolled to form a surface on which to lie or sit) and the mat as a high-status gift article.

The twentieth century has seen the transformation of Pattamadai mats into ritual and craft objects, and into gifts suitable for royalty, presidents, prime ministers and parliaments. The transformation is effected both as a result of the materiality of the Pattamadai mat, and the embedding of the mat in the discourses and practices of the craft worlds. It has had important consequences for the producers. The mat for the Queen brought both the mats and the Labbais of Pattamadai into the purview of the craft worlds. Furthermore, the mats allow those actors in Pattamadai who are able, to access networks from which they would normally be barred. These include powerful industrialists, politicians and Brahmins. The mats became agents in transcending the spatial and temporal and political constraints of the weavers.

But, as Abdul's enjoyment of the joke shows, weavers at least are fully aware of the irony of making a gift of a mat (normally a low-status article) to an august assembly. In the next chapter I examine Pattamadai mats as craft objects for sale, and suggest that, in dedicated craft bazaars, certain tensions become apparent. These arise from the gap between the idealised construction of craft and the commodification of craft objects in the market place.

8 Selling Gifts: Matts in the Market

In this chapter I focus on the mat as an object for sale which competes with other kinds of commodity in the marketplace. Described by a buyer as 'objects with souls,'[1] craft 'inhabits an ironic position: that of a commodity that rebels against the market-place' (Hickey, 1997: 97). Arguably, crafts and craft production have, since the nineteenth century, always been defined in opposition to industrialisation and commoditisation. Notwithstanding this, in commercial craft production the craft object has to be sold if the craft tradition is to live.

The craft object is central to the craft development project. The need for, and access to, money constitutes a central concern for actors in monetised economies. This is as true of artisanal groups as it is of others. In order to make a livelihood from craft production, the artisan needs to sell his products regularly, realise a viable income from each sale, and be assured of regular sales in the future. This is recognised by those who seek to develop crafts. Despite the

[1] A craft buyer's view cited in Craft Enterprises document, 'Our philosophy regarding handcrafted corporate gifts', n.d.

discursive construction of the craft object as a gift and its partial decommodification as an essential ritual good, the marketing of the craft object remains an important concern.[2] 'The craft skill and the product—its identification, development, production and marketing—are the catalyst to help traditional craftspeople regain their place in the Indian economic mainstream and development process' (Dastkar publicity material).[3]

However, as Tyabji points out, it is not simple to sell crafts in an urban India which is already overcrowded with commodities.[4] The artisan has to be re-educated and the object refashioned according to the terms demanded by a modern market.[5]

One of the most noteworthy aspects of the consumption of craft objects in India, though not confined to it, is the phenomenon of ethnic chic. This not only brings craft into the realm of fashion, but also turns craft objects into indicators which can be used to reveal the socio-political ideals of those who buy, use and display craft objects on their bodies or in their homes. Commentators are wryly cynical about the phenomenon:

> The craze for 'ethnic' is something that adds an artificial rural touch to our mundane, mechanical lives. Just like Granny's secret recipe for colic, or indigestion, the 'chatti-chattai-charpoy'[6] formula of mud pots, grass mats and string beds, are added liberally whenever there is a need to make a statement about tradition being an

[2] For a development oriented view of craft bazaars, see Raj (n.d.).

[3] Dastkar is among the leading NGOs in India working with craft development. The Dastkar website can be found on http://www.coop4coop.org/highlight/dastkar/index.htm.

[4] Tyabji, 'Dastkar and the marketing of craft: a subsidized con trick or a success story?', *The Economic Times*, 10/08/1994.

[5] Often, the services of a designer are required to translate the wishes of the buyer into the imagination and skill-base of the producer. See Rees (1997) and Tyabji (CAPART Magazine, 01/10/1995) for two very different discussions of what it means to design for crafts in the 'West' and in contemporary India.

[6] The *chatti, chattai, charpai* formula uses one Tamil word (*chatti*) in conjunction with two Hindi words. This is a good indication of the inclusive and pan-Indian concept of traditional craft.

> important part of the way we present ourselves. No hotel lobby, no airport arrival lounge, no MD's [Managing Director's] grandiose granite-lined waiting room, modern villa masquerading as a farm-house, or designer wedding, could possibly survive without some reference being made to the craft tradition. (Geeta Doctor, 'Craft in contemporary design', *The Hindu, Folio*, 21/03/1999)

The term 'ethnic chic' is used by Greenough (1995) and Tarlo (1996) to discuss the adoption by members of urban middle and upper class in India, of clothing, furnishings and other objects from different parts of the country. Tarlo, especially, highlights the fact that consumption of 'ethnic products' often involves their exoticisation and their characterisation as the 'primitive other' (ibid.: 311). Other writers use the term to refer to a return to Indian roots through the conscious adoption of traditional objects and clothing (Narasimhan, 1999). Here, the consumption of traditional craft products may be linked to 'the search for a lost identity' (see Campbell, 1997). However, the 'lost identity' may itself be a creation of the present. As Durrans pointed out with reference to the Festival of India in Britain, 'Tradition is the unifying factor only as an abstraction; in detail, most traditions are particular and regional or local' (1982: 16).

It is now possible to see mats used in many contexts in urban India. Large numbers of mats were used to decorate the auditorium stage at the Music Academy in Madras during the 1999–2000 classical music festival. Mats are converted into, and used as, window blinds, they are used on dining tables, and can be seen decorating walls and doors. They also replace rugs on floors. A Madras-based dance company, Arangham Trust, used korai mats and palm leaf masks in a dance production *Gajaana* in such a way as to bring 'the simplicity and beauty of craft rhythms into the dance arena' (Chari, 'Weaving Craft into Dance' in *The Hindu*, 15/02/1998).

The decontextualisation of mats should also be seen in the context of the declining use of mats in urban well-to-do Tamil houses. Sleeping or sitting on mats is increasingly seen as an 'old-fashioned' or rural option. Because the possession and use of furniture is governed in part by economic considerations, it is also people who cannot afford furniture who *need* to use mats. The exception is in other 'traditional activities' like south Indian classical music where people do sit on mats that they spread out on the floor when they sing, play an instrument or attend music lessons. These activities are very common in certain sections of Tamil society. Otherwise, like earthenware pots, mats, while being low-status goods when put to their intended use, become 'craft objects' able to project a certain image of the user when diverted to other contexts. They thus become symbols in conspicuous consumption and join the galaxy of objects used in self-conscious ways to portray socio-political aspirations and ideals. The demand for decontextualised mats is so high that at a sale of Pattamadai mats in a north Indian city, a Tamil visitor said, seemingly without irony, 'I do not want a mattish mat' (Tamil: *enakku paish pai vendam*, 2000).

The manner in which craft objects are marketed emphasises their rural origins, even if this may not actually be the case. As has already been said, a leading craft shop describes Pattamadai, a busy bustling town of over 13,000 people, as a 'sleepy hamlet' (Dakshinachitra, Madras). This is less a pointed statement about the shop's dissemination of inaccurate information and more a remark about how crafts, by the very nature of their discursive construction, have to be from places which have been left behind in the rat race of modernity because, 'Handicrafts were not symbols of employment generation alone but also functioned as indicators of a different style of life, of a different value system' (Varadarajan, 1990: 376).

At the same time, the craft object is also purchased in ways that Veblen (1994 (1899)) would recognise as the subversion of the ideal of craft by conspicuous consumption. One man bought a superfine mat because, 'It is exclusive and I want exclusive accessories for my exclusive fibre-glass holiday cabin.'

Selling Pattamadai Mats

The fine and especially superfine mats from Pattamadai have long been items of elite consumption and difficult to market.

> A mat of very superior composition and considerable reputation is produced at Pattamadai...In spite of their artistic merits, however,

it is difficult to see that the mats are of much practical value... they are by their very fineness and delicacy less suitable than the ordinary coarser articles. There is unfortunately no real demand for them' (Pate, 1917: 219).

By 1929, there appears to be a specialised, if small, market for Pattamadai mats. The *Report on the survey of cottage industries* says of them, 'These mats are exquisitely fine and the workmanship is splendid...they can be folded and carried in a coat pocket. These are purchased mostly by Europeans, high officials, tourists and wealthy landlords, chiefly for decoration as wall hangings of apartments' (Rao, 1929: 149).

In the 1960s superfine Pattamadai mats were being bought by the state government as gifts for visiting dignitaries; Nambiar nevertheless identifies a shift from high-quality to medium-quality mat weaving (1964). This is congruent with my analysis in the previous chapters that the superfine mats open new doors for the (relatively) cheaper fine mats also made by the weavers. But it also echoes a trend seen throughout the nation, and is seen by those who seek to develop the superfine mat industry as a response to dwindling local markets for highly specialised products especially as new, and often cheaper, alternatives become available. Organising craft bazaars in urban areas aimed at the wealthy, and inviting selected craft producers to sell their products is seen as an answer to this ongoing problem. The craft bazaar is often likened to the village fair in craft development literature. Its main imputed advantages are that it will eliminate exploitation of producers by middlemen and allow exchange of ideas and information between the buyer and seller who might not otherwise meet (see for instance, Raj, n.d. for a general discussion on craft bazaars. Also see Mehmood and Aazam, 2002, for a very positive portrayal of one particular craft bazaar).

Craft Enterprises describes certain kinds of bazaars it organises as 'sacred spaces' where 'the two spheres—the urban new and the rural old' can see and perhaps learn from each other ('Our Philosophy of the Home Bazaar', 1998). While bazaars can incorporate these elements, and are certainly important in terms of revenue generated for craft producers who attend them, I argue, through a detailed examination of one specific craft bazaar held in New Delhi from 8 to 14 December 1999, that craft bazaars can also be seen as arenas where ways of imaging crafts are both reinforced and contested. In their serious speech acts, organisers of bazaars draw on several of the images of craft objects and producers identified in Chapter 1. These are often echoed in newspaper reports that cover the events. However, within the bazaar itself, the tensions between the idealised image of the craftsperson and the buyer who is seeking a bargain can be pronounced.

My approach in this chapter follows the extended case study method developed by Max Gluckman (1958). While there have been criticisms of Gluckman's method, (see A Long, 1992), the extended case study is nevertheless useful as a means of analysing a series of interactions that are bounded in time, and interpreting them in the light of larger social mores.

Bazaars and marketplaces are important sites of anthropological enquiry. Following Geertz (1973), Gell analyses the market as an enacted text whose meaning can be construed by specifying its context. Gell writes of a weekly market in central India,

> The market is a paradigm of social relations; interaction in the market-place is coloured by factors external to the market-place, so that a tribal interlacing with a market trader does not see him simply as the purveyor of some good that he has in mind to buy, but as a representative of a category relatively ranked in accordance with a sociological scheme of values. (Gell, 1999b: 112)

In this chapter I look at a one-off craft bazaar to which specially selected sellers are invited in accordance with bureaucratic regulations and norms and where the sellers, as much as what they have come to sell, are discursively and visually constructed as 'traditional'. The dedicated craft bazaar is a space where the totality of craft—object+person+idea—is made visible. It is an orchestrated space, but at the same time it is a place where commodity-like craft objects are exchanged for money. This also makes it a contested space.

'The Master's Best, Yours to Possess'[7]

The Master Creation '99 exhibition was held in December 1999 at Dilli Haat in Delhi.[8] Only craft producers who had won national awards were invited by the National Handicrafts Board to attend the bazaar. Invitations to the bazaar, in English, arrived less than four weeks before the event, leaving little time for invitees to prepare stock. Unless the person who received the invitation was also a trader, or closely associated with a trader, (s)he had to buy or borrow objects from other producers to sell at the bazaar.

An invitation to the Master Creation bazaar was sent to Beevi in Pattamadai. Train fares would be paid for the national award winner and one companion. Mohammad decided to accompany Beevi. Fathima, Beevi's sister, also decided to travel with them even though she would have to pay for herself. She had never been to Delhi and this was a good opportunity. Fatima would help Beevi and Mohammad at the mat stall and then the three of them would see the sights and also take a day trip to Agra to see the Taj Mahal before returning to Pattamadai. The group took with them stock worth around Rs 1,30,000, including ten superfine mats. The majority of the stock comprised fine mats in different sizes and small 'novelty objects' made from mats. They hired a van to transport their stock from Pattamadai to Tirunelveli and boarded a train to Madras. Their train from Madras to Delhi would not leave until the next day, so they spent the night in a hotel and took the northbound train the next day. The group arrived in Delhi the day before the bazaar, found lodgings near the venue and set up their stall. Travelling with large bundles of mats was difficult, but they did not want to send their mats unaccompanied to Delhi, in case they did not get there in time for the bazaar. Mohammad knew that railway police might well make them open

[7] All publicity materials for Master Creation '99 featured this slogan.

[8] The Dilli Haat complex was especially designed for marketing of craft products. See Tyabji (*First City*, Feb. 1999) and Joshua (*The Hindu, Folio*, 21/03/1999) for descriptions of Dilli Haat. Also see Compendium of Handicraft Schemes (1998) for a description of proposals to create urban haats (markets) for craft promotion throughout the country on the basis of the success of Dilli Haat.

their bundles, given that the group was visibly Muslim and that they were travelling in December, but he was willing to risk the inconvenience and unpleasantness. However, and despite their protestations, the official in charge of reimbursing travel allowances refused to reimburse them for their over-night stop in Madras, or for the cost of transporting their stock from the train station to the hotel and back again. He said they should have booked their stock all the way to Delhi from Tirunelveli.

Large posters emphasising the presence of national award winners who would be bringing their 'handcrafted creations' for exhibition and sale were prominently displayed just outside the venue. On the evening that the bazaar opened, richly caparisoned elephants and camels paraded through the central aisles between stalls. The president of India, his wife, attendant dignitaries, guards and others graced the opening with their presence. The craftspersons, enjoined in their invitation letters to be dressed in 'traditional costumes' and to behave decorously for the duration of the bazaar, were fully aware that it was their status as national awardees which merited this singular attention. At the same time, they were also aware that after the glamour of the opening day, they would have to bargain, extort and cajole visitors to sell their stock, the main reason for which they were at the bazaar. They would also have to deal with suspicious government officials in getting their monies reimbursed or their daily allowances.[9]

Entry to the bazaar was free. Buyers thronged the space while sellers exhibited their wares in stalls allocated to them by the organisers. I attended the bazaar throughout and spent the largest part of each day in the mat stall. Mohammad and Fathima were usually behind the counter and Beevi and I sat just outside the counter to the left of it.[10] Mostly I was content to observe and

[9] The suspicion seemed mutual. I noticed at the bazaar that artisans rarely revealed their takings for the day to the officials who came round to collect details for their records at the end of each day.

[10] Initially, I had intended to conduct formal interviews with people who came to the stall, but gave up the plan as few people seemed interested in talking to me rather than browsing through the different exhibits.

chat when business was slack but when it got busy, I would be pulled into displaying and selling mats, and translating between English and Hindi and Tamil.[11]

There were 75 crafts stalls in the bazaar, of which two sold mats. The second mat stall has Sitalpati mats from West Bengal. The craft producer had been asked to bring her mat-making equipment with her and demonstrate her skill. She, as well as her mats, was being exhibited.

The Pattamadai mat stall was located off the central aisle and was flanked on either side by a group of woodworkers from Ghaziabad (near Delhi) and by woollen shawl and garment weavers and embroiderers from Kashmir. The average price of the woodworkers' products was about Rs 200 and the average price of products in the Kashmir woollen goods stall was about Rs 4,000.[12] The most expensive Pattamadai superfine mat in the stall was around Rs 1,600; fine mats were priced between Rs 200 and Rs 1,000; the cheapest set of tablemats was about Rs 100; and the small fans were around Rs 25 each.

The fans and the table mats sold quite quickly as did the 2' × 4' mats meant for display on walls. The larger sleeping mats did not sell well.[13] The use of mats as objects to lie on and keep rolled up in a corner of the room when not in use, is not common in urban north India. A couple of comments are worth recounting. Two Tamil women said, in response to my question, that they used to sleep on mats when they lived in Tamilnadu. Since moving to Delhi, however, they had found that no one of their acquaintance slept on the floor on a mat, preferring to sleep on cots even in

[11] Beevi and Fathima spoke only Tamil and Mohammad's English and Hindi, though adequate for simple conversations, were insufficient for longer discussions. Mohammad, however, had a stock set of phrases in Hindi and English about the glory of India's craft tradition and the beauty of Pattamadai mats that he used to good effect throughout.

[12] This does not include one very fine shawl that was priced at Rs 2,00,000.

[13] These were all at least six feet in length and two-and-a-half to three feet in width.

summer. They too had stopped sleeping on mats: 'It looks bad if we sleep on the floor, even servants sleep on cots here.'

Some buyers bought large mats to use in place of floor rugs. Bold combinations, especially black and white mats, sold well for this purpose. Buyers described them as 'contemporary yet ethnic' and enthused that they were reminiscent of 'bold tribal designs'. All the superfine mats were sold, many to interior designers who were executing commissions. At the end of the bazaar, the group from Pattamadai was left with some unsold stock entirely comprising large mats. All three were unanimous in their feeling that all those mats would have sold had the bazaar been in Madras or Bangalore, where the use of large mats was known and appreciated. 'People here are very modern (*nagarigam*),' commented Mohammad, 'they will not use mats to sit or lie on.'

The reason Mohammad had these large unsaleable mats, despite knowing what the north Indian market would want, was that the bazaar invitation had arrived only a few weeks before the bazaar. He could not commission as many small mats as he would have liked to have brought. He had, therefore, brought a selection of mats he had in his shop and stock room.

In craft bazaars, Mohammad sells the mats as beautiful examples of India's handicraft tradition—*Bharat ki hastakala ka sunderta* (Hindi)—and as floor and wall decorations. These were mats especially made for the urban market that sought ethnic chic. Indeed, the largest part of the stock comprised reproductions of colour-ways and designs commissioned in Pattamadai by designers from outside Pattamadai, including those employed by wholesale and export buyers. The few 'traditional' mats that had the plain bodies and borders comprising stripes in two colours, usually red and green, which are normally seen in houses in Pattamadai and elsewhere in rural Tamilnadu, were the ones that did not sell.

A few buyers did not bargain. They chose their mats, paid the price and left. Some said that they were very pleased to buy craft products made by a national award winner. A few asked who the award winner was, and thanked Beevi for having made the object they had bought as she smiled politely (she had, in fact, made only a small proportion of the mats being sold).

My presence in the stall influenced the nature of interactions between sellers and some prospective buyers. Many buyers automatically assumed that I was 'in charge' of the craftspeople and would address all their comments to me. This was invariably the case unless they were bargaining, in which case they would address Mohammad or the women directly and quite often rather aggressively. When Mohammad proved inflexible about the price, customers would often turn to me to ask if the price was a fair one and if they could believe the craftsperson. It was as if they sought legitimacy from me for the craftspeople. This was probably because I spoke English, was dressed in handloom sarees,[14] and my general appearance clearly indicated my urban background. I was accorded the role of the urban-based craft expert or NGO employee who was 'helping the poor craftspeople.'[15]

There is one case in particular that seems worthy of mention. An American, who probably worked in Delhi (he had an identity card on a chain round his neck and did not seem, either in dress or in manner, a tourist), stopped at the stall and was shown some superfine mats by Mohammad. He chose two mats and started bargaining to bring the price down. Mohammad merely said 'fixed price' and started dealing with other customers. The man continued trying to bargain with Beevi, who speaks no English, and she turned to me for translation. At her request I told him that the price was fixed and that it was a fair price, accurately reflecting the amount of work and skill that went into the mats in question. On my intervention, the man turned to me and said, 'Oh come on, after all they just do this while they are sitting around with nothing else to do.'[16]

[14] In urban India, handloom sarees tend to be identified with people who work in NGOs and also with those who have left-leaning ideals.

[15] NGO activists who work with craftspeople confirmed that the same thing regularly happened with them.

[16] Hickey writes of a conversation overheard in a glass-blower's studio in Canada. Admiring the objects on display, a man says to his wife, 'God, these things are beautiful. I just don't know where these people get the time to make them.' The wife responds, 'Well, they don't work' (Flanders, 1981: 93, cited in Hickey, 1997: 87). Neither can

The man had clearly bought into the rhetoric of craft being a way of life, not work, and was using it to get a better price. I pointed out that this was how Beevi and the others earned their livelihood, to which he retorted, 'I think *you* won't let them lower the price,' insinuating that the craftspersons were being exploited by me and that I controlled the prices. He then turned back to Mohammad and tried bargaining with him again, but to no avail. Mohammad refused to respond, not even repositioning the mats as examples of an ancient craft heritage. The man wanted the mats though, and finally bought two mats and left. Mohammad rebuked me later, 'Don't talk to someone like him. His desire for the mats will make him buy one. Talk will just prolong the process.' Both cases, the first where I was seen as the helper of the craftspeople in the stall, and the second where I was cast in the role of the exploitative middleman, reflect the larger ways in which craft producers are depicted in craft discourses: as helpless and 'empowered' not through their own agency but by the good offices of educated middle-class 'social workers', or as helpless and innocent and, therefore, open to exploitation by outsiders.

Participation in 'Master Creation' was by invitation only. The craftspersons in the bazaar had already been through two stages of legitimisation—both as national award winners and as invited participants in the bazaar. But, while there is no doubt that one person in the stall is a 'master-craftsperson', the very presence of an obvious outsider in the stall detracts from the craftsperson. This is not unusual in the context of such markets. Beevi's reaction to people asking me if the price was a fair one and if the craftspeople could be trusted was philosophical and insightful: 'If [someone like] you says it, they get some satisfaction' (*neenga sonna avangallukku thripthi kidaikkum*).

Buyers bring their own impressions and ideas about crafts and craftspeople to the bazaars. These, in turn, affect the ways in which sellers market their wares. Mohammad, for instance, has successfully positioned Pattamadai mats within a market enchanted with 'ethnic

---

conceive that the glass blower is a professional who earns his living through his studio.

chic' and where the domestic uses of mats in rural Tamilnadu do not apply. For Mohammad, the craft bazaar is important both in terms of sales and publicity. He does not allow any bargaining at his stall and meets any attempt to bargain with the response, 'This is the work of India's craftsmen. See how beautiful it is and how fine the work is. You don't have to buy it, just look at it.' He can say this in both English and Hindi. By refusing to engage in any discussions about the prices of mats and concentrating instead on crafts as a national resource, he is able to refocus the buyer's gaze on the object as a tangible manifestation of larger principles. When the buyer persists in bargaining, Mohammad ignores him. At the same time, both he and the two women bargained long and hard with artisans in other stalls when they wanted to buy objects, often claiming that other stalls were selling objects at inflated prices. However, when not exclaiming at the 'high prices' charged by another stall holder, Mohammad and his daughters established friendly relations with neighbouring stall holders. It was Ramadan, and the Ghaziabadi Muslim wooden toy makers would borrow mats to say their prayers. The Tamil saree weaver, who did not speak a word of English, would sometimes come over to the Pattamadai stall and ask if either Mohammad or I could go over and translate between him and a potential customer. If we were free, one of us often did go with him. Different craft producers were in competition with each other, but were also willing to help each other as co-sojourners in a strange place. They were not willing, however, to see each other's objects as special or as specimens of India's craft tradition, only to *refer* to their own in these terms. Speech is used pragmatically.

How should we understand these contradictory views in the light of the interactions between craftspersons and buyers and between craftspersons? As Askegaard and Firat point out, 'Social reality is built upon a semiotic system that is much larger than verbal language' (1997: 123). Despite the rhetoric surrounding the bazaar, including the posters advertising 'the Master's best', non-verbal signs contribute to the larger picture of craftspersons. These include officials' treatment of craftspersons which sometimes borders on the terse. It is affected by the craft producer's clothing, which is, by request of the organisers, 'traditional' and therefore old-fashioned, especially in the case of the men. In spaces like these in Delhi, where Hindi and English are spoken, when the craft producer does not have these languages, communication between buyer and seller or seller and bureaucrat is difficult. Sometimes, as in the case of the saree weaver from Tamilnadu, it is simply impossible. The low status, often based on considerations of caste, accorded throughout India, to those who work with their hands is also a contributing factor.

My detailed description of the 'master creation' bazaar has to be seen in the context of the preceding chapters which emphasised the gaps between the ways in which craft is imagined in India, the fragmented and contradictory application of the abstraction, and the multiple realities of craft producer's lives. In his analysis of the Festival of India in Great Britain, Durrans (1992) makes some general points about cultural exhibitions which are applicable to the above discussion. Durrans identifies cultural exhibitions as sites where meanings are constructed and contested rather than imposed. He locates this in the fundamental asymmetry between participants and in the fact that such exhibitions serve broad political and economic aims which may not be equally acceptable to all parties (ibid.).

Craft bazaars, which bring together pragmatic and idealistic concerns, are fundamentally contested sites. This is partly because the juxtapositions are often so odd: the market perforce puts a price on what are discursively constructed as 'priceless examples of national culture'. As Hickey suggests, 'The attributes that [define] the "vocation versus profession distinction"...are made to support the sales transaction. Rather than the craft object being commodified, marketing is inverted' (ibid.: 95). At least this is what producer-traders and development agents often seek to do at the point of sale; depending on their mood, budget or inclination, buyers resist or acquiesce.

By refusing to engage in any discussions about the prices of mats and concentrating instead on crafts as materialising the nation's heritage, Mohammad is able to refocus the buyer's gaze on the object as a tangible manifestation of larger principles. When the buyer persists in bargaining, Mohammad ignores him. At the same time, he is willing to bargain with artisans in other stalls at the same bazaars, often claiming that they are selling objects at inflated prices. This clearly indicates the ways in which he consciously engages with dominant ways of engaging with the ideology of craft to his own benefit, while simultaneously being cynical of, and undermining, similar efforts by other artisans. But he is not doing anything different from most other people in the bazaar.

In spaces such as the master creations bazaar, the tension between the craft object as 'object+person+idea' and the object as 'thing without person' (or commodity) becomes most apparent. Sellers seek to emphasise the former and buyers the latter. This is especially true where artisans sell their own wares and where prospective buyers try and bargain prices down. That buyers do not bargain with people whom they perceive to be of the same social status as them or of higher social status, for instance, urban educated elites, but will bargain with weavers who are *known* as socially inferior (people who work with their hands, hailing from villages, not speaking English, wearing, often by special request of craft bazaar organisers, their 'traditional', i.e. old-fashioned clothing), is revealing of the way in which the weaver becomes only partially acceptable because of the objects he makes that others covet. The only way out of this play of unequal social relations is to emphasise the identification of craft producer as person+object+idea and craft object as object+person+idea, in both cases the totality stands for traditional people and values, communities, and embodied national heritage. In short, successful trading by a craft producer requires the ability to objectify one's self effectively and to impress upon the viewer the composite that is craft. Conversely, successfully striking a bargain requires the separation of person from thing—something that even the artisan in pursuit of a bargain does not scruple to try and achieve.

The next, and penultimate, chapter returns to Pattamadai to focus on technology. Through a detailed discussion of various attempts to improve the mat weaving loom, I will seek to show how it is in the actual processes of production that craft practice becomes inseparable from the social lives of the producers.

9 Technological Matters

The type of technology used is a crucial part of the marketing process for those objects termed as 'craft products' (Cable *et al*, 1986; Ennew, 1982). Technology in craft production is often simple; that is to say, producers can produce most tools themselves or source them locally, easily and cheaply. They can also make modifications to the tools or processes. This is certainly true of the mat weaving loom, which is essentially a straightforward construction. The 1964 census gazetteer on the Pattamadai mat industry gives us a detailed description of weaving and related processes as does the 1917 *Gazetteer of the Tinnevelly district* (Pate, 1917). Comparing these descriptions to what weavers do today, it is possible to note a number of changes. Most seem concerned with simplifying the work of weaving. For instance, in 1964 weavers were preparing the yarn for the warp in their houses. In 1997 they were buying pre-prepared yarn from the local shops, which stock it for this purpose. There are also innovations that more directly affect the structure of the fabric. Thus the creation of the shed by lifting alternate warp threads has been simplified so that two warp threads at a time are lifted rather than one. This makes the laying out of the loom quicker, but makes the mats slightly thicker. Most such innovations have come from within the group with one weaver making a change, which becomes more widely adopted as its benefits are perceived.

Few changes have, however, been made to the basic structure of the loom. This, despite the fact that there have been a number of governmental and other attempts to modify and improve the loom since the 1970s. One could perhaps say that weavers who use this type of loom, and who have seen it used by preceding generations, view it as the 'natural' way to weave. Anthropological analyses of attempts to change the loom can reveal much about the way weaving skill is transmitted and acquired, 'techniques of the body' (Mauss, 1935: 97), the motivations and methods of development agents, and different actors' responses to interventions.

This chapter focuses on a set of attempts to improve the loom, placing the technical firmly within the social, in which term I include the political and the economic. I do not, however, see the relationship between the social and the technical as evidence of the unchanging nature of Indian craft. Thus, I sharply disagree with, for instance, Dhamija's analysis of the *Nakshabanda* weavers of Varanasi,

> The weaver and the *Nakshabandas* perform their actions without a conscious awareness of the deep significance of their every gesture, every act, choice of space and the movement of the material, equipment and their posture. If you question them as to why something is done, the answer is, 'It is our tradition. It is what my mother taught me and it is what my mother learnt from my nani [grandmother] and thus it has always been' (1999: 45).[1]

Dhamija deems no further exploration necessary, instead suggesting that 'the integrated approach to the art of weaving makes it a timeless process of a way of life of a community' (Dhamija, 1999: 46). I would suggest that people are aware of the advantages, reasons and significance of some of the things they do and see

[1] The translation into the archaic turn of phrase 'thus it has always been' is interesting for its implication of timelessness.

others as 'natural' or 'normal', not paying them much thought. This is something one can learn through paying close attention to, and perhaps learning, the actual processes of weaving.

On another note, a number of studies dealing with production (particularly artisanal production) in India have tended to concentrate on symbolic systems underlying production. These include the ritual processes related to production and analyses wherein action on the material world is analysed primarily in terms of how it is mapped onto a belief system (see especially Brouwer, 1995; Mehta, 1997. Exceptions include Bundgaard, 1999; Wilkinson-Weber, 1999. Some very detailed and thorough descriptions of artisanal tools and their uses have been carried out in India by Fischer and Shah, 1970.[2]). While it is undeniable and deeply interesting that among some groups, weaving is an ontological act or process, this is by no means the case for all weaving groups in India. The main disadvantage of generalising the former finding is that the craft producer often ends up being viewed as a conduit through which timeless traditions are transmitted and not as someone living in this world, making decisions and working through various, sometimes competing, concerns.

By neglecting technical details and taking them as 'given', I suggest that the scholar only reinforces an artificial distinction between 'social' and 'technical'. Vital insights relating to processes of decision-making and negotiation remain overlooked. Unfortunately, however, despite detailed descriptions of aspects of production in early studies, and more recent pleas for its inclusion by Pfaffenberger (1992),

[2] I have already discussed the census monographs of 1961 in Chapter 1. These are noteworthy for their detailed descriptions of production processes, which come out of the larger colonial traditions of documentation. The 1961 monograph on the fine mat weaving industry of Pattamadai has been an invaluable resource in more ways than one. One of the most beautifully written works which deals sensitively with issues of craft, workmanship and technology is that written by a wood turner in England (Pye, 1968). This sets a standard that would be very satisfying to emulate, but can only be the outcome of total immersion in the production process.

and Lemonnier (1993), technology is still relatively overlooked by anthropologists (Lemonnier, 1993: 7), though recent work focusing on it includes Ingold (2001), Marchand (2001), Pfaffenberger (1992, 2001).[3] Suchman (2001) suggests that the growing attention in the fields of social/cultural anthropology to materiality (see Chapter 7), and to the ways in which artefacts construct social persons as much as the other way around, has animated a related discussion in the field of social studies of science and technology, especially within the framework of 'actor-network-theory' (see for instance, Latour, 1993; 2005) wherein heterogeneous networks comprising human and non-human agents form the object of study. Here, through the principle of generalised symmetry, the concern has been to try and theorise relations of technology and society in a way that avoids determinism, or the reduction of either category to the terms of the other. Rather, the focus is on a seamless web of technology and society whose 'elements are more and less malleable, alignments more and less stable' (Suchman, 2001: 165). While I am not approaching the question of the loom through the framework of the actor-network-theory, I nevertheless want to retain one wonderful image from Latour (2006: 17–8). He recounts a suggestion that at the end of the Iraq war, when the liberating forces have triumphed, a pneumatic parliament be parachuted into Iraq. This, when opened up, will enable instant democracy. The absurdity of course comes from the idea that a technology can operate without reference to the situatedness of the practices in which it is embedded. From an analysis of attempts to improve the loom in Pattamadai, it becomes clear that in addition to the elements recognised as relevant, i.e. loom components, other artefacts and assemblages and a complex of other factors—political, economic, social and what Ingold refers to as skilled practice (2001)—present themselves as equally important.

[3] For discussions relating to technology and its implications on industrial and gender organisation in the Indian, though not necessarily artisanal context, see the edited volume *The worlds of Indian industrial labour* (Parry et al, 1999), especially the papers by Engelshoven, Kapadia and Knorringa. Also see Baud (1991).

For Ingold, it is not possible to regard skill, say in craftwork, or in weaving as is our concern, as simply a technique of the body or of the knowing mind that directs the body in its use of tools to achieve a desired end. Rather, skilled practice is 'immanent in the activity itself, in the gestural synergy of human being, tool and raw material' (2001: 20). Ingold follows Bateson to argue that what we need to consider in thinking about the woodsman cutting a tree is the entire man-axe-tree system. 'Skill, in short, is a property not of the individual human body as a bio-physical entity, a thing-in-itself, but of the total field of relations constituted by the presence of the organism-person, indissolubly body and mind, in a richly structured environment' (ibid.: 21). I have no argument with Ingold's perceptive and well-argued plea for a more situated anthropology of technology. The constant and minute adjustments made by the weaver in the weaving of a mat in accordance to the requirements of the body, the loom and the raw material, the working out of problems in the process of weaving—these are all testimony to the skilled practice of weaving, mastery over which may be attained only through doing. But, I would suggest, the weaver on the loom is also thinking about other things as he or she works: keeping a peripheral eye on the children in the house, aware of the smells and requirements of cooking, uneasiness about the damage done to an already inflamed eye by close attention to weaving, the nagging pain in the small of the back, worrying about how to raise money for the next ROSCA payment or the marriage of a household member. The holism of the man-axe-tree system is complicated by the other thoughts that tease the edges of one's attention and at times draw it away. I would also make a further plea against the depoliticisation inherent in Ingold's approach. Weaver's attention to their work, their pride in it, the way in which in the act of weaving the loom becomes an extension of the body—these do not take away from the ambivalence weavers feel about having to do this work at all, more so if this is a person's sole means of livelihood. Here come into play unequal relations of power between weavers and traders, and between them and the development mechanism, the valorised anachronism that is traditional craft in India, the general disdain for manual work, the lack of financial security, and a host of other things.

Technologies of production not only involve means to produce material objects, but also social relations. Technological choices (Lemonnier, 1993: 7) are as dependent on social and political structures and ideas about work and the body, as on physical constraints and desired action on the material world.[4] In Pattamadai, the ways in which people (individually and collectively) approach the mat weaving loom, access to raw material and other 'technical matters' reveals much about skilled practice, the ways in which the household reproduces itself, the ways in which different individuals and households regard mat weaving, and also the ways in which weavers and traders engage with development agents, the state and interested others. I will explore these through a detailed study of attempts to 'improve' mat weaving loom in Pattamadai.

Who Wants a Better Loom?

In an interview, the district collector of Tirunelveli district discussed technology for 'traditional industries' in the following terms:

> ...We are now concentrating on pottery, Pattamadai fine mat weaving, cane manufacture and brass vessels...all traditionally famous in Tirunelveli...we can help with technology [through] CRENEO [a Central government assisted centre for rural development and technology]...they [the weavers] have to access some latest technology, particularly in the dyeing of fibres...also for some technological upgradation we can send them for some training to places like Chennai [Madras] etc. I am getting some funds...so that I can help in any sort of training for improving the fine mat technology. (Dhanavel, IAS, 05/02/2000)[5]

[4] Lemonnier uses the term 'technological choices' to refer to the process of sorting out possibilities on which the development of a technical system is based. However, he qualifies the use of the term 'choices' in this context and emphasises that the term rarely implies a formally deliberated decision making process (1993: 6–7).

[5] It was this same district collector who sanctioned funds for the construction of a new weaving shed in the grounds of the cooperative society (Chapter 4). Indeed, it is almost unheard of for the cooperative

There are two main ways of looking at technology in the context of artisanal production. The first is the assumption that the introduction of 'modernising technology', usually taken to mean mechanisation, will, through increased production improve the weaver's economic condition and, therefore, his quality of life. This is what Fairhead and Leach aptly characterise as an 'off the shelf narrative' (1997). The second focuses directly on the issue of quality of life and argues that improved technology, by reducing drudgery and improving posture among other things, will make weaving a more attractive and viable option by eliminating occupation-related health conditions. Many initiatives to introduce better technology in India come from governmental and non-governmental agencies. 'Experts' are commissioned to design new technologies. This is, of course, problematic, both in terms of effectiveness and in terms of economics as expensive technologies, often imported into situations without much understanding of local needs and ideas, fail to 'take off'.[6] Sometimes technological changes are introduced by local entrepreneurs. These may be more likely to gain acceptance, though the benefits of their introduction may not be spread evenly over all the people involved in their adoption.[7]

While no specific measures relating to 'improved technology' were discussed in the interview which introduced this section,

---

society, traders or weavers to reject government funds offered to them even if the funds are meant for inappropriate or undesired purposes.

[6] For some examples from around the world, see Crewe (1997); Pfaffenberger (1993). Indeed, as Crewe shows, the 'beneficiaries' are frequently never even consulted about their preferences and needs.

[7] Where new technology is expensive and the investment required to acquire and install it is high, the returns to the capitalist are correspondingly high. This may be reflected in increased wages to workers, but the proportion by which the worker's wages rise is rarely matched by the increase in profits due to new technology. The powerloom mat industry is a case in point. While a coarse mat weaver can make a mat a day on a handloom and makes a daily income of Rs 15 from piece rate sales; a powerloom can produce up to 125 mats a day, but the powerloom mat worker only earns Rs 45 a day in wages ('Useful work of art', *The Hindu*, 09/10/1995).

it was clear that 'technological upgradation', especially involving 'latest technology', was a very high priority for the district collector and for the government agencies he represented. This has been a long-standing concern. It is in this context that we must look at the Bangalore-based Regional Design and Technical Development Centre's (RD&TDC) 1979 project for the development of an 'improved' mat weaving loom. The loom prototype which emerged from this process was based on cloth weaving frame looms and, according to weavers and also Lila who had seen it, did not take into account the ways in which cloth weaving and mat weaving differ, most importantly the nature of the raw materials. Following a short trial period when it was placed in the cooperative society building for weavers to try, it was dismantled and removed to Bangalore and stored. But the problem with the 'improved loom' was not merely that it was not adapted well enough for mat weaving.

This first attempt to modify the loom was followed by others, some more sensitive than others as will be seen. But, and it is important to note this, no weaver I ever spoke to said he or she wanted a new and improved loom. What weavers did want was some intervention and assistance, especially in sourcing to find loom components.

One of the first things that some superfine mat weavers asked of Craft Enterprises was that the NGO find a reliable source of new *achu*. The superfine mat *achu*, as was discussed in Chapter 4, has a wooden frame and metal 'eyes' through which warp threads are passed. It has a two-fold purpose—first, to ensure that the warp threads are evenly spaced; second, it is used to beat back woven weft strands, thereby tightening the construction of the fabric. The *achu* used in fine and coarse mat weaving is made entirely of wood. Local carpenters can easily run up these wooden *achu*. The wood and metal ones require more skill and experience, especially in the case of those *achu* that have upto 140 'eyes' per handspan and that are used to weave the highest quality mats in Pattamadai, i.e. those containing 140 warp threads in every handspan. Superfine mat *achu* had not been replaced for over twenty years as no local artisans could be found to make them. Weavers were reluctant to use old worn out *achu*, especially ones with splinters and broken 'eyes' as these could potentially damage mats on the loom. Many weavers had, therefore, stopped weaving 140-count mats. No wonder this was an important issue that weavers wanted addressed. The search for new *achu* is not restricted to weavers. Traders too are keen to increase their stock, both for use in weaving sheds and in order to benefit from lending *achu* to weavers who will then supply mats to them. In 2001, when the mat weaving society in the neighbouring town of Veeravanallur had an auction to dispose of various loom parts, two traders from Pattamadai competed against each other to purchase the 50-count *achu*.

One of the reasons it is difficult to acquire even second hand *achu* is the fact that even in households where weaving is not normally carried on, people see weaving as a resource that they can turn to in times of trouble. They thus store their loom components and are reluctant to dispose of them. When anti-Muslim riots broke out in Bombay in 1991–2, many Labbais from Pattamadai who lived and worked in Bombay returned to Pattamadai. Some took up weaving and earned their living for a time producing mats. Equally, people move between fine and superfine mat weaving if they feel the need or desire. Hasina who used to weave 50-count mats switched to weaving superfine mats as a *coolie* weaver. When I asked why, she said that she suffered from asthma, and found that the force required to push back the reed in 50-count mats after each weft strand was inserted, was worsening her condition. On the advice of the local general practitioner, she switched to superfine mat weaving where less force is required as the weft strands are finer and break if too much force is applied.

In keeping with the weavers' request for new *achu*, in 1996 a textile (saree) reed maker who was willing to manufacture superfine mat reeds was located by Lila. *Achu* used in handloom cloth weaving and in mat weaving are quite similar, though textile *achu* tend to be finer with more 'eyes'. This similarity not something that the mat weavers or even traders recognise. Even though there are cloth weavers in Pattamadai, contact between the two groups is rare, collaborations unknown. In fact, the first such collaboration between cloth and mat weavers of Pattamadai was initiated by Craft Enterprises in their quest for an improved loom. This perhaps is the difference between being wholly embedded in a set of production practices as the weavers are, and between the development agent's experience of not only making connections but also seeing the 'traditional craft sector' as one entity. But we are running ahead of our story now.

In October 1996, the first set of workable reeds made by the textile reed maker for 100-, 120- and 140-count mats were delivered to superfine weavers in Pattamadai. These reeds were not of very high standard as the reed maker was unused to making reeds for mat looms. They were distributed free of cost to those weavers who wanted them. Despite their poor quality, the new reeds were crucial in reviving the weaving of 140-count mats and increasing production of 100- and 120-count mats. While weavers and Craft Enterprises agreed that the new reeds were not as good as the old ones in terms of positioning of the 'eyes', etc., they still acknowledged the importance of having new *achu*. Subsequently Craft Enterprises (November–December 2000) found another maker and commissioned new and better quality *achu*, which were sold to the weavers at the manufacturer's price of Rs 500 for a set of three—one each of 100-count, 120-count and 140-count. Some weavers were willing to make this investment.[8]

Following the success of the *achu* initiative and from the partial success of the natural dyes initiative,[9] Craft Enterprises decided that the next big project they would tackle was that of improving the loom. While, as in the case of natural dyes, it was Mohammad who first suggested that the NGO work on a new loom, Lila had her own reasons to attempt to design and produce a modified ergonomic loom. For her the main problem with the existing loom was that weavers were suggesting that it caused health problems—back and

[8] The same weavers were, however, unwilling to invest a similar sum in laying down stocks of korai following another of Craft Enterprises' initiatives (see Venkatesan, 2001, Chapter 7). Clearly they felt that they could source their own korai and pay small amounts of money for this as and when required rather than block up space and capital.

[9] Discussed in Chapter 6.

knee pain, stomach trouble, eye-strain, etc.[10] This was what needed to be addressed:

> ...After a few years of weaving, everyone complains of back, eye and knee problems...But there was not enough clarity from the community on why the loom had to be redesigned. They insisted on a more 'productive' loom for higher output rather than rectifying the physical discomfort due to bad posture forced by the loom...A brief has been formulated to design a more ergonomic loom which would allow the weaver to stand and weave within a 2ft range thereby reducing the strain on the back shoulders and eyes. (Project Report, 1998: 50)

Before we go into the ways in which Lila and Craft Enterprises worked on this brief, I want to briefly discuss Mohammad's role in sparking off the NGO's interest in this project as well as in introduction of the natural dyes. When Craft Enterprises first came to Pattamadai, they saw Mohammad as an important community leader through whom they could reach the weavers. As we saw in Chapter 5, relationships within the mat weaving industry are far more complex and divisive than the community model posits. Perhaps Mohammad suggested these two projects as a way of approaching the quagmire of new alliances, aspirations and interventions which the arrival of Craft Enterprises precipitated. He may also have hoped to actively benefit from the presence of the NGO. For Mohammad, who was used to other NGOs which worked with and through him, and did not have a permanent presence in Pattamadai, Craft Enterprises represented a potential opportunity to tap into new markets and the kinds of resources that NGOs (either their own or government aided) could bring in the form of training programmes, workshops, etc.

Mohammad's attitude towards funded workshops is not dissimilar to that of the cooperative society or of the other traders in the town. Training programmes and attempts to improve technologies bring certain advantages in their wake. These include daily stipends for participation in the programme, stipends for trainers, opportunities for publicity through media coverage and the chance

[10] See Chapter 4.

to meet important government officials who often inaugurate such programmes. The programmes often work through the cooperative society or through one weaver/trader who is expected to enrol others in the scheme. In many cases, the person who is mediating the programme chooses participants on the basis of their personal relationship with him/her. They thus reinforce existing power and patronage structures.

In December 2000, a twelve-day dye and mat weaving workshop was organised by a government agency (RD&TDC) and held in the mat weavers' cooperative society building in Pattamadai.[11] Each participant was paid a stipend of Rs 70 per day to compensate for the loss of productive time due to participation in the workshop. 'Experts' from RD&TDC attended the workshop and showed weavers how to dye korai using different vegetable dyes. The frame loom prototype designed by the RD&TDC for mat weaving was brought to Pattamadai for trials when the workshop began and remained in the cooperative society, at the request of the president, for another two months. When I was in Pattamadai in January 2001, I visited the cooperative to look at the loom. It was not in use. The shed was empty except for a woman who sat in one of the doorways of the weaving shed, rolling beedis. The president of the cooperative society,[12] who had seen me from his office, came into the shed and demonstrated the use of the loom. He does not normally weave. When I asked him if other weavers came to try the loom, he did not reply directly and only said, 'We can all weave.' Discussing the workshop, one weaver said, 'When the RD&TDC staff were present and were giving money for loom trials, there were people willing to weave, but now no one will go there. The loom will just lie there for the two months. But it looks good if the society keeps it' (Ali, January 2001).

[11] I was not in Pattamadai during the workshop but arrived shortly afterwards and was told about it by different people, some of whom had participated.

[12] He had been the vice-president during my last visit in 1999–2000 and had recently become president after the retirement of the earlier incumbent in late 2000.

While the workshop organisers attempted to be inclusive in the choice of participants by including in the list of proposed participants, weavers who worked with Craft Enterprises, the two national award winners and members identified by the cooperative society, internal politics and power structures determined the list of actual participants. Among those who did not participate was Beevi, the first national award winner, who, though on the proposed list, was not invited by the office bearers of the cooperative society on whose grounds the workshop was held. This reflected a rivalry at the time between the cooperative society and Mohammad, who is Beevi's father. As the workshop was initiated on Craft Enterprises' suggestion, which also had a hand in its organisation, four Craft Enterprises weavers participated in it. The other participants included the president of the society and others nominated by him, of whom few weave.

In January 2001, hardly any of the weavers who attended the workshop were willing to try the new dyes in their homes. 'Give us orders and we will make mats using these dyes' was the standard response even from Craft Enterprises weavers who are assured of a steady market for every one of their mats. The value of the workshop seemed to lie in the publicity it generated. *The Hindu*, for instance, carried an article on the mat weaving industry and the 'need for taking special efforts to protect and revive the dying Pattamadai superfine mat weaving industry,' and praised the various government agencies and officials for their efforts (11/12/2000).[13] The daily stipend of Rs 70, and the certificates of attendance distributed to participants also formed important incentives. Even the samples of korai dyed in the workshop were not given to weavers or left in the society but taken back to the RD&TDC office in Bangalore.

[13] The superfine mat weaving industry is not dying, largely due to the efforts of Craft Enterprises who have found new and regular markets for these mats and raised piece rates, as a result of which more weavers are taking up superfine mat weaving. The fact that press and government discourses focus on the 'dying industry' reflects both the meta-narratives on crafts in India, and the fact that local actors engage with these discourses in their 'serious speech acts' to media and government personnel.

The workshop, like other attempts to improve technology, thus had limited success with regard to its aim of increasing knowledge and use of natural dyes in Pattamadai, but was nonetheless of value to some local and other actors who participated in it.

Lila's close association with weavers and the fact that some weavers bypassed the traders to associate themselves with Craft Enterprises meant that Mohammad did not feel that the attempts to improve the loom or to introduce natural dyes would benefit him or his business. Thus, once the NGO took up the challenge of improving the loom and designed and made two loom prototypes in December 1998 and December 1999 respectively, Mohammad disassociated himself from the project and did not even want to look at the loom prototypes which were being tested by various weavers in Pattamadai. Neither the cooperative nor the other traders showed interest in the modified loom and trials to test prototypes. When Lila requested space in the unused first floor of the cooperative building to erect the first of the two loom prototypes, the president and vice-president refused permission. Once he had ascertained that the loom trials were 'not a training scheme,' the vice-president of the cooperative society also declined on its behalf to participate in them. This is in contrast to the cooperative society's response to the prospect of government-run loom trial and training schemes such as the one discussed above. Mohammad too refused to mediate between the cooperative and Craft Enterprises in this matter, though he had played the role of mediator on other occasions (Pattamadai Report, October–November 1998). Eventually Craft Enterprises hired a room in which to place this loom so that weavers could try it out. The lack of interest on the part of traders and the office bearers of the cooperative society appears to lie in the fact that there were few benefits to be gained by them in the short term from the loom modification project. Equally, Mohammad runs down natural dyes as damaging the korai and therefore the mats. Visitors to his shop who enquire about natural dyes are shown a raggedy mat with patchy colours and told that this is what happens when natural dyes are used. When challenged and shown other natural-dyed mats (as I have once done), Mohammad argues that cultivated korai, which the majority of weavers use in fine mat weaving, cannot take the long soaking times that is required for natural dyeing; wild korai used in superfine mat weaving can, but it is expensive and harder to find. For the majority of weavers, he says, natural dyes do not work. And indeed they do not, but mostly because it takes more effort and time to source and use natural dyes. Also, the colours are subdued and go against the dominant local aesthetic which favours bright and vibrant colours.

The Craft Enterprises Looms

The first Craft Enterprises loom was designed by Lila and Badrinarayan, an ergonomics consultant based in Bangalore. Badrinarayan along with Raghu Anantanarayanan, a yoga practitioner and one of the members of the NGO's steering group, visited Pattamadai for a couple of days in January 1998. They filmed weavers on their looms and also talked to weavers. A cloth weaver was also consulted. A loom was subsequently made in Bangalore and transported to Pattamadai, installed and tested for two months from December 1998. However, the prototype, in addition to being expensive, focused more on ergonomic design than on the particular needs of mat weaving. Based on the responses of weavers, Lila decided that it needed further modification.

> We studied the new loom [the first prototype] and the traditional loom and evolved a holistic guideline for designing the next model upright sitting posture for comfortable weaving; details of structure to be simplified for manufacturing locally; should fit into existing spaces and conditions; should use existing practices in processes related to weaving such as warping and packing. (Pattamadai Report, end 1999)

Based on these guidelines and using her considerable knowledge of the weaving process, Lila constructed a scaled down model of the loom (she referred to this as her 'toy loom') on which she successfully wove a tiny 4" × 9" 120-count mat. The small size of the loom meant that it could be carried to weavers' houses in Pattamadai for demonstration. It also meant that the loom could be used to try out different warping configurations without spending huge amounts of time on the protracted task of laying out a warp on the full-size loom. (The laying out of the warp with even tension throughout is one of the most crucial aspects of not just fine and superfine mat weaving but of weaving in general.)

When the small mat and the loom were brought to Pattamadai, they met with a mixture of responses. According to Lila, 'the toy loom...caught everyone's attention...but the real significance of the new loom in testing warp configurations was not seen at all...' (Pattamadai Report, April 1999). Only one weaver (Abdul) showed a thorough understanding of the purpose of the toy loom and he suggested a few changes be made to the model (ibid.).[14] The small mat which Lila wove, however, helped shape local actors' perceptions about Lila, her abilities and her commitment to the project in Pattamadai. The son of Meeran, one of the traders, said to me,

> My father said, 'We call ourselves superfine mat weavers, yet see what she has managed to do.' She has woven a superfine mat by herself. (Sulaiman, Pattamadai, January 2000)

Meeran still did not like the threat that he felt the NGO represented to his interests, but he was able to appreciate what he saw as a genuine achievement.[15]

A full-size version of the second Craft Enterprises loom prototype, which was based on Lila's learnings from the 'toy loom' and the local actors' responses to it, was set up in the front yard of Abdul's house in early 2000. All along, Lila and I had long conversations about it, and I watched the new loom being developed and refined.

[14] Abdul is one of the few weavers' whose entire household income comes from superfine mat weaving. He is keenly interested in the technology of weaving and discourses at length about different kinds of mat weaving, including powerloom mat weaving. It was he who tried out the RD&TDC frame loom in Bangalore at the behest of Craft Enterprises. Nonetheless, Abdul has not taught his sons how to weave, nor does he indicate that he might do so in the future.

[15] When I asked to be taught how to weave and began with the process of warping at the house of one of the weavers, it took several attempts before I could tie one of the basic knots. The elderly weaver who was teaching me said, 'You can read and write but you cannot even tie a knot! Lila can do all this.'

We were both curious to see what would happen, possibly for different reasons. Lila's new loom was ambitious and, I think, a technical masterpiece. It was the product of a genuine and informed understanding of the technical processes of weaving.

Loom trials were carried out in the last fortnight of January 2000. Weavers who came forward to try the loom were compensated for their time with cash payments made by Craft Enterprises. These rates were agreed at a meeting where Lila and the weavers who worked with the NGO were present (I was also present as were several excited children). While the loom trials were open to anyone who was interested, weavers closely associated with Craft Enterprises were strongly encouraged by Lila to come at fixed times and work on the loom. The mood at the meeting seemed positive, with weavers promising to work on the loom and encourage others to come as well, yet by the time the trials were actually underway shortly after, the enthusiasm seemed to have fizzled out. Talking to them, I felt that they were not totally convinced about the need to modify the loom.

In Pattamadai, in January 2001, I saw the new loom folded up in a corner of the verandah of Abdul's house where it had been tested a year earlier. I asked him if he had used it after the trials in January 2000 and received a non-committal answer: 'It is okay, but not suitable' (*paravaillai, anal othuvarallai*). Today the loom continues to sit in a corner in another location, unused and dormant. As Lila ruefully said, 'It did not meet their psychological needs.'

Challenging the Body

Lila designed the second loom with sensitivity and using her considerable knowledge about the weaving process gained through actually sitting down and weaving in the houses of weavers. I will attempt to tease out why responses to the loom were unenthusiastic. Craft Enterprises' concern with loom modification stems from their understanding that the mat weaving loom, though well adapted for coarse mat weaving, is not entirely suitable for the comparatively recent practice of superfine mat weaving. This is not necessarily a view that weavers share. I suggest that the new loom challenges existing body practices, both at the loom and in other situations. This makes it unlikely to find acceptance among established weavers who are accustomed to the 'traditional' loom.

In Chapter 4, I described the weaving process. The weaver sits on a low stool placed underneath the warp. As one section is woven, the stool is moved under it and the weaver sits on the newly woven section in order to continue weaving the next bit. The weaver thus travels the length of the mat as (s)he weaves it. At no stage in the weaving process is any part of the mat hidden from the weaver's or the packer's eyes.

One chief difference between the loom already in use in Pattamadai and the modified loom is the latter's height. Designed as a loom for a weaver to sit on a bench (instead of on a low stool placed directly under the warp and just before the section to be woven), the new loom imposes certain changes in the lay out of the mat as it is being woven. Instead of the entire warp being laid out in front of the weaver so that the whole mat (and its skeleton prior to weaving) is visible, the warp in the modified loom is rolled up underneath the loom at the end furthest from the weaver. After the weaver weaves and packs a section of the mat, (s)he rolls up the finished section underneath the warp nearest to her. As the mat progresses, the rolled up warp gradually unfolds before the weaver, is woven, packed and rolled up again.

It can be seen at once that the modified loom challenges the entire visual perception of the loom: first, by virtue of being raised a few feet above ground level; and second, because it is not (indeed the fact that the weaver sits *at* it rather than *on* it means that it cannot be) as long as the 'traditional' loom, the warp and finished sections of mat are rolled up underneath it. Experienced weavers who are used to the other loom find it difficult to adjust to the modified one on several counts.

Most weavers rarely sit on chairs or benches. All activities (sitting, sleeping, cooking, etc.) are performed at floor level. Furniture in houses is minimal, with mats being unrolled to form sitting or sleeping spaces, and cooking equipment is also placed on the floor. The 'traditional' loom is also placed at ground level and, therefore, is in keeping with other activities. The elevated loom occupies physical

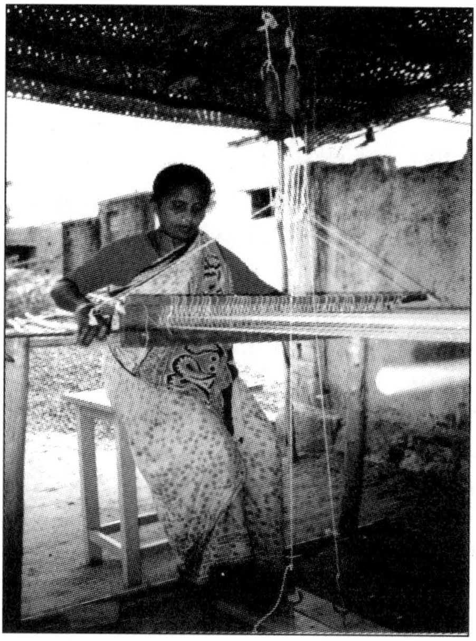

Hasan Fathima sits at the prototype new loom.
Photo: Soumhya Venkatesan.

space differently and requires some mental adjustment. Second, both weavers and buyers value symmetry within a mat with regard to its body, borders and patterns. When a mat is laid out fully for the weavers' inspection through every stage of its making, it is possible for an experienced person to ensure symmetry by making minute adjustments in packing. This option is considerably harder in a mat that is partially rolled up. The weaver has to pay more regard to the exact *number* of weft strands in different colours used throughout the mat, something that they tend to measure with their eyes. Nor, in a household with many members, does a single person sit on the loom exclusively. Should the person on the loom get up to attend to some task, someone else might move over to the loom and carry on weaving. The fact that the entire mat (woven and yet to be woven sections) is visible to everyone considerably aids this way of working. Finally, weavers are not used to sitting with their legs dangling (as from a chair) and one common complaint during the trials was that the new loom caused pins and needles in the legs.

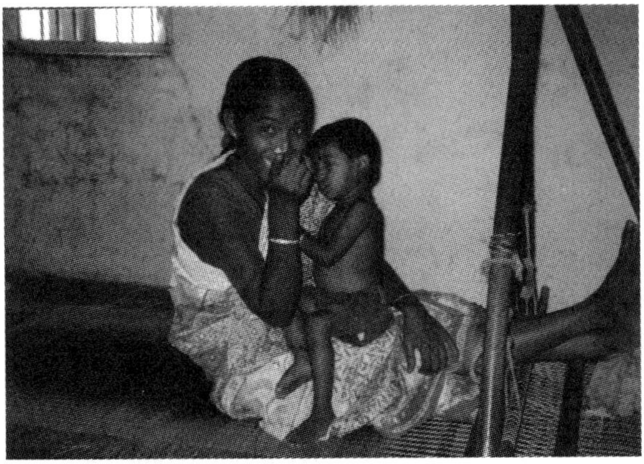

Regina on the loom with her child.
Photo: Soumhya Venkatesan.

Following Bourdieu, Wilk suggests that when standards are taken for granted, people operate on unspoken shared understanding and physical perception or habitus. This includes the concept of 'comfort' (2001: 115). Wilk identifies this as naturalisation. Submersive naturalisation, he argues, 'maintains the status quo by keeping needs..."inscribed" in the habitus by continually asserting that the existing order is natural.' It is furthermore deeply embedded in bodily practice and habit, profoundly shaping the 'sense of the possibility of any new tool, and new options are never considered' (ibid.). Submersive naturalisation is not passive, though it may appear so. People actively choose what they are accustomed to and feel comfortable with. Repressive naturalisation, on the other hand, actively maintains the status quo through disincentivising or actively discouraging change. Mohammad's and the cooperative society's attitudes towards the new loom, and Mohammad's attitude towards natural dyes may be seen in this light.

But, Wilk suggests, the possibility of change does exist and may override naturalisation as new ideas, possibilities, objects and experiences challenge older ways of doing things. Innovations, as we have seen, have emerged from within the weaving group, which have made the weaving process less time-consuming and labour intensive. And indeed, for younger people who are more used to sitting on chairs in schools, the modified loom seemed to fewer problems. Additionally, a less experienced weaver, more so a non-weaver, has fewer expectations of how a loom ought to be and may be more open to innovation. It is not surprising that Lila wondered if subsequent loom trials should involve younger people rather than experienced weavers.

The greatest enthusiasm, in fact, was generated by teenage girls who, giggling and chattering, came to see and try the new loom. Several of these girls were skilled in korai preparation but had not spent much time actually weaving on the traditional loom.

The new loom, however, does not merely challenge naturalised bodily practices. It challenges ideas about weaving that are prevalent throughout the Labbai group. Weaving, it must be reiterated, is seen as a resource on which not much money is spent. Furthermore, few people weave all the time. A few hours here and there in a day, interspersed with other activities, is the norm. People sometimes take days off weaving if there is a marriage in the house or some other opportunity comes up, or if they can afford it. Then the loom, even with a half-done mat on it, is rolled up and put away. This is one of the advantages of household-based self-employed artisanal work, as Nita Kumar points out in her study of artisans in Banaras (1988). The new Craft Enterprises loom is posited on a greater number of weaving hours and the greater productivity that ensues from this without damaging people's health. It occupies more space than the traditional loom, having a whole new component of height. It is harder to roll up and put away. Moreover, even if it did suit working patterns, it is expensive, costing around Rs 3000 or the price of two superfine mats. When there is a loom that works, why spend money on a new loom that does not confer any huge advantage? For weavers, it is not the *loom* that causes back and eye problems, it is *weaving*: an occupation that, as we have seen, people feel extremely ambivalent about. A trader, who though scornful of the entire project albeit curious about it, gave his own reasons for its failure. 'This is women's work,' he said, 'and women are not good at picking up new things.' This, even though he was fully aware that several male weavers were participating in the trial. I read his statement as one that positions weaving firmly in the sphere of women—weak, defenceless people who do not have many choices but make the best of what they have, without seeking to improve their lot. What he was saying was that people who could successfully work with new ideas, incorporate new technologies and take advantage of new opportunities would not be weavers.

The area near the loom prototype was also full of very small girls who made their own 'toy looms' using bricks, old toothbrushes and combs. The brick forms the base, something that does not exist in a full-size loom. The comb acts as the *achu* and the broken toothbrush with a hole on one end as the 'needle' to thread weft strands through the warp. This leads me to my final point.

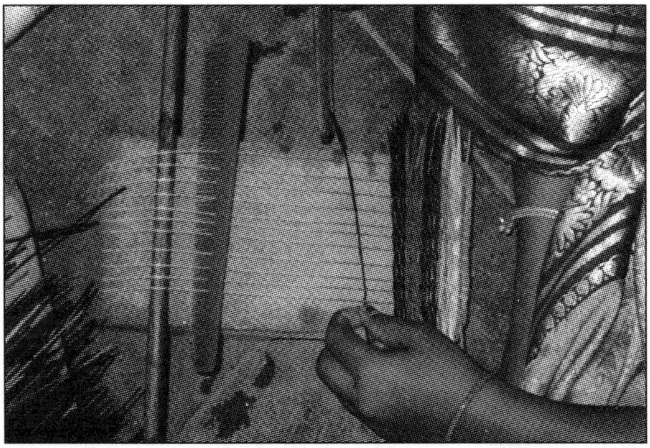

A brick-stick-comb-and-old-toothbrush loom.
Photo: Soumhya Venkatesan.

The mat weaving loom is very easy to construct using materials that are available at hand, or in the carpenters' yards in Pattamadai. Wooden poles form the tripod and define the spatial limits of the loom at either end. The shed is created by inserting a smooth stick through the warp, separating it into two vertical layers. The *kuchali* or 'needle' used to insert weft strands through the warp is also made using a smooth stick with a hole on one end. The only component that is difficult to source is the *achu* and this is what weavers wanted from Craft Enterprises. Apart from this, the loom is easy and cheap to make. Like the brick-toothbrush-and-comb looms made by the little girls from things available at hand, the traditional loom too does not require much effort or investment. The new loom has a few more complicated parts: pedals to move the warp up or down replace the tripod, a roller device to roll up and unroll woven sections and unwoven warp respectively, a frame to lift the warp off the ground, and a high stool or bench. All of these have to be bought or somehow acquired, stored and maintained. This requires time, money and storage space, and is more than most weavers are willing to spare. Even teenage girls who are excited by the new loom and perhaps willing to use it, I suggest, may not be given the opportunity, resources or encouragement by other members of their households to incorporate the new loom into their weaving practice.

In this chapter I have sought to extend Ingold's notion of skilled practice through a detailed analysis of the economic, social and political dimensions of artisanal work. While it is true that weavers find their traditional loom natural and most suitable for their work, they also make their choices on economic and social grounds. 'Improving technology' is an attractive proposition for many kinds of actor—from the top-down initiatives imposed by government schemes and quotas, to the kinds of opportunities that traders envisage from workshops and training schemes, and the desire to make things better for weavers that drives initiatives like the development of a new loom by Craft Enterprises. Sometimes, these different motivations intersect briefly as they did when Mohammad suggested that Craft Enterprises 'improve' the loom. Weavers too participate in these attempts to improve technology, though it is difficult to say whether this participation is motivated by loyalty, the desire to experiment, a genuine feeling that some change is required, or perhaps all of these, to varying degrees and for different individuals. The anthropology of technology here extends to an anthropology of people at work and the myriad complexities of social life that this entails.

10 Conclusion

Throughout this book, I have asked the questions: why does craft matter in contemporary India, and to whom? Around this powerful concept and the words and images that make it up, several different networks coalesce—between artisans, development agents, the state, and different members of the craft worlds: philanthropists, patrons, consumers and concerned individuals and institutions. Together, sometimes acting in harmony, sometimes not, and bringing their various concerns, hopes and aspirations for themselves and others, the different agents who make up the networks make craft valued in both material and ideological terms. Craft is both an idea and a thing—indeed, the things identified as craft objects are agentive and seminal in the workings of the applied abstraction that is 'traditional Indian craft'. The application of this abstraction often comes in the form of development initiated by the state or by non-governmental agencies. As I have shown, there are many different kinds of development and also different ways of engaging with it, whether on the part of the objects of development or the agents of development. Keeping at its centre the question of 'craft' in India, and moving from the large (the nation, heritage, development) to the small (the weavers, particular development agents) to the large again, this book has explored the different spheres within which value is created, contested, transformed and recreated.

This book has shown how value emerges not only in consumption and exchange but also in the relations and processes of production that give rise to the objects that are exchanged and consumed. Value can be a function of development; indeed, because of the way in which craft objects in India are doubly produced—both physically and through words and images—development discourses and practices are crucial in the continuing importance of craft.

I suggested early on in the book that the concern with craft in India forms part of a utopian vision that seeks to harmoniously connect past and present, tradition and modernity, heritage and progress, the ritual of the maker with the imperatives of the marketplace, and diverse sections of Indian society. For Foucault, 'utopias are sites with no real place...They present society itself in perfected form...Utopias are fundamentally unreal places.' (Foucault, 1967; trans. Miskowiec, 1986: 24).[1] The heterotopia, on the other hand, is a 'kind of effectively enacted utopia in which the real sites, all the other sites that can be found within the culture, are simultaneously represented, contested and inverted' (ibid.). If a utopia is a vision of a perfect order, the heterotopia is an attempt to realise a particular utopia.

Foucault identifies six principles of the heterotopia: first, that there is probably not a single culture in the world that does not constitute heterotopias. Second, the heterotopia is historically constituted. That is to say, a given society at different historical moments can make the same heterotopia function in very different fashions. Third, the heterotopia is 'capable of juxtaposing in a

[1] The text, entitled 'Des espaces autres' and published by the French journal *Architecture-Mouvement-Continuite* in October 1984, was the basis of a lecture given by Michel Foucault in March 1967. Although not reviewed for publication by the author and thus not part of the official corpus of his work, the manuscript was released into the public domain for an exhibition in Berlin shortly before Michel Foucault's death. The version I am using was translated by Jay Miskowiec and published in 1986.

single real place several spaces, several sites that are in themselves incompatible.' Fourth, heterotopias have a complex relation with time. The museum for Foucault is a heterotopia that indefinitely accumulates time. This is contrasted with the heterotopia that is connected to time flowing, passing, transitory: the festival or the carnival. Fifth, heterotopias always presuppose a system of opening and closing that both isolates them and makes them penetrable. The heterotopia is not freely accessible to anyone and everyone. It has its own forms of barriers and gate-keeping. Even when a heterotopia looks open to anyone, it is not. Finally, heterotopias 'have a function in relation to all the space that remains'. That is to say, that the role of the heterotopia might be either to create a space that exposes the illusory nature of other spaces of everyday human life or to create another real space that is 'perfect' in comparison to the messy, jumbled spaces of our lives. This latter is the heterotopia of compensation.

Craft in India is a heterotopia in Foucauldian terms. Indeed, one could describe craft as a compensatory, patchworked, accumulative, restricted and restrictive heterotopia. Today, when 'Our experience of the world is...that of a network that connects points and intersects with its own skein' (ibid.: 22) the heterotopia that is craft is made up of a large network (one without end?) that connects artisans, traders, development agents, the nation, the world, the past, the present, the market, the home, the ritual space and the public space. Craft is the mirror through which this network sees itself. The mirror shows something that is both here, and not here. And, just outside its frame continue all the concerns that press upon the different people who are gazing into it.

Furthermore, like the heterotopia Foucault describes, and as I have shown throughout this book, the various points that make up the network are not necessarily compatible nor do they function outside the particular historical moment that is India today, with its material and human resources, its messiness, hierarchies, inequalities, complications and differences, the colonial past and the anti-colonial movement, and the ideological, pragmatic and other concerns that drive various people.

Craft matters has mostly been a book about people who engage with development—some not all the time and not necessarily directly, and others much of the time. It is not a book that seeks to decry development as inherently exploitative or self-seeking. Rather it seeks to show how development forms an organising paradigm for action in the world. Pattamadai is one of hundreds of craft villages and towns in India and the complex nature of its craft industry is by no means unique. With development continuing to remain an important mode of acting in the world, and given the economic and cultural significance of craft in contemporary India, the fields of craft production and development merit further and more detailed anthropological analyses. These must take into account the diverse concerns of, and strategies open to, groups which practice craft as one of their livelihood choices. They must also take into account the varied histories of different actors—be they producers, development agents, the state or, indeed, the craft objects themselves.

This book has sought to understand the processes and particular ways in which poor, rural, hereditary artisans like the weavers become visible as craft producers within the Indian state and within development. It shows how the weavers, like other artisans, are created as particular kinds of subject—'traditional craft producers' (person+object+idea)—and simultaneously as objects of national and international concern. It demonstrates why artisans, of whom there are over twenty million in India, actively and passively participate in the shaping and continued currency of images about them that they recognise as, at best, partially representative of what they do and why. It is only in this form that access to the heterotopia of craft and the benefits of belonging is possible. Those who can 'talk the talk', and 'work the image' are reflected clearly in the mirror, while those unable or unwilling to do so retreat to the margins even as the things they make find their way into the image.

In *The Indian craftsman*, Coomaraswamy relates the tale of a sultan who falls in love with a girl and asks her father for her hand in marriage. The father refuses to permit the marriage unless the sultan learns a handicraft for, according to him, although a handicraft might not enrich the craftsman, it 'veileth poverty' while kingship, despite its advantages, is not a stable profession and in it 'there is no trust.' Keen to marry the girl, the sultan learns the craft of mat-making and 'wove these articles of various colours, both plain and striped' (1909: 28–9). Coomaraswamy does not tell us but we must presume that the marriage takes place and all the characters live happily ever after, and that the new bridegroom does not lose his throne.

The people with whom I work in Pattamadai would recognise this story, although not necessarily in the way Coomaraswamy intended it. For him, it is a salutary tale about the value of craft, the ability to create beautiful things that gladden the eye, and the wisdom of the father of the sultan's beloved, the knowledge and faith he has in an embodied skill that one cannot lose in a fickle world. The Labbais of Pattamadai know that weaving is a resource, a skill that they have or can acquire, and that they can turn to in times of need. They also know they make beautiful things that other people desire, though this desire has to be worked at. Their objects can also open doors and, like the Queen's mat, bring unforeseen opportunities. But, they do not want to be solely bound to craft practice. It cannot satisfy all their needs, wants or aspirations for themselves and their children. Craft can, however, open some opportunities and some people are quick to realise this. The traders and some weavers come up to the mirror often and create themselves within it as craft producers. Most other weavers are at the edges of the frame, peering into it occasionally and not always comfortably. But they are necessary to sustain the network. It is their skill in making physical objects that forms the bedrock for the image in the mirror.

Craft development is somewhat different from most other kinds of development in that at its centre are physical objects and technologies that have the ability to enchant, to pin dreams on. This is what brings development agents to producers; yet few producers are enchanted by the things they make, nor do the majority pin their dreams on to them. Mat weaving is a livelihood. Craft, like kingship, is unreliable. It is subject to the vagaries of fashion, funding and the ever-shifting gaze of development. But it is potentially rewarding. Often, it is the money craft (both as physical object and as image) can bring in that keeps the majority of weavers producing mats on a regular basis.

For the myriad others interested in craft—concerned individuals, members of various organisations, including non-governmental and governmental agencies, and the Indian state itself—the heterotopia that is craft offers a space to try and create a world where traditional skills can survive, where the nation can feel pride in itself, where weaker members of the state can be helped, and where people are happy to stay in their villages, work, contribute to the economy and overcome their various hardships. While artisans are known to have the skills, they are not seen to have the knowledge to use their skills effectively. It is this knowledge that members of the craft worlds strive to impart through development projects, schemes and incentives, some more sensitively than others. The tension, and the challenge for those who seek to develop craft, is that not all artisans are *craft producers*, nor are all craft producers *artisans*.

Appendix

Newspaper and Magazine Articles

Some of the following have been cited in the main text and are in the Bibliography. All the articles listed here pertain to aspects of the Pattamadai mat weaving industry and were published in newspapers and magazines. Some do not specify names of authors. I have collated them here to indicate the extent of media attention generated by national awards and more generally by craft. The reader will notice that a majority of these are from *The Hindu.* This is a national newspaper based in Madras and, therefore, covers news from Tamilnadu in more detail than other English language newspapers. A significant proportion of these were showed to me by weavers and traders in Pattamadai who also kindly allowed me to photocopy them. Again, the fact that they preserve newspaper and magazine cuttings shows how aware they are of the advantages of publicity.

In English

'Pattamadai mat weaving industry changes its colour'. *The Hindu.* 22/11/2005.

Soma Basu. 'The carpet makers'. *The Hindu Magazine.* 14/08/2005.

Pushpa Chari. 'The wonder of the Pattamadai mat'. *The Hindu.* 25/02/1996.

Pushpa Chari. 'Weaving craft into dance'. *The Hindu.* 15/02/1998.

Pushpa Chari. 'Traditional motifs in trendy style'. *The Hindu.* 27/04/2001.

Aditi De. 'Craft: shifting sands'. *The Hindu.* 09/06/2002.

Geeta Doctor. 'South Indian grass mats'. *Inside Outside.* October 1994.

Geeta Doctor. 'Craft in contemporary design'. *The Hindu, Folio.* 21/03/1999.

Syed Muthahar. 'Matchless quality'. *The Hindu.* 21/10/1994.

Syed Muthahar. 'University bid to revive dying skill'. *The Hindu.* 23/11/1995.

R Y Narayanan. 'CII turns white knight, moves into rural households'. *The Hindu Business Line.* 29/11/2001.

Lakshmi Sundaram. 'Rural interlude: mats from Pattamadai' [pictured a mat with the caption: 'a queenly gift']. *The Hindu.* 24/02/2002.

S Venkatraman. 'Mat weaving faces extinction'. *Women's Era.* 15/02/1996.

'States' crafts on display'. *Hindustan Times.* 09/12/1992.

'Craftspersons to be honoured'. *Hindustan Times.* 04/03/1994.

'Craftspersons awarded'. *The Hindu.* 06/03/1994.

'Mat-weaving industry faces extinction'. *The Hindu.* 04/03/1995.

'Training institute urged for Pattamadai mat-weavers'. *The Hindu.* 08/11/1996.

'Reporter's diary'. *The Hindu.* 27/10/1997.

'DRIP will prove a different project'. *The Hindu.* 22/03/1999.

Mamta Reddy Kailkhuria. 'Crafted to perfection: This stuff can beautify your home'. *The Economic Times.* 16/01/2000.

'Call to revive mat weaving industry'. *The Hindu.* 11/12/2000.

'Reporter's diary'. *The Hindu.* 11/12/2000.

In Tamil

(Translations are my own; these are not exact translations but rather seek to preserve the spirit of the headline.)

'The Pattamadai mat that was presented to Gorbachev (*Gorbachevukku parisallikkapatta Pattamadai Pai*)'. *Junior Vikadan.* 28/01/1987.

'Zeal in weaving silk mats: national award for Pattamadai girl, president awards it to her in Delhi next month (*Pattu pai nesavu seyvadhil saadhanai: Pattamadai pennukku desiya virudhu! Adutha maadham Delhiyil janadhipathi vazhangugirar*)'. *Dinathandhi.* 17/02/1994

'Congratulatory ceremony for girl who won the national award (*Desiya virudhu perra pennukku paaraattu vizha*)'. *Nellai Kadhiravan.* 15/3/1994.

'National award for Pattamadai girl (*Pattamadai pennukku desiya virudhu*)'. *Dinakaran.* 16/03/1994.

'Beevi's zeal in mat weaving (*Pai pinnuvadhil sadhanai Pattamadai Beevikku*)'. *Marumalarchi.* 10/04/1994.

'National award got by a girl (*Pennal kidaitha desiya virudhu*)'. *Dinamalar.* 10/04/1994.

'Zeal in braiding mats: Pattamadai Muslim girl receives award from president (*Pai pinnuvadhil saadhanai: Pattamadai Muslim penn janaadhipadhiyidam virudhu perra*)'. *Dinathandi.* 25/4/1994.

T Vallavan. 'Pattamadai mats: viewers praise [but] the town cries (*Pattamadai paigall: paar pugazhuvadhu, oor azhuvudhu*)'. *Vannmagan.* 26/12/1994.

'Workers' plea for grants to support the Pattamadai mat industry (*Nalivadaindhu varum Pattamadai pai thozhilukku arasu maniyathudan kadan uthavi thozhilallargell korikkai*)'. *Dinakaran,* 01/12/1996.

'Pattamadai mats that accumulate awards (*Virudhugall Kuvikkum Pattamadai pai*)'. *Dinakaran.* 10/12/1996.

'The achievements of the Pattamadai mat (*Pattamadai paayin perumaigall*)'. *Nellai Thamizhmurasu,* special issue on Pattamadai. 31/3/2000.

Bibliography

Books, Book Sections and Journal Papers

Ahmad, ed. 1976. *Family, kinship and marriage among Muslims in India.* New Delhi: Manohar.

Ahmad, Imtiaz, ed. 1973. *Caste and social stratification among the Muslims.* New Delhi: Manohar.

Amalraj, V A. 1990. 'Cultivated sedges of South India for mat weaving industry'. *Journal of Economic and Taxonomic* Botany, 14 (3): 629–31.

Ananthanarayanan, Ragu. 1999. *Pathamadai: a parable of social change and leadership.* Madras: Faces.

Appadurai, Arjun, ed. 1986. *The social life of things: commodities in cultural perspective.* Cambridge: Cambridge University Press.

Ardener, Shirley. 1964. 'The comparative study of rotating credit associations'. *Journal of the Royal Anthropological Institute,* XCIV: 201–29.

Ardener, Shirley, and Sandra Burman, eds. 1996 (1995). *Money-Go-Rounds: the importance of Rotating Savings and Credit Associations for women.* Oxford: Berg.

Arterburne, Yvonne J. 1982. *The loom of interdependence: silk weaving cooperatives in Kanchipuram.* New Delhi: Hindustan.

Ashraf, Nehal. 1997. 'Islam and Dowry'. *Man in India,* 77 (4): 409–16.

Askegaard, Soren, and A Fuat Firat. 1997. 'Towards a critique of material culture, consumption and markets' in *Experiencing material culture in the Western World*, edited by S Pearce. London: Leicester University Press.

Austin, J L. 1962. *How to do things with words*. Oxford: Oxford University Press.

Ayyar, Jagadisa. 1998. *South Indian customs*. New Delhi: Rupa.

Baker, Christopher John. 1984. *An Indian rural economy, 1880–1955: the Tamilnad countryside*. Oxford: Clarendon Press.

Bakewell, Lisa. 1998. 'Image acts'. *American Anthropologist*, 100 (1): 22–32.

Banerjee, Mukulika and Daniel Miller. 2003. *The sari*. Oxford: Berg.

Battaglia, Debbora. 1997. 'Ambiguating agency: the case of Malinowski's ghost'. *American Anthropologist*, 99 (3): 505–10.

Baud, I. 1991. 'The impact of changing technology on the gender division of labour' in *Indian women in a changing industrial scenario*, edited by N Banerjee. New Delhi: Sage.

Bayly, C A. 1986. 'The origins of swadeshi (home industry): cloth and Indian society, 1700–1930' in *The social life of things: commodities in cultural perspective*, edited by A Appadurai. Cambridge: Cambridge University Press.

Bayly, Susan. 1989. *Saints, goddesses and kings: Muslims and Christians in South Indian society, 1700–1900*. Cambridge: Cambridge University Press.

———. 1999. *Caste, society and politics in India from the eighteenth century to the modern age*. Cambridge: Cambridge University Press.

Bean, Susan. 1999. 'The art of clay sculpture in Bengal' in *Maker and meaning: craft and society*. Dakshinachitra. Madras: Madras Craft Foundation.

Becker, Howard S. 1982. *Art worlds*. Berkeley: University of California Press.

Beteille, Andre. 1974. *Studies in agrarian structure*. New Delhi: Oxford University Press.

———. 1979. 'Homo Hierarchicus, Homo Equalis'. *Modern Asian Studies*, 13 (4): 529–48.

———. 1991. *Society and politics in India: essays in a comparitive perspective*. London: The Athlone Press.

———. 1996 (1965). *Caste, class and power: changing patterns of stratification in a Tanjore village*. New Delhi: Oxford University Press.

———. 1997 (1996). 'Caste in contemporary India' in *Caste today*, edited by C J Fuller. New Delhi: Oxford India Paperbacks.

Birdwood, G M. 1880. *The industrial arts of India.* South Kensington Museum art handbooks. London: Chapman and Hall.

Brantlinger, Patrick. 1996. 'A postindustrial prelude to postcolonialism: John Ruskin, William Morris, and Gandhism' in *Critical Enquiry*, 22 (3): 466–485.

Breckenridge, Carol A. 1986. 'The social use of everyday objects in Hindu South India' in *Dimensions of Indian art: Pupul Jayakar seventy*, edited by L Chandra, J Jain and A Prasad. Delhi: Agam Kala Prakashan.

Brouwer, Jan. 1995. *The makers of the world: caste, craft and mind of South Indian artisans.* Delhi: Oxford University Press.

———. 1996. 'Units of production in South India: an explanation of artisan's choices' in *Institutions and economic change in South Asia*, edited by B Stein and S Subrahmanyam. Delhi: Oxford University Press.

———. 1999. 'South Indian craftsmen and the indigenous economic concepts underlying their production and marketing practises' in *Maker and meaning: craft and society*. Madras: Madras Craft Foundation.

Bundgaard, Helle. 1996. 'Handicraft awards and their changing significance: a case study from Orissa, India'. *Folk: Journal of the Danish Ethnographic Society*, 38: 107–24.

———. 1999. *Indian art worlds in contention: local, regional and national discourses on Orissa Patta paintings.* Richmond: Curzon.

Cable, V, A Weston, and L C Jain. 1986. *The commerce of culture: experience of Indian handicrafts.* New Delhi: Lancer.

Calasso, Roberto, and (trans.) Tim Parks. 1999. *Ka.* London: Vintage.

Campbell, Colin. 1987. *The romantic ethic and the spirit of modern consumersim.* Oxford: Basil Blackwell.

———. 1997. 'The romantic ethic and the spirit of modern consumerism: reflections on the reception of a thesis concerning the origin of the continuing desire for goods' in *Experiencing material culture in the western world*, edited by S Pearce. London: Leicester University Press.

Carrier, James G, and Josiah McC Heyman. 1997. 'Consumption and political economy'. *Journal of the Royal Anthropological Institute*, 3 (2): 355–73.

Channa, Subhadra. 1988. 'What to do with the informal sector of the Indian economy: reflections from case studies'. *Man in India*, 68 (2): 186–99.

Chattopadhyay, Kamaladevi. 1963. *Indian handicrafts.* Bombay: Allied Publishers.

———. 1980. *India's craft tradition*. New Delhi: Publications Division, Government of India.

———. 1995. *Handicrafts of India*. New Delhi: Indian Council of Cultural Relations. Original edition, 1975.

Cohn, Bernard S. 1996. *Colonialism and its forms of knowledge*. Princeton: Princeton University Press.

Coomaraswamy, Ananda Kentish. 1905. *Borrowed plumes*. Colombo: Manasa.

———. 1909. *The Indian craftsman*. London: Probsthain.

———. 1912. *Art and swadeshi*. Madras: Ganesh.

———. 1956. 'The Christian and Oriental, or True, Philosophy of Art' in *Christian and Oriental Philosophy of Art*. New York: Doner.

Coote, Jeremy, and Anthony Shelton, eds. 1992. *Anthropology, art and aesthetics*. Oxford: Clarendon.

Craig, David, and Doug Porter. 1997. 'Framing participation: development projects, professionals and organisations' in *Development and patronage*, edited by D Eade. Oxford: Oxfam (UK and Ireland).

Crewe, Emma. 1997. 'The silent traditions of developing cooks' in *Discourses of development: anthropological perspectives*, edited by R L Grillo and R D Stirrat. Oxford: Berg.

Curtis, Donal. 1991. *Beyond government: organisations for common benefit*. London: Macmillan.

Dalmia, Yashodhara. 1988. *The painted world of the Warlis: art and ritual of the Warli tribes of Maharashtra*. New Delhi: Lalit Kala Akademi.

Dhamija, Jasleen. 1999. 'The Nakshabandas of Varanasi: the interlinkages between family, society and space' in *Maker and meaning: craft and society*. Madras: Madras Craft Foundation.

Dirks, Nicholas. 1997. 'Recasting Tamil society: the politics of caste and race in contemporary southern India' in *Caste today*, edited by C Fuller. Delhi: Oxford India Paperbacks.

Dore, Ronald, and Zoe Mars, eds. 1981. *Community development*. London: Croom Helm.

Dormer, Peter, ed. 1997. *The culture of craft*. Manchester: Manchester University Press.

Dumont, Louis. 1980. *Homo Hierarchicus: the caste system and its implications*. Chicago: University of Chicago Press.

Durrans, Brian. 1982. *Handicrafts, ideology and the Festival of India*. South Asia Research, 2 (1): 13–22.

———. 1992. 'Competitive Pragmatism: Organising the 1982 Festival of India in Berlin'. *History and Anthropology*, 6 (1): 23–45.

Duvvury, Vasumathy K. 1991. *Play, symbolism and ritual: a study of Tamil Brahmin women's rites of passage*. New York: Lang.

Engelshoven, Miranda. 1999. 'Diamonds and Patels: A report on the diamond industry of Surat' in *The worlds of Indian industrial labour*, edited by J Parry, J Breman and K Kapadia. New Delhi: Sage.

Ennew, Judith. 1982. 'Harris tweed: construction, retention and representation of a cottage industry' in *From craft to industry: the ethnography of proto-industrial craft production*, edited by E N Goody. Cambridge: Cambridge University Press.

Fairhead, James, and Melissa Leach. 1997. 'Webs of power and the construction of environmental policy problems: forest loss in New Guinea' in *Discourses of development: anthropological perspectives*, edited by R L Grillo and R D Stirrat. Oxford: Berg.

Fanselow, Frank S. 1989. 'Muslim society in Tamilnadu (India): an historical perspective'. *Journal of the Institiute of Muslim Minority Affairs*, 10: 1, January: 265–89.

———. 1997. 'The disinvention of caste among Tamil Muslims' in *Caste today*, edited by C J Fuller. New Delhi: Oxford India Paperbacks.

Fessler, Daniel M T. 2002. 'Windfall and socially distributed willpower: the psychocultural dynamics of rotating savings and credit associations in a Bengkulu village'. *Ethos*, 30 (1–2): 25–48.

Fischer, E, and H Shah. 1970. *Rural craftsmen and their work*. Ahmedabad: National Institute of Design.

Fisher, Allyn Johnston. 1972. 'The All India Handicrafts Board and the development of handicrafts in India'. Unpublished PhD thesis. Sociology department, University of Syracuse, Syracuse.

Foucault, Michel, and Jay Miskowiec. 1986. 'Of other spaces'. *Diacritics*, 16 (1): 22–7.

Fuller, Christopher John, ed. 1997. *Caste today*. New Delhi: Oxford India Paperbacks.

Gandhi, Mohandas Karamchand. 1956. *Sarvodaya*. Translated by V G Desai. Ahmadabad: Navjivan. Original edition, 1908.

Gardner, Katy, and David Lewis. 1996. *Anthropology, development and the post-modern challenge*. London: Pluto.

Geertz, Clifford. 1973. 'Deep play: notes on the Balinese cockfight' in *The interpretation of cultures*, edited by C Geertz. New York: Basic Books.

Gell, Alfred. 1998. *Art and agency*. Oxford: Clarendon Press.

———. 1999a. 'The technology of enchantment and the enchantment of technology' in *The art of anthropology: essays and diagrams*, edited by E Hirsch. London: Athlone.

———. 1999b. 'The market wheel: symbolic aspects of an Indian tribal market' in *The art of anthropology: essays and diagrams*, edited by E Hirsch. London: Athlone.

Giddens, Anthony. 1984. *The constitution of society: an outline of the theory of structuration*. Cambridge: Polity.

Gluckman, Max. 1958. Analysis of a social situation in modern Zululand. *Rhodes Livingstone Papers*, Vol. 28. Manchester: Manchester University Press.

Good, Anthony. 1982. 'The actor and the act: categories of prestation in South India'. *Man* (N S), 17 (1): 23–41.

———. 1991. *The female bridegroom: a comparative study of life-cycle rituals in South India and Sri Lanka*. Oxford: Clarendon Press.

Goody, Esther N, ed. 1982. *From craft to industry: the ethnography of proto-industrial cloth production*. Cambridge: Cambridge University Press.

Gopal, Meena. 1999. 'Disempowered despite wage work: women workers in beedi industry'. *Economic and Political Weekly: review of women studies* (April 17–24): n.p.

Gopal, Sarvepalli, ed. 1993. *Anatomy of a confrontation: the rise of communal politics in India*. London: Zed.

Goswami, Manu. 2004. *Producing India: from colonial economy to national space*. Delhi: Permanent Black.

Gray, John N, and David J Mearns, eds. 1989. *Society from the inside out: anthropological perspectives on the South Asian household*. New Delhi: Sage.

Green, Sarah F. 1997. *Urban amazons: lesbian feminism and beyond in the gender, sexuality and identity battles of London*. London: Macmillan.

Greenhalgh, Paul. 1997. 'The history of craft' in *The culture of craft*, edited by P Dormer. Manchester: Manchester University Press.

Greenough, Paul. 1995. 'Nation, economy and tradition displayed: the Indian Crafts Museum, New Delhi' in *Consuming modernity: public culture in a South Asian world*, edited by C A Breckenridge. Minneapolis: University of Minnesota Press.

Gregory, C A. 1997. *Savage money: the anthropology and politics of commodity exchange*. London: Routledge.

Grillo, R D and R L Stirrat, eds. 1997. *Discourses of development: anthropological perspectives*. Oxford: Berg.

Guha-Thakurta, Tapati. 1992. *The making of a new 'Indian' art: artists, aesthetics and nationalism in Bengal, c. 1850–1920*. Cambridge: Cambridge University Press.

Hanchett. 1988. *Coloured rice*. Delhi.

Harriss-White, B, S Janakarajan, D Jayaraj, and K Nagaraj. n.d. *Socio-economic factors underlying growth of silk-weaving in the Arni region: a preliminary study*. Madras: Madras Institute of Developmental Studies. Oxford: Queen Elizabeth House.

Havell, E B. 1986. *The basis for artistic and industrial revival in India*. Delhi: Usha. Original edition, 1912.

Haynes, Douglas E. 1993. The labour process in the Bombay handloom industry. Paper read at seminar on 'Cloth, the world economy and the artisan' at Dartmouth College, Hanover, USA.

———. 1996. 'The dynamics of continuity in Indian domestic industry: Jari manufacture in Surat, 1900–1947' in *Cloth and commerce: textiles in colonial India*, edited by T Roy. New Delhi: Sage.

———. 1996. 'The logic of the artisan firm in a capitalist economy: handloom weavers and technological change in Western India, 1880–1947' in *Institutions and economic change in South Asia*, edited by B Stein and S Subrahmanyam. Delhi: Oxford University Press.

Hecht, Anna. 1989. *The art of the loom: weaving, spinning and dyeing across the world*. London: British Museum Publications.

Henare, Amiria. 2005. *Museums, anthropology and imperial exchange*. Cambridge: Cambridge University Press.

Herzfeld, Michael. 2004. *The body impolitic: artisans and artifice in the global hierarchy of value*. Chicago: University of Chicago Press.

Hickey, Gloria. 1997. 'Craft within a consuming society' in *The culture of craft*, edited by P Dormer. Manchester: Manchester University Press.

Hobsbawm, Eric, and Terence Ranger, eds. 1993 (1983). *The invention of tradition*. Cambridge: Cambridge University Press.

Holland, Dorothy, and Kevin Leander. 2004. Ethnographic studies of positioning and subjectivity: an introduction. *Ethos*, 32 (2): 127–39.

Ingold, Tim. 2001. 'Beyond art and technology: the anthropology of skill' in *Anthropological perspectives on technology*, edited by M B Schiffer. Albuquerque: University of New Mexico Press.

Jayakar, Pupul. 1989. *The Earth Mother*. New Delhi: Penguin.

Jeffery, Patricia, and Roger Jeffery. 2002. 'A population out of control? Myths about Muslim fertility in contemporary India'. *World Development*, 30 (10): 1805–22.

Jhala, Jayasinghji. 2006. 'Journey with Ganesh: telling stories of objects acting in the world and being acted upon in the world'. *South Asian Popular Culture*, 4 (1): 35–47.

Jodhka, Surinder S. 1999. 'Community and identities: interrogating contemporary discourses on India'. *Economic and Political Weekly*, 34 (41): 2957–63.

Kaladhar, K. 1996. 'Designing financial services for rural poor'. *Economic and Political Weekly*, 31 (39): 117–22.

Kapadia, Karin. 1999. 'Gender ideologies and the formation of rural industrial classes in South India today' in *The worlds of Indian industrial labour*, edited by J Parry, J Breman and K Kapadia. New Delhi: Sage.

Knorringa, Peter. 1999. 'Artisan labour in the Agra footwear industry: continued informality and changing threats' in *The worlds of Indian industrial labour*, edited by J Parry, J Breman and K Kapadia. Delhi: Sage.

Kumar, Nita. 1988. *The artisans of Banaras: popular culture and identity, 1880–1986*. Princeton: Princeton University Press.

Latour, Bruno. 1993. *We have never been modern*. Translated by C Porter. Cambridge, Mass.: Harvard University Press.

Latour, Bruno, and Peter Weibel, eds. 2005. *Making things public: atmospheres of democracy*. Cambridge, Mass.: MIT Press.

Lemonnier, Pierre, ed. 1993. Technological choices: transformation in material cultures since the Neolithic, Material Cultures. London, New York: Routledge.

Liebl, Maureen, and Tirthankar Roy. 2004. 'Handmade in India'. *Economic and Political Weekly*, 38 (51 and 52): 5366–76.

Long, Andrew. 1992. 'Goods, knowledge and beer' in *Battlefields of knowledge: the interlocking of theory and practise in social research and development*, edited by N Long and A Long. London: Routledge.

———. 1992b. 'From paradigm lost to paradigm regained? The case for an actor-oriented sociology of development' in *Battlefields of knowledge: the interlocking of theory and practise in social research and development*, edited by N Long and A Long. London: Routledge.

Long, Norman, and Ann Long, eds. 1992a. *Battlefields of knowledge: the interlocking of theory and practise in social research theory and development*. London: Routledge.

Long, Norman, and Paul Richardson. 1978. 'Informal sector, petty commodity production and the social relations of small-scale enterprise' in *The new economic anthropology*, edited by J Clammer. London: Macmillan.

Ludden, David. 1989. *Peasant history in South India*. Delhi: Oxford University Press.

———. 1996. 'Caste society and units of production in early-modern South India' in *Institutions and economic change in South Asia*, edited by B Stein and S Subrahmanyam. Delhi: Oxford University Press.

———, ed. 1996. *Contesting the nation: religion, community, and the politics of democracy in India*. Philadelphia: University of Pennsylvania Press.

Mabro, Judy. 1996. *Veiled half-truths: western travelers' perception of Middle Eastern women*. London: I B Tauris.

Marchand, Trevor. 2001. *Minaret buidling and apprenticeship in Yemen*. Richmond: Curzon.

Mayoux, Linda, and Shri Anand. 1996 (1995). 'Gender inequality, ROSCAs and sectoral employment strategies: questions from the South Indian silk industry' in *Money-Go-Rounds: the importance of rotating savings and credit associations for women*, edited by S Ardener and S Burman. Oxford: Berg.

Mehmood, Faraaz, and Gulrez Aazam. 2002. 'Shilpgram in Udaipur'. *Economic and Political Weekly*, 37 (42): 4278.

Mehta, Deepak. 1997. *Work, ritual, biography*. New Delhi: Oxford University Press.

Mehta, Rustam. 1960. *Handicrafts and industrial arts of India*. Bombay: D B Taraporevala Sons.

Meis, Maria. 1982. *The lace makers of Narsapur: Indian housewives produce for the world market*. London: Zed Press.

Mines, Mattison. 1973. 'Social stratification among Muslim Tamils in Tamilnadu' in *Caste and social stratification among the Muslims in India*, edited by I Ahmad. New Delhi: Manohar.

———. 1976. 'Urbanization, Family Structure and the Muslim Merchants of Tamilnadu' in *Family, kinship and marriage among Muslims in India*, edited by I Ahmad: Columbia.

———. 1984. *The warrior merchants: textiles, trade and territory in South India*. Cambridge: Cambridge University Press.

———. 1994. *Public faces, private voices: community and individuality in South India*. Berkeley, London: University of California Press.

Misra, Sanjiv. 1993. *India's textile sector: a policy analysis*. New Delhi: Sage.

Mitter, Partha. 1977. *Much maligned monsters: History of European reactions to Indian art*. Oxford: Clarendon Press.

———. 1994. *Art and nationalism in colonial India, 1850–1922: Occidental orientations*. Cambridge: Cambridge University Press.

More, J B P. 1997. *The political evolution of Muslims in Tamilnadu and Madras, 1930–1947*. Madras: Orient Longman.

Mosse, David. 1997. 'Tank irrigation development in Tamilnadu' in *Discourses of development: anthropological perspectives*, edited by R L Grillo and R D Stirrat. Oxford: Berg.

Nambiar, P K. 1964. *Fine mats of Pattamadai*. Vol. IX, Madras, part VII-A-IV, handicrafts and artisans of Madras State. *Census of India 1961*. Madras: Census of India.

Narasimhan, Sakuntala. 1999. *Kamaladevi Chattopadhyay: the romantic rebel*. New Delhi: Sterling.

Neve, Geert de. 2002. 'Weaving rugs for IKEA: the dynamics of subcontracting work for the global market in rural Tamilnadu'. *Centre of South Asian Studies Occasional Paper 4*. Cambridge: Centre of South Asian Studies, University of Cambridge.

———. 2007. 'We are all sondukarar (relatives)! Kinship and its morality in an urban industry of Tamilnadu, South India'. *Modern Asian Studies*, 41.

Nuijten, Monique. 1992. 'Local organization as organizing practices' in *Battlefields of knowledge: the interlocking of theory and practise in social research and development*, edited by N Long and A Long. London: Routledge.

Padmanabha, P. 1978. 'Indian census and anthropological investigations'. Paper read at tenth international congress of anthropological and ethnological sciences.

Pandey, R. 1993. *Hindu samskaras*. New Delhi: Manoharlal. Original edition, 1969.

Pandian, Jacob. 1978. 'The Hindu caste system and Muslim ethnicity: the Labbai of a Tamil village in South India'. *Ethnohistory*, 25 (2): 141–57.

Parry, Jonathan, Jan Breman, and Karin Kapadia, eds. 1999. *The worlds of Indian industrial labour*. New Delhi: Sage.

Pate, H R. 1917. *Gazetteer of the Tinnevelly district*. Vol. 1, Madras District Gazetteers. Madras: Government Press.

Pfaffenberger, Bryan. 1992. 'Social anthropology of technology'. *Annual Review of* Anthropology, 21: 491–516.

———. 1993. 'The factory as artefact' in *Technological changes: transformation in material culture since the Neolithic*, edited by Lemonnier. London, New York: Routledge.

———. 2001. 'Symbols do not create meanings—activities do or, why symbolic anthropology needs the anthropology of technology' in *Anthropological perspectives on technology*, edited by M B Schiffer. Albuquerque: University of New Mexico Press.

Pinney, Christopher, and Nicholas Thomas, eds. 2001. *Beyond aesthetics: art and the technologies of enchantment*. Oxford: Berg.

Prasad, Leela. 2007. *Poetics of conduct: oral narrative and moral being in a South Indian town*. New York: Columbia University Press.

Pye, David. 1968. *The nature and art of workmanship*. Cambridge: Cambridge University Press.

Quigley, Declan. 1993. *The interpretation of caste*. Oxford: Clarendon Press.

Racine, Jean Luc, ed. 1997. *Peasant moorings: village ties and mobility rationales in South India*. New Delhi: Sage.

Raj, J E. n.d. *Livelihood systems: the importance of sales exhibitions in marketing craft products*. New Delhi: ActionAid.

Rajasekhar, D. 2002. 'Economic programmes and poverty reduction: NGO experiences from Tamilnadu'. *Economic and Political Weekly*, 37 (29): 3063–8.

Rao, C V Ramachandra. 1980. *A K Coomaraswamy (an inspirer of Indian renaissance) & other cultural causerie*. Nellore: Manasa.

Rao, Narayana. 1929. *Report on survey of cottage industries*. Madras: Government Press.

Rees, Helen. 1997. 'Patterns of making: thinking and making in industrial design' in *The culture of craft*, edited by P Dormer. Manchester: Manchester University Press.

Risley, H H. 1891. 'Ethnographic researches in India'. *The Journal of the Anthropological Institute of Great Britain and Northern Ireland*, 20: 290–2.

———. 1891. 'The study of ethnology in India'. *The Journal of the Anthropological Institute of Great Britain and Northern Ireland*, 20: 235–63.

Rorty, Richard. 1999. *Philosophy and social hope*. London: Penguin.

Roy, Tirthankar. 1993. *Artisans and industrialization: Indian weaving in the twentieth century*. Delhi: Oxford University Press.

———, ed. 1996. *Cloth and commerce: textiles in colonial India*. New Delhi: Sage.

Ruskin, John. 1862 (1987). 'Unto this last' in *Unto this last and other writings*, edited by C Wilmer. London: Penguin.

Said, Edward. 1978. *Orientalism*. London: Routledge and Kegan Paul.

Sethi, Raj Mohini. 1996 (1995). 'Women's ROSCAs in contemporary Indian society' in *Money-Go-Rounds: the importance of rotating savings and credit associations for women*, edited by S Ardener and S Burman. Oxford: Berg.

Sethi, Rajeev. 1989. 'Towards a cultural policy: dialogues on continuity and change' in *Contemporary Indian tradition: voices on culture, nature and the challenges of change*, edited by C M Borden. Washington: Smithsonian Institution Press.

Shah, Haku. 1999. 'Tradition and training in craft' in *Maker and meaning: craft and society*. Madras: Madras Craft Foundation.

Sills, D L, ed. 1968. *International encyclopaedia of social sciences*. New York: MacMillan.

Simmel, Georg. 1950. 'The stranger' in *The sociology of Georg Simmel*, edited by K Wolff. New York: The Free Press.

Singh, B P. 1998. *India's culture: the state, the arts and beyond*. Delhi: Oxford University Press.

Solanki, S S. 2002. 'Migration of rural artisans'. *Economic and Political Weekly*, 37 (35): 3579–80.

Specker, Konrad. 1996. 'Madras handlooms in the nineteenth century' in *Cloth and commerce: textiles in colonial India*, edited by T Roy. New Delhi: Sage.

Srinivas, M N. 1966. *Social change in modern India*. Berkeley: University of California Press.

Srinivas, M N. 1976. *The remembered village*. Berkeley: University of California Press.

SRUTI. 1995. *India's artisans: a status report*. New Delhi: Society for Rural, Urban and Tribal Initiative.

Stein, Burton, ed. 1978. *South Indian temples; an analytical reconsideration*. New Delhi: Vikas.

Suchman, Lucy. 2001. 'Building bridges: practice-based ethnographies' in *Anthropological perspectives on technology*, edited by M B Schiffer. Albuquerque: University of New Mexico Press.

Sundar, Pushpa. 1995. *Patrons and philistines*. Delhi: Oxford University Press.

Swallow, Deborah A. 1982. 'Production and control in the Indian garment export industry' in *From craft to industry: the ethnography of proto-industrial cloth production*, edited by E Goody. Cambridge: Cambridge University Press.

Tarlo, Emma. 1996. *Clothing matters: dress and identity in India*. London: Hurst.

Thurston, Edgar. 1907. *Ethnographic notes in Southern India*. Madras: Government Press.

Thurston, Edgar, and K Rangachari. 1909. *Castes and tribes of Southern India*. Madras: Government Press.

Tsing, A L. 2004. *Friction: an ethnography of global connection*. Princeton: Princeton University Press.

Ufford, Philip Quarles van. 1993. 'Knowledge and ignorance in the practices of development policy' in *An anthropological critique of development: the growth of ignorance*, edited by M Hobart. London: Routledge.

Upadhya, Carol. 2001. 'The concept of community in Indian social sciences: an anthropological perspective' in *Community and identities: contemporary discourses on culture and politics in India*, edited by S S Jodhka. New Delhi: Sage.

Varadarajan, Lotika. 1990. 'Whither culture?' in *India: creating a modern nation*, edited by J Masselos. New Delhi: Sterling.

Varadarajan, Siddharth, ed. 2002. *Gujarat: the making of a tragedy*. New Delhi: Penguin.

Venkatesan, Soumhya. 1994. The process and effects of the commercialisation of Warli painting. MA, History of Art, National Museum Institute for the History of Art, Conservation and Museology, Delhi.

———. 2002a. Crafting culture: Pattamadai mats from South India, a catalogue to supplement the exhibition of the same name at the University of Cambridge Museum of Archaeology and Anthropology. Cambridge: University of Cambridge Museum of Archaeology and Anthropology.

———. 2002b. Crafting discourse: mat weaving in Pattamadai town, South India. PhD, Social Anthropology, University of Cambridge, Cambridge.

———. 2006. 'Shifting balances in a 'craft community': the mat weavers of Pattamadai, South India'. *Contributions to Indian Sociology* (n.s), 40 (1).

Walker, Benjamin. 1995. *The Hindu world.* New Delhi: Indus-Harper Collins. Original edition, 1968.

Watt, George. 1904. *Indian art at Delhi 1903*, official catalogue of the Delhi exhibition, 1902–1903. London: John Murray.

White, Jenny. 2000. 'Kinship, reciprocity and the world market' in *Dividends of kinship*, edited by P Schweitzer. London: Routledge.

Wikan, Unni. 1992. 'Beyond the words: the power of resonance'. *American Anthropologist*, 19 (3): 460–82.

Wilk, Richard R. 2001. 'Towards an anthropology of needs' in *Anthropological perspectives on technology*, edited by M B Schiffer. Albuquerque: University of New Mexico Press.

Wilkinson-Weber, Clare. 1999. *Embroidering lives.* Albany: State University of New York Press.

Yanagisawa, Haruka. 1996. 'The handloom industry and its market structure: the case of the Madras Presidency in the first half of the twentieth century' in *Cloth and commerce: textiles in colonial India*, edited by T Roy. New Delhi: Sage.

Yarrow, T. 2008. Paired opposites: dualism in development and anthropology. *Critique of Anthropology* 28(4): 426–45.

Reports, Some Unpublished and With no Named Author

1995. Proposal for reviving fine korai mats at Pathamadai, Tamilnadu. Foundation for the advancement of crafts skills and enterprises/ Confederation of Indian Industry.

1998. Status report. Foundation for the Advancement of Crafts Enterprises and Skills.

1999. Designing organisations for craft development: reflections from the FACES experience. Paper presented to the Maker and meaning: craft and society, Dakshina Chitra, Madras, 1999.

Government of India, Ninth Five Year Plan, 1997–2002.

Office of the Development Commissioner (Handicrafts), Government of India. 1998. Compendium of handicraft schemes.

Office of the Development Commissioner (Handicrafts), Government of India. 1999. National awards for master craftspersons and weavers, 1996 and 1997.

MAFOI. 1996. Socio economic study of four crafts in South India. MAFOI/FACES.

Mohapatra, S K. 1989. Report of task force on handicrafts for the VIII five year plan. Office of the Development Commissioner, Handicrafts, Ministry of Textiles, Government of India.

National Council for Applied Economic Research. 1995. Evaluation of handicrafts training programmes. Project sponsored by the Office of the Development Commissioner (Handicrafts).

SRUTI. 1995. *India's artisans: a status report.* Society for Rural, Urban and Tribal Initiative.

Newspaper and Magazine Articles

In English

04/03/1995. 'Mat-weaving industry faces extinction'. *The Hindu*. Madras.

08/11/1996. 'Training institute urged for Pattamadai mat-weavers'. *The Hindu*. Madras.

27/10/1997. 'Reporter's diary'. *The Hindu.* Madras.
11/12/2000. 'Call to revive mat weaving industry'. *The Hindu.* Madras.
11/12/2000. 'Reporter's diary'. *The Hindu.* Madras.
Chari, P. 25/02/1996. 'The wonder of the Pattamadai mat'. *The Hindu.* Madras.
Chari, P. 15/02/1998. 'Weaving craft into dance'. *The Hindu.* Madras.
Doctor, G. 21/03/1999. 'Craft in contemporary design'. Folio, *The Hindu.* Madras.
Ganapathy, V. 09/10/1995. 'Useful work of art'. *The Hindu.* Madras.
Gangadharan, V. 25/01/2000. 'Pocketful of business: new markets beckon grass mats of Tamilnadu'. *Rediff Business Special.* (http://www.rediff.com/business/2000/jan/25mats.htm)
Muthahar, S. 21/10/1994. 'Matchless quality'. *The Hindu.* Madras.
Muthahar, S. 23/11/1995. 'University bid to revive dying skill'. *The Hindu.*
Muthahar, S. 17/12/2000. 'Target of hate'. *The Hindu.* Madras.
Raghuraman, G. 09/02/1998. 'Making hay in the sunshine...' *The Hindu.* Madras.
Subramanian. T S. 14–27/09/2002. 'Promise and potential'. *Frontline*, volume 19, issue 19. Madras.
Tyabji, Laila. 10/08/1994. 'Dastkar and the marketing of craft: a subsidized con trick or a success story?' *The Economic Times.*
———. 10/08/1994b. 'Indian textiles 1947–1997: tradition, culture & aesthetics—technology, employment & economics'. CAPART Magazine.
———. 2003. 'The problem'. *Seminar*, 523 (Celebrating crafts): 12–6.

In Tamil

01/12/1996. 'Workers' plea for grants to support the Pattamadai mat industry'. (*Nalivadaindhu varum Pattamadai pai thozhilukku arasu maniyathudan kadan uthavi thozhilallargell korikkai*). *Dinakaran.* Tirunelveli.
16/11/1986. Jokes section. *Kalkanndu.*

Index

actor-network-theory, 246
actor-oriented framework, 166–7
All India Handicrafts Board, 4, 32, 147, 175, 212
anthropology
  and development, 14–17
  of technology, brief overview, 243–8
  apprenticeship training scheme, 128, 173, 187
arena model of development, 167
Art and agency, 19, 37, 191, 210–15
art versus craft, 22–3, 27–30, 210–16
Arts and Crafts Movement, 23–5, 28
Ayodhya, 63

Bayly, S, 27, 48, 52*n*, 58*n*, 198
beedi rolling, 80–1, 83–5, 87, 98, 126–9, 173, 254
Birdwood, Sir George, 25, 27–8, 40
Bombay, 25*n*, 58, 70, 92, 98, 100, 206, 222, 251
Brahmin(s), 10–11, 47, 50–3, 59, 64, 75, 109, 193–8, 202–7, 222–3, 226
Breckenridge, C, 191–2, 204
burkha, 96–7. *See also* clothing

Cambridge University Museum of Archaeology and Anthropology (CUMAA), 14–15, 109, 117
  exhibition, Crafting culture: Pattamadai mats from South India, 14–15, 109
Census (1961) publication on the fine mats of Pattamadai (Nambiar 1964), 12*n*, 31, 73, 108*n*, 112*n*, 146–7, 156*n*, 195, 212, 218, 232, 245*n*
Censuses and Gazetteers, 31–2, 159, 195, 243. *See also* Pate, H R
Charles, Prince and Princess Diana, 219, 222–4
Chattopadhyay, Kamaladevi, 4, 104, 146, 171, 212–13
Chennai, *see* Madras
clothing, 37, 43, 81, 97, 153–4, 192, 204, 230, 240, 242
  importance of white clothing, 186
  'devout Muslim's uniform', 153

community, 18, 23, 44*n*, 58–9, 91, 98, 140, 145, 147, 149, 151, 165, 172, 181, 220, 244
'craft community', 4, 7, 94–5, 138, 158–9, 161–2, 166–9, 178, 180, 186, 214
coolie loom/*coolie* weaving, 86–7, 251
Coomaraswamy, Ananda, 25, 27–8, 172*n*, 269–70
cooperative competition, 13, 16, 18
craft bazaar, 33, 35*n*, 37–8, 41, 70, 124, 129, 133–4, 143, 173, 180, 182, 213, 227, 232–3, 237, 240–2
craft worlds, 10, 18, 38, 45, 129, 133, 136–7, 140, 142–3, 149, 170–1, 177, 179–80, 183, 193, 207–8, 213–6, 226, 271
creative opportunism, 140

decorative arts, 22–4, 29*n*, 30
Delhi Exhibition (1903), 2, 30, 103
discourse, 28, 35–6, 88*n*, 94, 128, 138, 150, 154*n*, 165–8, 174, 179, 185, 188, 199, 226, 239, 255, 258*n*, 267
divorce/*talaq*, 77, 86–8, 223
dowry, 78–9, 81, 93, 97–8
Duvvury, V, 196–7

Elizabeth, Queen, 1–3
coronation of, 1–3, 146, 212
coronation gift, 2–3
coronation mat, 216
the mat for the Queen, 2, 7, 15
Mr Rangan, 1–4, 212, 214, 219, 223
ethnic chic, 229–30, 237

Fanselow, F, 48, 57*n*, 58
Foucault, M, 20, 267–8
discourse, 35*n*

Gandhi, M K, 24*n*, 29
Gell, A, 7, 19, 37, 191, 210–15, 233
Gray, J N and Mearns, D J, 72–3
Greenhalgh, P, 22–4, 30
Gregory, C A, 192

Havell, E B, 25, 27–8
Herzfeld, M, 38, 45
heterotopia, 20, 267–9, 271
The Hindu, 28, 40–1, 96, 106, 150, 185, 216, 230, 255, 272
Hindu-Muslim relations, 9, 56, 62–71, 206
anti-Muslim riots, in Bombay, 70, 251; in Gujarat, 63
demolition of Babri Masjid, 63
September 11, 62
and marriage mats, 202–5
Holland, D, and Leander, K, 67–8

image act, 39
images of craft, 6, 18, 20, 39–45, 100, 133, 140–1, 160, 180, 233, 266–7
Ingold, T, 20, 246–7, 265
'inside-out' versus 'outside-in' approach, 72–3

Jodhka, S, 165

Khadi, 29, 34*n*, 106
korai, 39, 51, 87, 105–9, 114, 116–22, 125, 128, 135–6, 148, 158, 171, 193*n*, 195–6, 199, 202, 230, 254–7, 263

Labbai(s), 2–3, 12, 18, 47, 50, 54, 56–61, 71–3, 80, 83, 85–6, 88–9, 91, 93–6, 100, 102, 104, 109–10, 124–7, 130–1, 133–5, 138–41, 143–51, 162–4, 178–80, 189, 193, 212, 216–19, 222–3, 226, 251, 263, 270; and Rauthers, 56–61
Labbai colony, 54, 61, 73, 86
lamination, 68
local traders, 18, 141, 195, 204, 216
Long, N, 166, 168

Madras, 1–2, 10, 28, 32, 41, 47, 100, 130, 134, 175, 180, 194–5, 198, 207, 218, 230, 234–5, 237, 248, 272
marriage mats, 19, 193–207
master craft producer, 128, 224
mat looms, 19–20, 26, 143, 147, 152, 189, 206, 242–54
  hand looms, 2, 34, 45, 53, 102; versus power looms, 102, 105–7, 147, 174
  'improved' loom, 181, 248–51
  Pattamadai loom, 49, 53, 74–6, 86–8, 108–14, 116, 118–21, 123, 127–31, 246, 257–65
mats, uses of, 19
  as utilitarian objects, 156
  as craft objects, 4, 124, 132–3, 208, 216, 227, 266. *See also* Pattamadai mats
Melapallayam, 58*n*, 83, 97
migration, 85
  within India, 35, 52, 73, 80
  to the Middle East, 80, 142–3
Mines, M, 59, 166
More, J B P, 56–8
Muslim, 2, 4–6, 9, 18–20, 33, 45, 47–8, 50–6, 62–72, 78, 88, 94–8, 103, 129, 135, 153, 187, 202, 205–6, 211, 216, 220–1, 235, 240, 251. *See also* Labbai, Rauthers

Nagercoil, 48
national awards for craft producers, 39*n*, 136–7, 158–9, 170–90, 207, 224–5, 234–5, 237, 239, 255, 272
natural dyes, 181–2, 186, 252–3, 256–7, 262

object+person+idea/person+object +idea, 7, 215, 233, 242, 269
organisational types for handicraft production, 124–5

Palayamkottai, 48
Pandian, J, 56–8
Papanasam, 48
Pate, H R, 32, 50, 103*n*, 104, 115*n*, 194*n*, 232, 243
Pattamadai, 48
Pattamadai mats
  fine mats, 2–3, 12, 14, 32, 102–8, 121, 123–4, 134, 137, 146–7, 149, 159, 181, 187, 195, 208–9, 218, 220, 225, 232, 234, 245*n*, 248, 256
  craft mats, 19, 134, 202, 208
  gift mats, 19, 217–23
  marriage mats, 19, 193–208
  old mat, 12, 74, 187
  pandhi pai , 103
  pattu pai, 198–9, 206
  superfine mats, 47, 105–10, 112, 119–21, 126, 132, 134, 138, 141, 144, 149, 155–60, 162–3, 176–7, 180, 185, 193, 198–9, 206*n*, 207, 216–18, 221, 224–6, 231–2, 234, 236–8, 250–1, 255, 257–9, 263
politics of work, 22–4
positioning, 65–72, 95, 133, 140, 187, 189, 213, 239
  social position, 66–7
purdah, 100. *See also burkha*, clothing

question of names, 13–15

Rauther(s), 47–8, 52, 54, 56–61. *See also* Muslim, Labbai
reed/*achu*, 2, 8, 102, 112, 114, 118–19, 208, 250–2, 264–5
Rolling Savings and Credit Associations (ROSCAs)/chit fund schemes, 74–5, 80, 85, 88–94, 142, 247

self-help groups, 94–5, 219–20, 222
selvi Jayalalithaa, 221

Simmel, G, 143, 155–6
subjectivity, 65, 68

Tamaraparani river, 39, 49, 108
Tirunelveli, 2, 32, 46–50, 55, 78, 83*n*, 96, 103, 130, 179, 201, 219, 234–5

Upadhya, C, 165–6

van Ufford, Q, 167

vernacular, 22–3
  crafts, 23
  -ism, 23–4

Western Ghats, 49
Wikan, U, 65–6
Wilk, R, 265, 269
women's household-based income generation, 80–8, 126
word images, 40*n*, 133
write-weave, 2, 122–3, 202